GRACE *in Motion*

The Intersection of Women's Ordination and Virginia Theological Seminary

JUDITH MAXWELL MCDANIEL

Judith McDaniel

Size 2
BV
4070
.P86
M33
2011

Dedication

FOR

JOANNA

WHO IS

GRACE...

IN MOTION

First published in the United States by:

RIVERPLACE COMMUNICATION ARTS, LLC
201 West Laurel Street
Brainerd, MN 56401
(218) 851-4843
www.RiverPlace-mn.com

ISBN 978-0-9831785-4-5
Printed in the United States of America
Publication date September 2011
FIRST EDITION

Cover Photo: B. Cayce Ramey

CONTENTS

FOREWORD

This is a book about the agency of God. Here we see evidence of the determination of the Holy Spirit to allow the gifts of all the baptized to be available to the Church. God's providence is at work in the lives documented in this book and in the slow recognition of a Church that responds to these lives.

Within the Anglican Communion, it was the Anglican Church of Canada which first passed legislation that permitted the ordination of women to the priesthood. The Episcopal Church followed one year later in 1976 at its General Convention, meeting in Minneapolis. Resolution B005 proposed making the ordination canons equally applicable to men and women for the three orders of bishop, priest and deacon. General Convention approved Resolution B005, and in the House of Bishops 95 voted for, 61 against with 2 abstaining. Thirty five years later, a woman priest serves as our Presiding Bishop, the Most Rev Dr Katharine Jefferts Schori; and there are many women serving at every level of our Church.

Although it is true that over the last thirty-five years there has been progress, it would be completely wrong to imagine that the journey has been easy. It took courage to keep on the way. As the vote to approve the ordination of women as priests would suggest, there have been a number of critics who challenged or maligned women's sense of call to priesthood. There have been moments of rejection, deep pain, and frustration.

Virginia Theological Seminary recognizes that for many women the journey through Seminary was difficult. As an institution we are culpable; we recognize our complicity in sin and seek forgiveness. We hope that the telling of the many individual stories in this book will be part of the healing. This remarkable book captures the joys, achievements, and miracles of ministry, while acknowledging both explicitly and implicitly the challenges which have been and are present along the way. Countless lives, often but not always in small parishes, have been changed by the woman who has been present as pastor, teacher, and priest.

The author, the Rev. Dr. Judith McDaniel, is by no means a detached historian. Judith's own journey is the story of women in the Episcopal Church who realized and responded to the call from God to pursue Holy Orders as a priest. Movingly, she speaks of the privilege of listening and documenting these remarkable stories. As she organized these interviews, the major theme that emerges is the grace of God.

As a Seminary, the grace of God manifested in the ministry of ordained women over these thirty-five years has been equally remarkable. My predecessor, the Very Rev. Martha J. Horne, was the first woman Dean and President in the Episcopal Seminaries. In 2011 our Faculty and our student body are almost exactly fifty/fifty men and women.

It would be wrong to imply that this story is over. There are still barriers which impede women in our Church. However, this book tells part of the story in a thoughtful and compelling way. Judith makes it possible for us to hear the voices of women priests as they have not been heard. There were moments on the journey when it all looked so difficult— and yet God found a way through, as did these women God called to be priests in God's Church. As we turn the pages, may we recover memories of the pain and the joy, the fear and the hope which is the story of women and the priesthood in the Episcopal Church.

The Very Rev Ian Markham
Ascension Day 2011

VIRGINIA THEOLOGICAL SEMINARY

PREFACE

The premise of this story is that any account of the relationship between women's ordination and Virginia Theological Seminary will necessarily involve some reconstruction of individual narratives of call and the steps the faculty of VTS took to respond to those calls. Without a record of the reflections of women and men who lived through those days of revolution in the Church, any manuscript attempting to record those events would be lifeless.

What took place was mutual ministry. Because there was only one lay woman at a time on the faculty for decades and an ordained woman was not called to be a professor until 1990, it was largely men on the faculty who listened to women's nascent sense of call. That those voices met is in itself a testament to grace, a response to something beyond what they had known before, and a gift to the Church.

For that gift and that response, we can only praise God.

GRACE in Motion

CHAPTER ONE

"So God created humankind [*adam*] in his image, in the image of God did he create it, male and female he created them."

Genesis 1:27
The Schocken Bible

This book contains a record of events, events many have characterized as a struggle for justice. The story told here, however, will offer an alternative vision: not an account of a struggle for justice or a depiction of rights—for no one, male or female, has a "right" to be ordained; nor an argument for equality—for men and women are not interchangeable but, instead, counterparts.[1] Rather, this narrative is intended to be a vehicle for meditation on the working of grace in our lives, the transformation of horizons that were too limited, and the significance of those conversions. The stories recorded here are those of the participants in these events, people who, upon reflection, discovered new life.

Thus, this book is a history of new life, a treasury of grace in motion. The new life recorded here revealed itself in the face of age-old customs as a fresh conception of reality, the creation of new thought for men and women and new life for the Church as the body of Christ. That new life was a gift to humankind from God, a movement of grace which freed men and women to express the fullness of their being and enabled them to further their understanding of the plenitude of God.

To trace the pattern of grace at work in human life can be an elusive pursuit. Sometimes grace moves in and out of life as softly as a baby's breath. Sometimes grace appears to move as shockingly as a startled cry. But grace is always in motion. Humans simply do not always perceive it.

For in the beginning God created *adam. Adam* is not the name of a man. *Adam* is man and woman. But early in human history, as depicted in the allegory of the garden of Eden, humans assumed the mantle of power, putting themselves in the place of God. Power, rather than stewardship of the gifts God gave us, began to determine the standards by which men and women lived; and

the fullness of creation was diminished in human minds. Lost to us was an appreciation of the necessity of the gifts both men and women bring, gifts that are each needed in order for the image of God to be apprehended.

This book, therefore, will sketch a pastiche of grace in the lives of women graduates of Virginia Seminary who were ordained and who, in their triumphs and tragedies, became icons of a movement toward wholeness and new life: grace in motion.

– Cultural Context –

The literature on the question of women's ordination is vast. Distributed from the first centuries of Christianity up to the present, this literature encompasses both learned theological argument and diatribe. The content of those arguments will not be explored here except when they pertain directly to the involvement of Virginia Theological Seminary in the evolution of the movement toward women's ordination. The fact that the argument is centuries old only serves to demonstrate that slowly, slowly does grace move the minds of men and women, for power differentials and their assumptions are deeply ingrained in our environments.

For an example as recent as the twentieth century, consider: The nineteenth amendment to the United States Constitution states, "The right of citizens of the United States to vote shall not be denied or abridged by the United States or by any state on account of sex," thus giving women the right to vote in secular political elections for the first time in this country in 1920. However, the possibility of women's having a voice in the governance of the Church continued to be fraught. The 1920 Lambeth Conference stated, "Women should be admitted to those Councils of the Church in which laymen are admitted,

[1] Genesis 2:18, "I will make him a helper corresponding to him." Schocken Bible.

and on equal terms."[2] But when the men of the Joint Commission on Woman's Work in the Church offered a resolution to the General Convention of 1922 which would have made women eligible for election as deputies, that resolution was defeated. When a similar resolution was presented in 1925, it was also defeated; and nothing further was heard about the possibility of women deputies until 1949.[3]

In 1946 at the Philadelphia General Convention, the Diocese of Missouri sent as one of its four lay deputies a woman. Elizabeth Dyer's presence was challenged, but she was seated. Steps were taken to assure that this not occur again; and when four women were elected by their own dioceses to attend the San Francisco General Convention of 1949, a resolution barring them from being seated was passed. However, this same convention passed a resolution asking for a report on the possibility of seating lay women as deputies to General Convention. That report was written by Mrs. Harold C. Kelleran, later known as Professor Marion M. Kelleran of Virginia Seminary. The report was presented to General Convention in 1952, and the motion to seat women as lay deputies to General Convention was defeated in the lay order in '52, '55, '58, '61, and '64. As the years went by, the laymen's votes against seating women

Mrs. Harold C. Kelleran

grew; and the language of sexual innuendo became more explicit, more ribald, more crude, and more obscene.[4] As Mrs. Kelleran testified in the Ecclesiastical Trial of the Rev. William A. Wendt in 1975, "This bitter experience colors my attitude toward the ordination of women going through the next Convention."[5]

> *He who learns must suffer*
> *And even in our sleep pain that cannot forget*
> *Falls drop by drop upon the heart,*
> *And in our own despite, against our will,*
> *Comes wisdom to us by the awful grace of God.*

wrote Aeschylus in the *Agamemnon*. Could it be said that the awful grace of God was at work in the minds and hearts of women and men during these years of struggle? Is struggle a theological category? Certainly there were men who supported the movement to give women decision-making voice and vote in the councils of the Church: The House of Bishops and the clergy order in the House of Deputies are on record as having voted in favor of seating women as lay deputies to General Convention long before the reality came to be. It was the lay men in the House of Deputies whose self-perception was impacted by the admission of lay women into their milieu of authority. Similarly, it was to be the clergy men whose self-image was at stake and whose votes slowed the movement toward women's ordination. Slowly, slowly, drop by drop does grace move via wisdom.

"In whose interests is this custom? Whom does this etiquette serve? Who benefits by this norm? Who is protected by this law? Who is being silenced? Who is being marginalized? Whose reality is being trivialized?

[2] *Encyclical Letter from the Bishops with the Resolutions and Reports*, 39.
[3] It is worth noting that women were excluded from the study process and the policy-making decisions regarding marriage in 1931, 1934, and 1937.
[4] Pamela W. Darling, *New Wine: the Story of Women Transforming Leadership and Power in the Episcopal Church* (Boston: Cowley Publications, 1994), 84.
[5] Ecclesiastical Court of the Diocese of Washington, The Board of Presenters v. The Rev. William A. Wendt, April 30, 1975-May 2, 1975, p. 297, Archives of the Episcopal Diocese of Washington, Mount St. Alban, Washington D.C. 20016.

Whose life is being forfeited?"[6] asked Alison Cheek years after women were admitted to holy orders. Such questions must always be asked if we are to be alert to the possibilities of grace in our midst, for lives are still being marginalized, trivialized, and forfeited around the globe; and deeply held assumptions need to be scrutinized for what they are: assumptions.

Marion Macdonald Kelleran, as she had identified herself in 1975, held a bachelor's degree from the University of Buffalo; but she was also a graduate of Windham House. Windham House in New York and St. Margaret's House in Berkeley, California, were graduate training schools for women church workers. Founded and funded by the Woman's Auxiliary in 1928, Windham House provided women the opportunity to study theology at General, Union, and Columbia Seminaries. But the first women students at Windham House heard lectures from the faculty of General only in the evenings at their residence away from the General close. Slowly they were allowed to sit outside classrooms, in the halls, to hear lectures at General.[7] By the early 1950's they were allowed to sit as an isolated group at the back of classrooms with men who were studying under the "old man's canon"; but they could not eat in the refectory and were provided only a single bathroom on campus. While there were women at Union Seminary who were headed toward ordination in the United Church of Christ and other denominations, the degrees of the Episcopal women were not from the seminaries but, depending on their major concentration, from Columbia Teacher's College.

Marion Kelleran began working for the Diocese of Washington as the Educational Consultant to Bishop Angus Dunn in 1946. Dean Alexander Zabriskie called her in 1949 to work one day a week at VTS as Visiting Instructor in Christian Education. In 1962 she was called by the Seminary to be Associate Professor of Pastoral Theology and Christian Education, the first woman on the faculty.[8] The Faculty Minutes of April 11, 1962 noted that the faculty two years before had passed a motion to add Kelleran to the faculty[9] and that she already was possessed of a national reputation, a fact elaborated in the Faculty Minutes of April 25, 1962, as follows: "Mrs. Kelleran is known throughout the church for her work in Christian Education both in the National Department and in summer conferences at Hood, Wellesley, Finger Lakes and Kanuga. She is past president of the Association of Professional Women Church Workers and is a member of the General Convention's Joint Commission on the Recruiting and Training of Women Workers."[10]

Although a brief synopsis of Marion Kelleran's ministry appeared in the *Virginia Seminary Journal* of March 1973—including the fact that as Vice-Chair of the Anglican Consultative Council, she is the only person to have declared the Archbishop of Canterbury out of order twice in the same meeting—there is no record of her personal experiences in the early years after her graduation from Windham House.

However, a Virginia Seminary adjunct professor in the 1990's, Joyce Glover, received a Master of Arts in religious education from Columbia Teacher's College via Windham House in 1951 and experienced a great deal of rejection, as did other women graduates of these training

[6] *Changing Women, Changing Church*, ed. Marie Louise Uhr (Newtown, Australia: Millennium Books, 1992), 126.
[7] Darling, p. 109.
[8] There had been previous female visiting instructors in "Public Reading and Speaking," Mrs. A. B. Rudd (1934-1944) and Mrs. A. E. Barton (1945-1947); but they were not part of the full-time faculty.
[9] Faculty Minutes, April 11, 1962, p. 1, item #6, RGV4 Faculty, Virginia Theological Seminary Archives, Bishop Payne Library, Alexandria, VA.
[10] Attachment: "Information Sheet."

schools. Approaching the first church by which she had been hired to be on staff after graduation, Glover was met  on the sidewalk by a contingent of approximately five older women. The first words out of their mouths were "we don't want you here." But it was not only women who denigrated female graduates from schools of theological studies. Many male clergy were just as antagonistic: At a weekend conference held at Chautauqua, New York, Glover was seated across the table at lunch from a priest who persisted in calling her "Doris." "Why are you calling me Doris?" asked Glover. "You know my name." He replied, "Oh, you Christian educated women are all the same. I know one who is Doris, therefore that'll be the name for all of you."[11]

Joyce Glover

To be categorized at all, particularly with the barbed insinuation that one's category is a nuisance, is at the very least demeaning. But it is also illustrative of the tendency to label as trouble-makers individuals who would seek to serve the Church in new ways, ways that do not conform to established patterns. In the mid-twentieth century professional women church workers could credibly claim with the author of Ecclesiastes, "In much wisdom is much grief; and he that increases knowledge increases sorrow."[12] Drop by slow drop comes wisdom by the awful grace of God.

Meanwhile the triennial meeting of the Woman's Auxiliary continued to petition the General Convention to eliminate the distinction between lay men and lay women. While their petitions were denied, the Convention gratefully accepted millions of dollars the women raised each triennial. The contributions of women to the work of the Church were not considered lay ministry. They were auxiliary. They had no committees or commissions. They were merely adjunct to the functioning boards of the Church. The men made all the decisions, and the women made all the coffee.

As can be seen in the case of Marion Kelleran, gradually women began to be appointed to commissions and committees that met *between* General Conventions; and in 1958 the Woman's Auxiliary changed its name to the General Division of Women's Work of the National Council and encouraged parish members to change their names to the Episcopal Church Women.[13] Note the language: No longer was a woma_n_'s place auxiliary, but rather wom_e_n were organizing as a group.

The *Virginia Seminary Journal* of March 1960 reported on the visit to the campus of Virginia Theological Seminary by the Executive Officers of the National Council on January 13-14: "Miss Francis [sic] Young, new to the National Council staff in December, is now Executive Director of Women's Work. In a good-natured way she chided the seminarians to treat women as people. She said that women are no longer just an Auxiliary to the Church. Women want to be treated as wives, teachers, professionals and not just cooks! 'It's time for women to stop selling cakes to one another and assume their role as part of the active lay ministry,' she asserted."[14]

[11] Interview with Joyce Glover, March 23, 2010.
[12] 1:18
[13] Darling, 87.
[14] *Virginia Seminary Journal,* March 1960, p. 14. Frances Young was a Windham House graduate.

The following December an article in the *Journal* mentioned seminarians' wives as able to take courses at the Seminary: "Many wives have already earned a variety of academic degrees, including the Bachelor in Divinity,"[15] wrote the president of the student wives' group. "Beginning this fall there is a study program planned over a three year span....This Christian study is by no means aimed to make the women assistant ministers, but rather to give the wives an opportunity to become better informed laywomen...."[16] It should be noted that any wife possessed of a Bachelor in Divinity had not earned it at Virginia Seminary.

The Faculty Minutes of Feb. 1, 1961, demonstrate both that inroads were being made by women seeking theological education and that old habits die hard: "The Dean reported on a meeting of the Joint Commission on Theological Education and on the meeting of Seminary Deans. A new and smaller Joint Commission will be appointed. A new division of Theological Education will be created which will have to do with the Seminaries, the training of women workers, continuing education and refresher courses, and with the financing and cost of Theological Education. The Dean fears that there may be a trend toward making this division of Theological Education a regulatory body....Marian Smallegan was recommended to the Rev. Philip Zabriskie as having had a good record while a student here at the Seminary."[17] "A request from the Wives' Group for a different course

Marian Smallegan & Class of '59

[15] p. 10.
[16] p. 11.
[17] p. 1.

next fall was discussed. Mr. Harvey was commissioned to ask Marion Kelleran to lead a study course for them on Christian Education."[18] At this point Marion Kelleran was a visiting instructor at VTS, only present on campus one day per week.

As can be seen by the reference to Marian Smallegan in the minutes of 1961, at about this time one or two women, apart from wives of students, were receiving some form of theological education at VTS. Records in the archives of Virginia Seminary indicate that a Miss Lily Kester was a part-time student at VTS from 1955-57, and that a Miss Floramae Hellwig audited courses from 1958-59. However, Marian Joyce Smallegan, A. B., M.A., was the first female full-time student to attend VTS. She received a Certificate of Work Accomplished, not a Bachelor in Divinity, in 1959 and is listed in the '58-59 & '59-60 Catalogues. On October 24, 1989, Marian Smallegan received an honorary Doctor in Divinity from Virginia Theological Seminary.

The career of Mary Lou Eaton at Virginia Seminary illustrates the transition that occurred at the Seminary in the 1960's. The Faculty Minutes of Sept. 6, 1962, report the following: "Mary Lou Eaton Titus – St. Agnes teacher wants to take OT.1 and NT.1.[19] She is to be accepted as a special student."[20] Nothing further is recorded in the minutes pertaining to this student until Sept. 7, 1967: "Mary Lou Eaton, who is in this program [the Master of Arts in Religion], will be an advanced student and complete the degree in one year [meaning with only one year's residence]"[21] because she took courses while a teacher at St. Agnes and during the summer of 1965

Mary Lou Eaton

worked at Union, NYC, accumulating the equivalent of a year's graduate work. And on Dec. 6, 1967: "Mary Lou Eaton Mary Lou will be the first graduate in our M.A.R. program. St. Stephen's School in Austin needs a Dean of Girls and an instructor in Sacred Studies. The Dean has talked with Mary Lou about this possibility but she is interested in a job which would involve more teaching and less administration. The Dean asked members of the faculty to keep their ears open for possibilities."[22] On Sept. 5, 1968: "M.A.R. (Mary Lou Eaton) The Dean called attention to the fact that Miss Mary Lou Eaton, our first M.A.R. alumna, does not yet have a job. The faculty was asked to let the Dean know of any possibilities of work for her that may come to their attention. He noted that the important thing in this connection is that we will have M.A.R. graduates who will be without a bishop to sponsor them and we may have to assume some responsibility of seeing to it that they secure jobs when they graduate."[23] Her letter of 1984 asking that a transcript be sent to St. Agnes School reports that she received a Master in Theological Studies degree in 1968. Could the shift from hesitant acceptance of the presence of women in the classroom to forthright promotion of

[18] p. 2.
[19] "OT. 1" was the introductory Old Testament course; "NT. 1," introductory New Testament.
[20] p. 2.
[21] p. 2.
[22] p. 5.
[23] p. 2.

their gifts at graduation be characterized as grace in motion? How did such a conversion come about?

In the Faculty Minutes of March 6/10, 1963, we read the following: "Miss Dorothy Stout. An English teacher in St. Margaret's School, Tokyo, Ken Heim has recommended that she audit courses here next year. Mr. Harvey read portions of her letter. It was the consensus of the meeting that there would be no objection to her auditing whatever courses she might be able to take. Mr. Price said that he would be glad to have her in ST 20."[24]

Phyllis Ingram

The 1963-64 Catalogue lists Dorothy Stout from Tokyo as a special student.

Then Phyllis Ingram applied for admission to the Bachelor in Divinity program as a full time student. A March 25, 1963, letter from Acting Dean T. Hudnall Harvey to the Rev. Michael A. Lynch reads, "While Mrs. Ingram is the first woman student to be accepted for the three-year program, I do not believe we should give this fact any publicity. It was necessary to secure special permission from the Board of Trustees for her to be enrolled. In giving this permission, the Board made it plain that her case was an individual exception and it has not yet thrown the doors open for any general applications from women. Any publicity relating to her acceptance here should be limited to a personal note about her own career in the local paper or parish bulletin."[25]

"Not [throwing] the doors open for any general applications from women" could better be understood by placing such a comment in the context of the Church at large and the society in general. Seminaries of the Church, like the oldest and best colleges many of which were founded for the purpose of educating clergy, were male bastions. For example, the Right Reverend Philip A. Smith (VTS '49, B.D.) and Dr. Raymond F. Glover (VTS '86, D.H.L) served as members of the faculty of VTS: Smith, from 1959-1970; Glover, from 1991-2000. Both speak of the unexamined privilege of growing up male in the Church. Both were choristers in all-male choirs, and both served as acolytes when girls were not allowed to do so. The cathedral in which Dr. Glover sang as a young boy also provided girls with a choir, though not with the same amount of training. Dr. Glover comments, "It was a male world and that is the world in which some of us were trained. That was the environment in which we grew. I, tragically, never questioned it; but now, of course, I would say, 'This is wrong.' The cultures in which we grew up were so different for boys and for girls."[26] However, both Bishop Smith and Dr. Glover encountered individuals who were the means of personal change and grace. Dr. Glover was sensitized over a long period of time by his

Raymond Glover

[24] p. 3. "ST" stands for "Systematic Theology."
[25] Letter from T. Hudnall Harvey to Michael A. Lynch, Faculty Minutes, R.G. V4, Virginia Theological Seminary Archives, Bishop Payne Library, Alexandria, Virginia
[26] Interview with Dr. Raymond Glover, March 23, 2010.

wife Joyce and, later, by articulate women who served with him on the Standing Commission on Church Music to produce *The Hymnal 1982* with its more inclusive language. Thus, change in the Church continued to come slowly.

On Dec. 4, 1963, the following item appears in the Faculty Minutes of VTS: "WOMEN STUDENTS. The Dean announced that word has got around that we are now taking women students and that the Chaplain of Sweet Briar has asked if he may suggest that graduates consider the possibility of coming to the seminary. The Dean asked what recommendation he should bring to the Board on this subject.

"There was a general discussion of the problem of training women for jobs in the Church. Mrs. Kelleran pointed out that our training schools for women will probably not continue in operation too much longer. She also noted the fact that clergy have difficulty working with women and often especially so if they have been students together in seminary. She also said that the chief need was for preparing women to work as Directors of Christian Education, which means that they must have an opportunity to do extensive work in the field of education. She recommended that before we take any further steps in developing a program for women, we talk with Mr. Kennedy at Union Seminary, New York, and with John Coburn [at that time, Dean of Episcopal Theological School].

"Consensus: We should continue our present policy of not encouraging women students but of making exceptions in special cases."[27] Apparently the Seminary did not feel adequately equipped to train people for careers in Christian Education and did not seriously consider the idea that women might want a seminary education for other purposes.

A "special case" was promptly made on Jan. 22, 1964: "Marjorie Leahy – She has been auditing courses for six years. Since the death of her husband she has been talking with Bishop Gibson and Mr. Bitsberger about overseas work.…A positive recommendation for work overseas. She is thoughtful and considerate and has done well in her work in parishes."[28]

Clearly the Seminary was teetering on the brink of something new, but they were moving two steps forward, then one step back; and the forces swirling about in the culture at large contributed to their unease.

The Feminine Mystique, authored by Betty Friedan, was published February 25, 1963, and the birth control pill became available that same year. 1964 saw other evidences of cultural revolution: The New York World's Fair introduced the touch tone telephone and the Ford Mustang, and the General Convention added the order of deaconess to the orders of ministry in the Church. 1964 also saw the beginning of some dioceses' permitting women to serve on vestries and as delegates to diocesan conventions.

The December 1964 *Journal* contains a record of the address delivered by VTS Associate Professor of Pastoral Theology and Christian Education Mrs. Harold C. Kelleran to the Triennial meeting of the Women of the Church on October 13, 1964, entitled "Women in Church and Society": "…training schools for women church workers…have recruiting problems…the dominant image is the romantic dream of husband and children."[29] "…the feminist movement [has gone into] decline…the life of feminism was strongest *when men and*

[27] p. 4.
[28] p. 1.
[29] p. 25.

women worked together on other social reform movements.… Parallel organizations for men and women remain the parish pattern in most places."[30] "When governments whether of state or church, have one sex—either one—making their laws and decisions, one may wonder about their appropriation of the principle of equality in one case, and of the doctrine of creation in the other.…This recommendation [of the report from the Joint Commission on the Structure of General Convention and Provinces] if adopted would *open the way* for the election of women as deputies to the Convention…[which was defeated] the last four conventions."[31] [emphases theirs].

But even at the Seminary, the issue of accepting women students was not resolved. The March 10, 1965, Faculty Minutes contain the following debate: "Admission of Women. The Dean announced that we are receiving applications for admission from women just out of college. If we admit them it will cut down the number of men since we have a ceiling on admissions of 65. On the other hand, it is possible that they would have much to contribute if they were to become teachers in secondary schools. He proposed that we might keep our ceiling of 65 on men and have a different program leading to the B.D.[32] with only minor differences for 4 or 5 women.

"Moved by Dr. Mollegen, seconded by Dr. Woolverton that we keep the ceiling of 65 on men and take in up to 5 women each year for a special program leading to a B.D.

"Discussion. There was a lengthy discussion of this proposal in which it was pointed out that the training schools for women are gradually being closed. Mrs. Kelleran pointed out, however, that if women were going

to teach they should probably have a different program from the one we are able to offer. The question of the increasing size of the class was also raised. Our previous decision to limit the class was based on an awareness of the fact that there is a kind of breaking point at 65, and that increases above this make it difficult to have the kind of relationship with students we would like to have.

"It was suggested that we might need extra help for such a program. Also, that we might consider the possibility of offering a different degree for women such as an M.A. It was pointed out that the B.D. now offers the possibility for teaching in some colleges. It was also suggested that we ought to get opinions from alumni who are teaching in secondary schools and further information from people like Dean Coburn and the heads of the women's training schools.

"The following amendment was offered by Mr. Pisani, seconded by Dr. Reid that the motion made by Dr. Mollegen will apply only to the current year and that we will review the question next year.

"The motion passed as amended. It was moved by Mrs. Kelleran, seconded by Dr. Booty that we refer this whole matter to the Curriculum Committee for study."[33]

The March 1965 *Journal* printed the February 18, 1965, Faculty Night Talk, "Idiolect and the Dictionary," by Marion M. Kelleran. Here it is important to realize that the rules of etiquette required that a widow be referred to as "Mrs. Harold C. Kelleran"; a divorced woman, as "Mrs. Marion M. Kelleran." In both cases, "Mrs." was required. Mrs. Harold C. Kelleran was a widow. To be recognized as her own person, simply Marion M. Kelleran, is a seismic shift in identity; but

[30] p. 26.
[31] p. 33.
[32] "B.D." stands for Bachelor in Divinity.
[33] pp. 3-4.

without any recorded evidence, it is difficult to know whether that change was due to cultural usage or an awakening on the part of the Seminary's *Journal* editor.

Faculty debate on the admission of women students continued. The Faculty Minutes of May 14-15, 1965, read as follows: "QUESTIONS REGARDING THE WOMEN'S TRAINING CENTERS (WIND-HAM HOUSE AND ST. MARGARET'S HOUSE): In response to what need did these centers come into being? Has this need changed? How are they constituted, staffed, financed? How many students are preparing at present to do what? What is the relationship of these students, if any, to their bishops? What standards govern the acceptance of these students? What standards, if any describe or govern their conditions of employment after graduation? What is the current demand in the church for trained and theologically educated women? Is the current supply greater or less than the need?

> How many of our accredited seminaries are open to women as regular students? How many such students are there, and in which seminaries? How many women students are enrolled in other than Episcopal Church seminaries? Where? How are women students in training center or seminary financed? What are the figures regarding the demand and supply of Deconesses? Where are they trained and educated? Where do they work? (Note: An extensive study is now in progress on the training and employment of women in professional positions in the church. Findings are expected to be published in December, 1965.)"[34]

St. Margaret's House was to close in 1966; Windham House, in 1967.

On Sept. 13, 1965, Bishop James Pike invested deaconess Phyllis Edwards with a deacon's stole and copy of the Gospels, recognizing her ministry as belonging to the order of deacons and precipitating the first crisis over women's ordination in the Episcopal Church. Pike came close to being tried for heresy, but he was prescient: The Lambeth Conference of 1968 recognized deaconesses as deacons.

It would not be until 1969 that barriers would be breached in the society at large. Yale and Princeton admitted women students for the first time that year, followed by Harvard in 1970. Columbia University waited until 1983 to admit women to its class of 1987. The loss to young women of even the possibility of applying to the best schools in the nation, to learn from the most pre-eminent scholars, to exchange perceptions with those who would control access to the corridors of power that determined the decisions of General Convention 1973 and 1976 and their world of ideas, politics, economics, and the Church is incalculable.

Meanwhile at the Seminary, Phyllis Ingram had been joined by Alison Cheek in applying for admission to the Bachelor in Divinity program at Virginia Theological Seminary for the Fall term of 1963. Thus, it is to the increasing enrollment of degree-seeking women students that we now turn.

[34] p. 4.

GRACE
in Motion

CHAPTER TWO

"My grace is sufficient for you, for my power
is made perfect in weakness."

2 Corinthians 12:9
Revised Standard Version

It could be said that we know grace immediately only in the sacraments, those outward and visible signs of inward and spiritual grace. For if grace is always in motion, yet seldom perceived, it must be in part because grace most often moves slowly, slowly. We detect the working of grace in our lives, if at all, by looking back on events from a distance in order to pull together occurrences that are seemingly disparate. For all the while God's power is working His/Her purposes out, though we with our finite knowledge cannot see the whole picture. Our weakness is supplemented by God's grace, empowering the purposes of God.

Three themes or common threads present themselves when we consider the stories of the first women ordained. First, there were those to whom came slow revelations, gradual perceptions of grace-filled moments, moments when one could say, "Yes, that is who I am," "yes" to opportunities or choices that may have been either easy or difficulty. Second, and rarer, were instant, life-changing occurrences: voices, appearances, serendipitous moments. Third, some had doors of blessing opened to them by mentors, had connections with people of importance in the Church, had legacies of entry that enabled them to be in the right place at the right time. Sometimes women reported two out of the three instances of grace, as if a second and very different example of call verified the first. Seldom, if ever, did they recount all three.

— The Advent of Women Students —

Although Bishop Payne Divinity School in Petersburg, Virginia, had established a degree-granting Department of Christian Education in 1945, had graduated women students from that program as early as 1947, 1948, 1949, and merged with Virginia Theological Seminary in 1953, the Alexandria campus moved more slowly toward the admission of women students.

Alison Cheek perceived grace calling her down the path that eventually led to ordination as a very long, slow process. As a parishioner at St. Alban's, Annandale, VA, she found herself increasingly asked to lead programs and projects undertaken by the women of the church. Because she consulted her rector about the growing number of discussions she was being asked to moderate, her rector suggested that she ask if she could take some courses at the Seminary. After a conversation with the secretary for admissions who indicated that she might be able to take a class, depending on the number of men who had signed up for it, Mrs. Cheek went back to her rector and said, "I would like to take some courses at the Seminary, but I would like to take them for credit." He said nothing, walked behind his desk to the telephone, dialed a number, and said, "Jess, I've got a parishioner who would like to come to Seminary." Then he grinned and said, "Well, Jess, I think I ought to tell you it's a woman." To his surprise Dean Trotter replied, "Oh, good! We have just been to the Board of Trustees to ask for an exception to the bylaws in order to admit the first woman for the B.D. degree, and it would be nice if she had some company."[1]

Bishop Gibson of Virginia indicated that he would sponsor Cheek for a year if she went through the same admission steps required of the men. Cheek admits that she filled out some forms with tongue in cheek: Number nine on her list of the ten books more recently read was "Mike Mulligan and His Steam Shovel" because she had to read that to her five-year-old every night to get her to bed. Her answer to "What journals do you read?" was *Good Housekeeping*. Nevertheless, she was admitted as a part-time student for the Fall term of 1963.

Her classmate, Phyllis Ingram, had a very strong

[1] Interview with Alison Cheek, May 13-16, 2010.

call to ordination and knew that was the direction she was headed even before entering Seminary. Alison Cheek, on the other hand, was not interested in ordination when she started studies at VTS. She comments, "I just wanted to get my theology into some kind of focus, and it took

Phyllis Ingram

Phyllis a little while to warm up to me because…she had this namby-pamby housewife as her classmate. It took my having to do better than she in a few classes for her to get over that [impression]. We became the best of friends and were right up until the time she died [in 1987]. I felt that I owed a lot to her because she was so adamant with the men, and she was feisty and would go to bat…."

The slow progress of grace came to a startling conclusion for Alison Cheek on retreat at the convent in Catonsville: "I don't talk about this normally, but I was there and I was lying on the bed in my little room. I had gotten very relaxed, almost in an auto-state of consciousness. I was praying, and I asked God what I was to do with my theological education; and this deep inner voice came back saying, 'I want you to be my priest,' and it scared the living daylights out of me. I went home and never told anybody, never talked about it, never told my husband ever. I thought everybody would think I was mad. I couldn't be ordained anyway, a priest, so I just put it aside and plodded on with my course. Then about a year or so later it came back to haunt me…so I set up a

meeting with Bishop Gibson."

The bishop was coming to northern Virginia for a confirmation and agreed to meet Cheek after the service. However, the place he picked for their meeting was not the rector's office but a Sunday school classroom filled only with tiny children's chairs. Squatting on the tiny chairs in the posture the bishop had chosen for the interview and reluctant to say anything about the inner voice she had heard, Cheek hesitantly stated her belief that she had a call to the priesthood. Gibson was not receptive and finished the interview by saying, "I don't think you know what you want." Cheek felt humiliated but also vastly relieved. Because she had four children at home, the youngest just starting kindergarten in 1963, Alison Cheek took six years to obtain her Bachelor in Divinity degree. On May 24, 1967, the Board of Trustees officially designated her a tutor on the faculty while she was still a student.[2] She taught Hebrew and Greek and is pictured in the December 1967 *Seminary Journal* in a photograph entitled "Virginia Seminary Faculty 1967-68" as well as among the faculty in the 1968-69 *Catalogue*. There were three other visiting teachers in 1967, but they are not pictured.

Meanwhile, her classmate Phyllis Ingram was about to become the first woman to receive a Bachelor in Divinity degree from Virginia Theological Seminary, graduating *cum laude* on May 26, 1966. But some startling evidences of grace were in the offing.

The Faculty Minutes of Feb. 16, 1966, read: "Phyllis Ingram Her son has one more year at St. Stephen's. She would like to stay on for a S.T.M.[3] in Biblical Studies. Her request was referred to Dr. Mollegen and Dr. Reid."[4] Then, without any forewarning comes a sur-

---

[2] Letter of May 26, 1967, from Jesse Trotter to Alison Cheek.
[3] "S.T.M." stands for Master in Sacred Theology.
[4] p. 1.

prising development: Faculty Minutes, March 16, 1966, "Phyllis Ingram – It was moved by Dr. Stanley, seconded by Dr. Rodgers that we recommend Phyllis Ingram for ordination. This motion failed 5-6.

"It was moved by Dr. Mollegen and seconded that in the event that Phyllis Ingram is accepted as a postulant for Holy Orders we certify to her personal, spiritual and academic qualifications for ordination. This motion carried with two dissents."[5]

The only allusion in seminary documents to the idea that women's ordination was a subject of discussion is in a March 1966 *Journal* article containing a Faculty Night Talk by Richard Reid, "How to be a Minister's Wife's Husband," in which Reid states, "I am not arguing here against the ordination of women. That is a separate topic which will have to be faced on its own merits."[6] While conversations with men who were seniors the year Phyllis Ingram entered seminary reveal no awareness on their part of the subject of women's ordination, Professor Emeritus Murray Newman recalls informal conversations on the topic amongst the faculty and remembers that the faculty were virtually unanimous in their support for women's ordination.[7] The

Richard Reid

Bishop of Rochester, George Barrett, had been appointed by Presiding Bishop John Hines to head a Committee to Study the Proper Place of Women in the Ministry of the Church in 1965,[8] and that report would subsequently urge the House of Bishops to take up the subject of women's ordination to the priesthood. So Professors Stanley, Rogers, and Mollegen were at the forefront of intellectual ferment on this subject.

The Faculty Minutes of May 13-14, 1966, note that Phyllis Ingram is to continue in the S.T.M. though the decision was made not to admit further S.T.M. candidates, male or female.[9]

Then on October 5, 1966, appears the following: "Phyllis Ingram The Dean reported that Phyllis plans to place her case for ordination before all the Bishops of the Church. He asked if the Seminary should not take some position in the matter of the ordination of women by a vote of faculty and perhaps Trustees.

"The action of the faculty from March 16, 1966 in which we certified to Phyllis' personal qualifications was read. It was pointed out, however, that the question of the ordination of women should be separated from any particular person.

"Dr. Mollegen commented that this is not the appropriate time to launch a campaign for the ordination of women. We have a chance of getting them [lay women as delegates] seated at General Convention next time. Dr. Kevin spoke of the ecumenical implications of this issue and urged that we support it independently of any individual involved.

"There was a further discussion of the strategy

[5] pp. 4-5.
[6] p. 31.
[7] Conversation June 8, 2010.
[8] Robert W. Prichard, A History of the Episcopal Church, (Wilton, CT: Morehouse Publishing, 1991), 255.
[9] p. 17. [Exceptions were made Jan. 4, '67.]

and whether this is the right time to take a stand. There was general agreement that there was no theological obstacle to the ordination of women.

"It was moved by Dr. Woolverton, seconded by Dr. Newman, that we declare that we see no theological objection to women in the ordained ministry of this Church and that we look forward to a time in the near future when women will be ordained. The vote on this motion was 15 yeas, 3 nos and 3 abstentions."[10]

The faculty would "look forward" for years before the ordination of women became a reality, and Phyllis Ingram despaired of waiting for that time. On Sept. 20, 1967, the Faculty Minutes record, "Phyllis Ingram has invited the faculty to attend her ordination to the ministry of the Congregational Christian Church, to be held in the Congregational Christian Church of Annandale, at 7:30 p.m., October 1, 1967."[11] In 1972 she applied to Andover Newton for a Doctor of Ministry degree.

That ambiguity about the place of women remained a factor on campus can be seen on both the part of the faculty in 1966 and in the *Catalogue* as late as 1969: On October 26, 1966, in a discussion of the decline in enrollment, the possibility of having an M.A. program was broached. "The Dean...commented on the problem of having women enrolled in such a program."[12] The "problem[s]" were logistical: Concerns were raised over issues of security and such mundane considerations as the lack of restroom facilities for women on campus.[13]

Nevertheless, planning for a new Master's degree program moved forward.

In the Nov. 23, 1966, Faculty Council meeting minutes, we read, "The Dean asked if we were to have such a program [an M.A.R.], would we not need a dorm for women students...perhaps making use of the top floor of Sparrow."[14] On Nov. 30, 1966, the Faculty meeting approved "the inauguration of a non-B.D. Graduate Program in Theological Studies."[15]

As the new year began, the Jan. 4, 1967, minutes note "Special Masters Program – The Secretary reported the action of the Faculty Council in establishing this program and stating that we would admit 60 students for the B.D. next year and no more than six for the newly instituted Masters Program."[16] On Feb. 15, 1967, one reads in the minutes, "M.A. in Religion This new program has been given the title as above and some publicity on it is ready to be mailed out."[17]

The Master of Arts in Religion began with the academic year 1967-1968, and both men and women were admitted to that program. The Faculty Minutes contain the following notation: Sept. 7, 1967 – "M.A.R. The Dean announced that Dr. Rightor (VTS '48) will be the advisor for these students."[18]

Planning for the next academic year began on May 1-3, 1968, with the following: "First there was a request from four women applicants who have been accepted for 1968-69 to live together in an apartment off

[10] pp. 2-3.
[11] p. 1.
[12] p. 3.
[13] Oct. 16, 1963, p. 2, Item #13 – "Ladies Room. Need for a ladies' room in Meade Hall." As late as 1979, men had to guard the outer doors of restrooms while the women went in because there were so few women's bathrooms on campus.
[14] pp. 2-3.
[15] p. p. 2.
[16] p. 6.
[17] p. 5. A description of the program for lay men and lay women can be found in the minutes of April 26, 1967.
[18] p. 2.

1967-1968 female M.A.R. students

campus....The Committee had decided that educationally this was acceptable but that financially the decision should be left to the administration and trustees to decide.... Dr. Stanley felt that the request from M.A.R. students to live off campus, should it be decided favorably by the administration and the Trustees, should include a letter from the Dean to parents of M.A.R. students stating that we were permitting them to live off campus but not encouraging them to do so."[19] But on May 29, 1968, "The Board ruled that all single students must live on campus."[20] And when the new academic year began, the minutes of September 5, 1968, read, "[The Dean] noted that the M.A.R. program has more than two times as many students as last year. This number includes two married men and nine unmarried women and one unmarried man."[21]

An article, written in 1972, by one of the women who entered the M.A.R. program at Virginia Seminary in the Fall of 1968 gives more specifics: "There were eight women students in Virginia Seminary in September, 1968, the largest number ever to be there. Three were returning for their second year and five of us were starting our first year. Of that five, one dropped out after two months, two dropped out before graduation, and two of us graduated after two years with a Master's Degree in Religion."[22] The title of Elisa DesPortes' article gives an indication of why the attrition rate was so high: "Bye, Bye, Miss American Pie!" "Bye, Bye …" was a 1971 song by Don McLean which gave voice to the social upheaval of the '60's: "So bye-bye, miss American pie. Drove my chevy to the levee, But the levee was dry. And them good old boys were drinkin' whiskey and rye singin' this'll be the day that I die, this'll be the day that I die" went the refrain.[23] Put a milder way, all the traditional standards of behavior were being questioned.

Elisa DesPortes

The '50's had been an idyllic time, a time when everything was clear. Not so any longer: Two Roman Catholic priests, Daniel and Philip Berrigan, were arrested in 1968 for destroying Selective Service files in Catonsville, MD. A Workshop on Racial Tension and Justice occurred at the Seminary on March 11, 1968, and hous-

[19] pp. 13-14.
[20] p. 3.
[21] p. 1.
[22] The Virginia Seminary Journal, Fall 1972, p. 7.
[23] There has been endless debate about the deeper meaning of verses containing such phrases as "Do you have faith in God above? If the Bible tells you so…Can music save your mortal soul?…A generation lost in space…I saw Satan laughing…And all the church bells were broken…The three men I admire the most, the Father, Son, and Holy Ghost caught the last train for the Coast."

ing was provided for the Poor People's Campaign.[24] A March 20, 1968, attachment to the Faculty Minutes marked "For Discussion Only NOT FOR PUBLICATION" from the American Association of Theological Schools summarized changes in the world and Church to which seminaries must respond including the adequacy and relevancy of seminaries educating *men* for priesthood/ministry. [emphasis mine] Demonstrations against the Vietnam War were rampant across the country including male students of the Seminary chaining themselves to the gates of the Pentagon and having to be bailed out by Academic Dean Richard Reid.

Ms. DesPortes expressed what the women students were feeling in this way: "'What's a nice girl like you doing in a place like this?' That was the motto of the women entering Virginia Seminary in 1968. It was a catchy slogan, a joke, but it was not funny....Virginia Seminary was not an easy or particularly happy experience for me. In fact, it was one of the most difficult confrontations—sometimes subtle and sometimes not so subtle—I have ever had....Over the next two years I would ask myself in times of exasperation, 'What's happening to me? I am so uncomfortable with myself and I used to be so normal.'"[25]

What was "normal" for women was in flux. The Special General Convention in South Bend in 1969 "struck the word 'male' from the lay reader canon altogether, making women eligible to read lessons, lead certain nonsacramental services, and administer the chalice on the same terms as men."[26] The Rev. Henry H. Rightor, Associate Professor of Pastoral Theology at VTS, became a

Henry Rightor

member of the newly-formed Joint Commission of the General Convention on Ordained and Licensed Ministries as well as a member of the committee on the laity of the Executive Council. In both capacities, he led the way in strategies that would help prepare the way for the ordination of women. But one would still find in the *Seminary Journal* such comments as "An elderly alumnus gave it as his opinion, a while back, that the highest compliment a man could receive would be to have his son follow him in the ministry. He himself had four daughters."[27]

Alison Cheek graduated *cum laude* with a B.D. in 1969 and went to work as a lay minister at Christ Church, Alexandria. She recalls, "I was put in charge of the pastoral ministry and really enjoyed that. I would go to visit a lot of parishioners who were shut-ins, who were just so pleased to see you. I would say to them all, 'Would you

Alison Cheek

---

[24] Faculty Minutes, May 15, 1968, pp. 2-3, RGV4 Faculty, Virginia Theological Seminary Archives, Bishop Payne Library, Alexandria, VA.
[25] Ibid.
[26] Darling, pp. 103-104, referencing *Special Convention Journal 1969*, 182-83. A "Special" General Convention is a gathering called at a time other than the normal three-year cycle of General Convention meetings.
[27] *The Seminary Journal*, October 1968, p. 21.

like to have the sacrament brought?' And they would say, 'Oh! Can you do that?' I would answer, 'No, I can't, but either of the men would be very willing to do it.' 'Oh, that's all right....'" would be the response. Cheek was allowed to preach three times in the two years she was at Christ Church. She began training with the Pastoral Counseling and Consulting Centers of greater Washington, the Washington Institute for Pastoral Psychotherapy, left Christ Church, and did Sunday work at her own parish, St. Alban's in Annandale, VA.

But ambivalence about the place of women in ministry remained in some quarters as can be seen in the 1969-70 *Catalogue* article entitled "Team Ministry": "A team ministry in today's idiom implies a partnership of two ordained ministers who, working together in a parish situation, have special areas of emphasis and interest. Still another use of the term is customary at the Virginia Seminary. Here the phrase describes a 'husband-wife' partnership; and this kind of team ministry spans the three years of a theological education. In this, the excitement of preparation for a life vocation is shared. The *girl* partner usually picks up a bit of theology just by listening, interacting, by sharing in formal wives' groups, or simply by being married. But the role of being a wife-member of such a team is greater than the opportunity to accumulate a bit of theology or biblical learning. The *girl* is the encourager. She is very often the breadwinner. She is often a mother. And most of all she is *queen* of a household."[28] [emphases mine] Certainly, the spouses of students deserved, and still deserve, encouragement in what is a trying three years. But what was "customary" at Virginia Seminary, and in the rest of the Episcopal Church, as revealed by language was that women were still subordinated.

The same catalogue has an article entitled "Mas-

ter's Program in Religion" by Miss Janis Moulton. The M.A.R. is now in its third year. She writes, "Some may return to careers in business and public affairs. Others will teach, or manage hardware stores, or join the staff of a daily newspaper. They'll be technologists, sociologists, directors of religious education. Some may try the Peace Corps or decide to add a year of Seminary education and head into the ordained ministry. For the lay men and women enrolled in the Master of Arts in Religion Program at Virginia Seminary, the choice of vocation is as wide as the Twentieth-Century world in which they live. Here is the program in which a *man* [emphasis mine] can test himself against the vocational ministry." Why the author did not say "a man or woman" can only be attributed to the unconscious assumption that women, by virtue of their gender, could not test a vocation to ordained ministry.

The Faculty Minutes of May 7, 1969, record the following discussion: "It was suggested that we might invite the M.A.R. *girls* to come to the Millwood meeting to discuss the problems of life in the dormitories. It was moved by Mr. Rightor, seconded by Dr. Newman, that we invite the M.A.R. *girls* to our Millwood Conference on Saturday morning....An amendment to the motion was offered that we invite the *girls* to come to the regular faculty meeting on Wednesday, May 14. The amended motion carried."[29] [emphases mine]

Elisa DesPortes discusses the problems of life in the dormitories referred to in the Faculty Minutes: "We were housed in a guest dorm called Moore Hall on the second floor. There were single rooms and one communal bath with urinals down one side and two showers. There was no bath tub. Every time I went to pee, I saw a wall of urinals, and I was reminded that I did not fit in. It felt

28 p. 26.
29 p. 3.

like I was in the men's room. I am not sure I had even seen a urinal before this time. Moore Hall was locked by the guest hostess at night; but there were no locks on the floors, and anyone could walk in or out at any time. There was no privacy. I felt like I was in a fish bowl and had no place to go to regroup or get away. There was no safe place....Male students came and went in Moore Hall and watched us through binoculars from the opposite dorm. The atmosphere on campus was very tense....The women's faculty advisor was Henry Rightor....He quoted to us a study when Radcliff integrated with Harvard. The study said that anything less than ¼ integration of a minority was 'emotional brutalization'....Even with this tension among the students there were romantic attachments that developed. Some ended up in marriage. I remember well walking to lunch one day with a professor who told me that the only reason I came to seminary was 'to catch a man.' This made me angry because I had no interest in being a clergy wife....In the Spring of my first year, 1969, all of us women students organized together and as a group went to see Philip Smith, the chaplain. We were at the boiling point. There was a lot of anger in that room. We let him have it, and bitterly complained about many things. What I remember most was the discussion of the living conditions. We had no privacy, no security, and we hated the urinals and wanted a bath tub. All of the sud-

Henry Rightor

den Phil became very animated. He said that Barbara (his wife) would never have put up with no bath tub. He got it! When we came back in the Fall of 1969, we were housed on the top floor of Sparrow, away from the men; and the door had a dead bolt lock for security. The bathroom had been completely redone with feminine vanities and a bathtub, besides showers. VTS was trying very hard. This made life on campus much more pleasant. My second year at VTS did not have the tension that the first year had."[30]

A number of women started theological studies in the M.A.R. program, then switched to the B.D. Among them was Nancy Hatch Wittig. Nancy Hatch entered the M.A.R. program along with Elizabeth (Betty) Powell Rosenberg in 1969, joining Elisa DesPortes and Nancy Wicks who were in their second year. These four were the only women students that year.

Nancy Hatch

Elisa DesPortes graduated with an M.A.R. in 1970 and, a month later, went to work on a research project with Loren Mead (VTS '55) and other clergymen fifteen to twenty years her senior. Project Test Pattern pioneered programs of parish renewal and church growth. DesPortes also served on the admissions committee of Inter-met, the urban seminary founded by John C. Fletcher (VTS '56). She married in 1973 and moved to New Haven, CT. She recalls, "That Fall I got a letter from an elder retired statesman who was in the VTS administration. He congratulated me on my marriage and stated that if I would like, he could intro-

[30] Written reflections from Elisa DesPortes Wheeler, Nov. 8, 2010.

duce me to some law firms where I might get a job as a secretary. I wrote him back that VTS did not teach me to type."

Nancy Hatch's sense of call had developed slowly through the years, and only in retrospect did she perceive where she was headed. While holding church for her teddy bears, wearing her father's stiff Navy collar backwards, when she was just a little child might have been the start of her religious imagination, it was living overseas for most of her growing up years with the Church as her constant that grounded her and helped her deal with the disruption of moving. Some of the churches this military family attended were without denominational affiliation, but that fact gave Hatch the sense that the Church was everywhere and always there for her. Returning to the family farm outside Leesburg, VA, Hatch found support and a model for ministry in the rector of the local Episcopal parish, Frank Moss, who was her mentor unaware. Finishing her last two years of college at Chapel Hill, she encountered a rector who had been threatened during the eruption of civil rights integration and lived through antiwar demonstrations. Pictures of clergy men and women religious on the front lines of civil rights caused her to think, "Yes, that's where the Church needs to be. The Church needs to be out in the highways and byways taking risks."[31]

As a child Elizabeth (Betty) Powell Rosenberg[32] was "always in touch with another level of being."[33] In college at Chapel Hill, North Carolina, she approached the rector of the Episcopal parish and asked his advice about books she might read pertaining to the search she was on. A year later, she was back in his office, talking to him about seminary.

She recalls, "One night, I woke up in the middle of the night, hearing my name; and I thought, 'Yeah, right, I am hearing my name. Like Samuel, you're right, you know. Like go back to sleep.' It happened again: 'You know, if this is really You, You are going to have to do it three times to convince me.' So, yes, there was a third time, and it hit me so hard I don't even remember making the decision; but I just rolled out of the bed onto my knees beside the bed. It was like, 'Okay. Here am I. What is it? Where am I going? Tell me.' It had something to do with seminary. It wasn't really clear exactly what yet...."

Several of the young men from the Episcopal parish at Chapel Hill were planning to attend a ministry weekend at VTS. Rosenberg had written VTS to say that she would like to attend that ministry weekend, and the Seminary had written back to say they could pay more attention to her if she came at another time when they could talk about the Master's program available to women. The men departed for VTS. Rosenberg "woke up in the middle of the night, and I could not stand it. I packed up and left at four in the morning and drove to Virginia Seminary. It was daylight by the time I got there. They were all [in Scott Lounge]. That's where I found my guys, and they were so welcoming. Well, they were a little shocked, but they were also very welcoming. I got to meet Phil Smith almost immediately. He was the chaplain at the time. He was a little miffed. He wasn't quite sure what to do with me, and he tried to come up with something I could do while *they* were having their meetings."

In the Spring of 1969 as part of her interview process, Rosenberg met Elisa DesPortes and remembers her counseling not coming to Virginia Seminary: "The phrase she used about how horrific the experience was was

---

[31] Interview, May 18, 2010.
[32] In August of 1991, Elizabeth Powell Rosenberg legally changed her name to Betty Powell.
[33] Interview of Betty Powell by Jennifer Andrews-Weckerly, April 7, 2011.

'emotional brutalization.' Later on after I had a lot of awful experiences, I began to see it as...spiritual brutalization." Among those experiences were men at the microphone in the refectory taking "Jimmy the Greek odds [on which] guys were going to get me"; a sketch distributed in liturgics practicum of a partially naked woman with the words "would you like to commune with her"; a total boycott on the part of the men of her liturgics section on the day on which she was to practice celebrating communion; a tea for the wives of seminarians to which the women students were invited and at which Rosenberg was accused of trying to steal the husband of one of the wives. Weak in the face of brute power, her strength would come from beyond herself.

At the May 27, 1970 Board of Trustees meeting, Mr. Thomas had discussed the possibility of the election of a woman to the Board.[34] The following Fall the Executive Committee, acting as the Nominating Committee, brought the name of Mrs. Theodore O. (Cynthia) Wedel. In 1952 Cynthia Wedel had become the first woman to address a joint session of the General Convention.[35] From 1955 to 1961, she was President of the ECW of the Diocese of Washington and one of four women members of the Executive Council of the Episcopal Church. From 1961 to 1963, along with fellow Episcopalian Eleanor Roosevelt, she was a member of the Presidential Commission on the Status of Women. From 1969 to 1972 she served as the first female President of the National Council of Churches and later headed the World Council of Churches. She was elected to the Board of Virginia Seminary on November 11, 1970, and served as a Trustee at Large from 1970 to 1975. While the name of a Mrs. Ellason Downs appears as a member of the Building and

Cynthia Wedel

Grounds Committee of the Board from 1957 to 1968, Cynthia Wedel was the first woman elected to the Board of VTS.

The Faculty Minutes of Nov. 18, 1970, reflect the additional action by the Board of Trustees that Fall to change the Bachelor in Divinity degree to Master in Divinity and the Master of Arts in Religion to Master in Theological Studies.

The 1970 General Convention had seen women seated as lay deputies for the first time and removed all distinctions between women and men as deacons, arguing—as Henry Rightor had repeatedly pointed out—that the language of the canons was gender inclusive and that no constitutional change was necessary. Moreover, the Triennial Meeting of the Women of the Church voted 222 to 45 for the ordination of women to the priesthood and episcopacy.[36] When women were allowed to be deacons by the Houston General Convention of 1970 but to go no farther, Mrs. Mollegen brought all kinds of sweets and fruit in a big paper bag, telling the women of Sparrow Hall, "I just want you all to know that it is going to change." It was then that Nancy Hatch discovered that Mrs. Mollegen was one of several women who had gone to [Union] seminary during WW II and ended up marrying clergymen, as had Cynthia Wedel.

[34] p. 12.
[35] *Journal of the General Convention of the Protestant Episcopal Church in the United States of America, Joint Session, Wednesday, September 10, 1952, p. 140.*
[36] *The Seminary Journal*, Fall 1972, p. 6.

Nancy Hatch and Elizabeth Rosenberg (Betty Powell) switched from the M.A.R./M.T.S. to the B.D./M.Div. program the second year they were at VTS, the Fall of 1970. Alison Cheek, meanwhile, had been an examiner for the canonical exams of the Diocese of Virginia. She reports that she wasn't worrying about ordination because she was growing and stretching through her work with the pastoral counseling centers. It was her rector, John Frizzell, who said to her one day, "Alison, we have got to get you ordained." So Alison Cheek and Nancy Hatch went through BACAM[37] together, becoming fast friends after that meeting.

Nancy Hatch recounts, "Some of the men [the BACAM examiners] behaved very poorly...." Alison Cheek recalls that the examiners "were awful to [Nancy] because she was going to marry a man who was training to become a Methodist minister. Heretic—she was a heretic to marry a Methodist." Hatch remembers, "One of the tragedies was that the psychiatrist for the Diocese of Virginia was there and not too much later went off and committed suicide. Part of the legend was that we [women] had caused that." Hatch found mentors for her slow but steady journey in the examples of Lee Tim Oi[38] and the deaconesses of West Virginia and Appalachia who ministered in remote villages.[39] Cheek, on the other hand, found such mentors as Sheldon Kopp and others of her colleagues in her psychotherapy practice.

Debates about the viability of having women students continued. On January 8, 1971, one reads in the Faculty Minutes, "Security on Campus – [The Dean] pointed out that the guard is needed, at least in part, because we have women students but that there is only a very small number of women. Perhaps it would be wiser to discontinue accepting women students. It was suggested that we might continue to enroll them but to ask them to live off campus."[40] And on February 17, 1971, "There was further discussion about the wisdom of having women students and requiring them to live in dormitories which seems to impose a burden on them. It was suggested that we might try to build up the number of women students."[41]

Even so, the faculty of Virginia Seminary had just voted at its meeting of February 3, 1971,[42] to recommend Alison Cheek for ordination to the diaconate.[43] The Faculty Minutes of January 19, 1972, record a milestone: "The Dean read an invitation to the faculty to attend the ordination to the diaconate of Alison Cheek which will be held on January 29th at St. Alban's Church. It was pointed out that Mrs. Cheek will be the first woman in the Diocese of Virginia to be ordained and is the first woman graduate of the Seminary to be ordained."[44]

At the 1975 Ecclesiastical Trial of William Wendt, Cheek testified, "When I went to seminary, the psychiatrist who screened me to be admitted to the Semi-

---

[37] The task of the Bishop's Advisory Committee on Admission to the Ministry was to recommend to the Commission on Ministry which persons should be admitted to postulancy and which should not.

[38] Ordained in China in 1944, renouncing her license, though not her priestly orders, after WWII rather than have her ordaining bishop be disciplined.

[39] See John Malcolm Ludlow, *Woman's Work in the Church: Historical Notes on Deaconesses and Sisterhoods* (Washington: Zenger Publishing Company, 1978) for an account of the sacrificial ministry of deaconesses.

[40] p. 2.

[41] p. 4.

[42] p. 3.

[43] See, also, letter from Asso. Dean Richard Reid, April 28, 1971, to Chairman of VA Standing Committee.

[44] p. 1.

nary later told me that he was quite sure I had a call to the priesthood and wanted to be a priest.

"But at that time, it was too scary for me to admit to such an unconventional vocation. So, when I began my seminary training, I protested that I didn't want to be a priest. But my classmates helped me by challenging me all the time and asking me was I one of these women who wanted to be a priest.

"So I had to pay attention to it. I had been in seminary, perhaps, about three years when I was able to own to myself that I did, indeed, have a call to the priesthood....I did not elect to become a Deaconess [at graduation in 1969] for two reasons – tremendous respect for the Deaconesses of the Church who were extremely offended about the way in which they had been treated since 1885. Also, my vocation was to the priesthood, not to the perpetual diaconate. After the General Convention began discussing ordination of women to the priesthood and clarified the canon on the Deacons, then I did apply to become a Deacon in the Diocese of Virginia....

"I remember that my Commission on Ministry asked me when I was being interviewed, before I became a Deacon, did I want to be a priest, and I told them that, yes, indeed, I did want to be a priest. They said, 'Well, good, because in this diocese, the Bishop does not favor perpetual Deacons.' So it was with the understanding that I wanted to be a priest that I was ordained Deacon.

"When the House of Deputies in 1973 voted against the resolution on the principle of the ordination of women to the priesthood, I found myself in a crisis of integrity. It felt very difficult to me to keep on belonging to a church that was saying that about women. Also during my years as a Deacon, I grew a great deal. I changed a lot in my thinking. This was due to the providence of the Church which, in a sense, rejected me so that I was forced out onto the boundaries.

"In training to be a psychotherapist, I began to work with women in some depth in psychotherapy. I began to experience not only my own pain and my own problems in being a woman in a man's church and a woman in a male-dominated society, but I began to work with the damage done to other women. So it became incredibly hard for me [after] the Louisville convention to stand up, Sunday after Sunday, in my parish church, do my work at the altar as a Deacon, visually representing what felt to me to be a church with an oppressive regime. And yet, I felt so deeply rooted in the Episcopal Church that somehow it was impossible for me to pull myself up by my roots."[45]

Thus, Cheek continued her private counseling practice after ordination to the diaconate, listening to the stories of many women; and her consciousness grew as she walked in the shoes of women with oppressions that she had known intellectually but hadn't really known emotionally. At the same time, because of her knowledge of Greek and Hebrew, she continued to do canonical exams in bible for young male graduates of seminary. She recalls, "I would be passing on all these men doing their canonicals and going to their services of ordination; and I remember Phil Smith was [the ordaining bishop] once, and he admonished me at the beginning of the service when we were lining up to process in. He said, 'Don't you go and lay hands. You are a deacon.' I remember how awful it felt when everybody got up from around me and left

[45] Ecclesiastical Court of the Diocese of Washington, The Board of Presenters v. The Rev. William A. Wendt, April 30, 1975-May 2, 1975, pp. 188-191, Archives of the Episcopal Diocese of Washington, Mt. St. Alban, Washington D.C. 20016.

me sitting in a pew and went and laid hands on these men who had come along after me."[46]

Powerless, she sat; and in that weakness, there was grace. That weakness cost her dearly, and that cost was grace. That weakness was grace because with each obstacle, she grew in faith. That weakness was grace because as she met each challenge, she became more open to the light. That weakness was grace because it made of her a witness.

[46] Interview with Alison Cheek, May 13-16, 2010.

GRACE
in Motion

CHAPTER THREE

"There is…one Lord, one faith, one baptism, one God and Father of us all, who is above all and through all and in all. But grace was given to each of us according to the measure of Christ's gift."

Ephesians 4:4-7
Revised Standard Version

A call to ordained ministry comes from God to individual men and women. The Church authorizes this call by the laying on of hands, indicating that the individual ordained is to be the bearer of a tradition. But what happens when an individual's sense of call through her relationship with God is in conflict with the religious imagination of the Church as an institution? Institutions inevitably assume more investment in maintaining the status quo, become more interested in preserving their entitlements than in enabling the gifts they were organized to empower.

Probabilism would hold that structures are formed by the conscience of the Church and follow it in order of importance, the conscience coming first. The women who were first ordained came to the point of breaking with the authority of General Convention to follow their own consciences, finding their sources of authority in the theologies of baptism and eucharist. They did not defy the creedal statements on which the Church is based nor the prayer offered at ordination which affirms that things cast down are being raised up, and things grown old are being made new. On the contrary, they embodied that prayer. They were faithful to the professions of the catechism regarding the sacraments: that all are adopted as members of Christ's body at baptism and, as an extension of baptism, all are united to Christ in the offering of eucharist. They did not seek to use the eucharist. They sought to share it more widely. They had no human models for the vision thrust upon them: They certainly did not want to be little men. All they had was insight granted them by grace.

– The run-up to 1974 –

Following the interpretation at the 1970 General Convention of canons governing ordination as gender inclusive, individuals interested in working for the ordination of women to the priesthood and episcopacy met in a number of locations around the country in a gathering thunderstorm of activity: Graymoor Conference Center, Kingston, NY, on Orthodox Easter weekend, April, 1970;[1] the Women's Institute of Boston Theological Institute in May 1970; Hood College in June 1970; and General Convention in Houston 1970.[2]

Nancy Hatch had married after her second year of seminary and, as Mrs. Wittig, followed her husband to Duke Divinity School where cross-registration with VTS allowed her to complete her studies and receive an M.Div. from Virginia in the Spring of 1972. However, with her marriage began a series of complications to her plans for ordination. As did male students, Nancy Hatch Wittig first had to obtain the consent of the Seminary to be married; but for her, controversy ensued: Wittig wanted permission to use the Consultation On Church Union liturgies. Having confirmed her, Bishop Gibson had been her hero for a number of years; but he appeared at the Seminary and started asking questions about who she was. As Wittig says, "He was very much a man of his own time so wasn't particularly supportive of women in seminary." Wittig obtained permission for the rites she desired but continued to be asked by Episcopal clergymen, "'Well, why don't you just become a Methodist?' and I would say, 'I am not a Methodist!' The only person who really understood that was Sid Sanders. He was chaplain [at VTS] and actually married us in the Chapel." The question of whether or not a woman could have a career and be married would be pressed by Commissions on Ministry, Standing Committees, and parishes in search of new lead-

---

[1] *Religious Institutions and Women's Leadership: New Roles Inside the Mainstream*, ed. Catherine Wessinger (Columbia: University of South Carolina Press, 1996), p. 225, fn 11.
[2] Huyck, p. 99. Huyck is mistaken about the location of Graymoor House.

ership for decades and decades and continues to this day. Not only is it often assumed that a husband cannot be a clergywoman's dependent, but also that child-bearing is an insurmountable barrier to the fulfilling of a woman's responsibilities as a leader. "Do you intend to have children?" is asked differently of women than men by screening committees, and parental leave is not often part of clergy employment negotiations.

The Fall of 1971, following her marriage, Nancy Wittig joined Betty Rosenberg (VTS '72) and Suzanne Hiatt in organizing the Episcopal Women's Caucus. Along with 57 other lay women and future clergywomen, they held a meeting at Virginia Theological Seminary on October 30.[3] Among the founding members were Elisa DesPortes (VTS M.A.R. '70, M.Div. '81), Patricia Merchant Park (VTS '74), Frances Young, Cynthia Wedel, and Marion Kelleran who had argued for women's ordination at the Anglican Consultative Council meeting in Kenya just three months before.[4] This caucus was to be the first of many such meetings sponsored by the Seminary.

Much of the tenor of October 30, 1971, came as a result of reaction to a copy of the address by the Rt. Rev. C. Kilmer Myers to the early October meeting of the House of Bishops in Pocono Manor, PA, in which he stated, "Initiative is, in itself, a male rather than a female attribute"[5] and that lacking the physical configuration to initiate was, in part, why women could not be ordained. Women in attendance spoke of their realization that it was the first time in their lives they had ever laughed at a man. The laughter, however, was soon followed by despair. Nancy Hatch Wittig reflects, "I think that it was that document that really coalesced a lot of different people from a lot of different parts of the country....The fact is we were all daughters of the Church, and we had grown up in the Church, and the Church had meant everything. But there are those crystallizing moments when you understand that "men" means really just MEN....As daughters of the Church we had heard ["men"] as inclusive, and when ["men"] didn't include us [long pause]....What gave it such power was we were daughters of the Church and had been in the Church and had thought that the gospel included us, and then we began to find out that it didn't; so there was a lot of righteous anger that propelled us....A great many of us were raised in the South, and we were taught to be ladies....You certainly don't go saying bad things about men in authority; but we were all well educated, and it was a very personal kind of thing in the sense that how was the Church going to deal with women in general? Did they really think with a male priesthood that the women sitting in the congregations were idiots? Some of them really did."

Reporting on interviews with Sue Hiatt and Marion Kelleran in her dissertation, "To Celebrate a Whole Priesthood: The History of Women's Ordination in the Episcopal Church," Heather Huyck records, "the women from California who had Myers as their bishop were 'devastated.' Marion Kelleran said:

Then the girls from California spoke. It still upsets me to think about them. They said, 'If my own bloodfather [sic] had rejected me it couldn't hurt worse. What do you do when denied by your father?' They had tears in their eyes.

Kelleran's reaction to their pain was to join the younger women sitting on the floor, a change symbolic of her decision that 'the only thing to do was to unite.'"[6]

[3] Ibid., p. 58.
[4] Ibid., p. 61.
[5] C. Kilmer Myers, quoted in *Christianity and Crisis*, December 13,1971, p. 275.
[6] Huyck, p. 62.

Out of this devastation came grace in the form of action. The women of the meeting sent a letter to Presiding Bishop John Hines citing the study being led by Bishop Barrett, the 1968 Lambeth resolution, and the work of the Rightor Committee. They wrote, "We deplore the action of the House of Bishops in forming yet another committee....We are convinced that further study constitutes <u>negative action</u> on this question."[7] In point of fact, the women themselves formed a steering committee which requested and received from the Board of Theological Education funding for six regional conferences. In typical southern fashion, the Alexandria conference of May 1972 took a more "low key" approach than the New York regional meeting's line of attack on the House of Bishops meeting in the Fall of 1972.[8] In his history of the Seminary, John Booty reports that the topic of discussion at VTS was "the 'changing role of women in the church,' with faculty and students in attendance from various seminaries."[9]

On September 6, 1972, Nancy Hatch Wittig (VTS '72) was recommended for candidacy by the faculty of Virginia Theological Seminary;[10] but because her husband had a job in New Jersey, she started the diocesan discernment process all over again in the Diocese of Newark with the encouragement of its bishop, George Rath.

The Fall of 1972 saw a new group of women enrollees at Virginia Theological Seminary—Mary Belfry, Betty Works, Victoria T. Hatch, and Blanche Lee Powell. Betty Works and Victoria Hatch each remember that there were only six or eight women students that year and that they had to deal with three prayer books in three years: the green book, the zebra book, and the blue book.

Works' experience was that women students were being sought out by Yale, Episcopal Theological School, and Virginia; so she was able to obtain a good scholarship by playing them off against each other! Works' parents had met and married at VTS in 1946: Her mother was the librarian from 1944 to 1948; and her father, a graduate of 1948. Though she was the daughter of a clergyman, Works had never particularly wanted to be a priest. She was, and continues to be, drawn to Christian Education and just wanted to go to seminary. She had had a life-changing experi-

Betty Works

ence in college, however, when she read Paul Tillich's *The Courage to Be*; and though she tried to talk to her college chaplain about the book, her father was the only person who really understood and helped her think through this exciting and strange encounter with new life.

Shortly after the seminary's 1972 academic year began, Virginia Suffragan Bishop Phil Smith was nominated for Bishop of New Hampshire. The day of the election, recounts Works, "I decided I would wander across to Bishop Smith's house across the street and knocked on the door. He greeted me with a big scowl, and he said, 'I just got elected. Your father just called me. Come in.' So there I am with the Bishop-elect, and I didn't know what to say. It was kind of fun. So he left [Virginia] and went off and became my Bishop." All her experiences at VTS were not so positive, however. In the refectory it seemed there was

[7] Ibid., p. 63.
[8] Ibid., p. 65.
[9] John E. Booty, *Mission and Ministry: A History of Virginia Theological Seminary* (Harrisburg, PA: Morehouse Publishing, 1995), 309.
[10] p. 3.

Left to right: Richard Reid, Bishop Gibson, Bishop Phil Smith

always a group of continuing education men: "They would treat us like we [women] were exhibits in a zoo or something – 'Why are you here, why are you wanting to go to seminary....' We didn't want to live like we were being interviewed for parish ministry every day."

Betty Works' most challenging experience during her seminary career was CPE: "Some people in my group ended up in in-patient psychiatric care afterwards. My particular supervisor would greet me in the morning; and he would get right into my face and say, 'Well, good morning, Miss Works, how are you?' in a very sexual tone. Looking back at it, I was being sexually harassed. I was twenty-two years old, and I thought I had to stay there for the twelve weeks and endure. It was horrible. When I got back, [Professor] Gordon Charlton did the debriefing; and he said, 'Betty, why didn't you call us and tell us what was going on?' And I said, 'It never occurred to me that there was an "out" if things were terrible.' He said, 'We would have told you to come home and forget about it.' Anyway, it taught me how tough I am."

"Tough" is an adjective often used to characterize the first women students at VTS; and it is usually accompanied by such phrases as "they had to be." Betty Works,

however, had had a life-changing experience and found that she was stronger than she knew.

Mary Belfry, on the other hand, was a young woman to whom revelations of a call to ordained ministry came very slowly. In an extensive interview published in the *Virginia Seminary Journal* of January 1986, she described the years leading up to her entrance to seminary in 1972 in these words: "It never occurred to me that I could be a minister myself, but I thought, It [sic] would be nice to be a minister's wife!... We had no career concept in 1962. Our only role models for career women were single women who were eccentric. You only had a career because you couldn't get married....I wanted a man to tell me what to do. It never occurred to me that I could figure it out for myself. The rector for whom I used to be parish secretary took me out for lunch one day and he said, 'What are you going to do?' I said I didn't know, and he said, 'I think you ought to go to seminary.' He told me that women's ordination was an issue now—I'd heard a little about it when I was in New Guinea—and was suddenly a possibility. My rector didn't *believe* in it, really, but he thought I ought to do something in the church. 'You ought to go to seminary,' he said, and other people said it—I think they were all envisioning my doing something with Christian education. I didn't have any better ideas, so I went."[11] Perhaps because she was from a culturally more traditional part of the country, it was her perception "that the male voices were the ones that were out loud, were public. Female voices were private. I had never been able to say things out loud, because I was a female. All of a sudden, I was in a world with a public issue. I didn't understand any of it; I didn't understand what a public issue was. I came here [to VTS], and here were all these women talking all this impassioned talk. I didn't know the language, I did not know that I had been and was being dis-

[11] pp. 2-3.

criminated against. Here I was with all these people with new ideas, and I couldn't cope with them, I couldn't understand. I fought my whole three years here and I never really understood why. I dragged my feet. In retrospect I see that what was working in me was my sense of 'either-or.' Either I would be a priest or I would be married, but never both."[12]

Belfry recalls that she was one of nine women students living on campus, not all M.Div. candidates. She reflects, "The seminary was growing in its understanding of what having women [students] was, and I certainly was growing in my understanding of what I was doing....The seminary's commitment to having women was enormously faithful, but I don't think they had a clue what that meant....They were trying to live with something new; and then there are those of us who came, some of us not knowing why; and you put those two muddles together, and it's amazing that we all kept on!"[13]

Mary Belfry contrasted female students who were fervent about their sense of vocation with some male and female students who "didn't know why they were there";[14] but it is worth noting that faculty minutes reflect that there have always been young students, both male and female, who were testing their vocations while enrolled and were ambivalent about their sense of direction.

Belfry was sensitive to the disparity between her own sense of vocation and that of more forceful female classmates, in part, because she and Blanche Lee Powell were the first two women seminarians to do field education at St. Patrick's Parish on Foxhall Road, Washington, D.C., where their distinctiveness was notable. They were called to St. Patrick's simultaneously, and it is remarkable

that they were. There was a third candidate for the position of seminarian there, a young man; and all three candidates were convinced that he would be chosen along with one of the women. That the rector, Kit Sherrill, perceived the benefits to his congregation of having women who were so different from each other as representative icons is a testament to grace.

A woman much more assertive than her classmate Mary Belfry, Blanche Lee Powell found herself hiking down a mountain in order to make early Holy Eucharist while a camp counselor. Once drawn to regular worship, that is where she wanted to be. While in graduate school in Madison, Wisconsin, she began to read everything available in the church library; visited a convent to test a possible vocation; discovered on a visit to Seabury Western that they "obviously...didn't want women";[15] and, finding Virginia Seminary a much more pleasant and welcoming place, entered VTS in pursuit of ordination, though still naïve about the resistance she would encounter in her own diocese. She joined the Episcopal Women's Caucus and found support coming from "all over the countryside" and from the majority of the faculty. She and Pat Park "would go in and talk with Cecil Woods because we needed to go to New York or we needed to go to Philadelphia or to Louisville or some place where the Caucus was meeting…and we didn't have any money. Sometimes he would give us some money, and he would tell

Blanche Lee Powell

[12] p. 3.
[13] Interview with Mary Belfry Hansley, June 4, 2010.
[14] Ibid.
[15] Interview with Blanche Lee Powell, July 10, 2010.

us we needed to be in class; and I remember saying to him, 'Dean Woods, you are right; but we also need to be at Louisville [at General Convention], and we have to be in Louisville. The only way you are going to keep me in this place is you are going to have to chain me, because I am going to be in Louisville one way or the other.' And we were....There were some tensions when our Caucus met at VTS: Some of our male seminarians were nervous. They didn't quite know what to do with this; and there was some resistance on the part of some classmates to our being ordained, period."[16]

Blanche Powell's journey to ordination, however, was to be even more complex: "I wasn't in seminary long before we were electing a new bishop in the Diocese of Milwaukee....I [received] a letter from Bishop Hallock. He wanted me to come back to Milwaukee and meet with him because we had elected a new bishop, Charles Gaskell, who was opposed to women's ordination....Bishop Hallock's letter to me had a face on it with this sad smile....He wanted to transfer me out of the Diocese of Milwaukee. I said, 'No, I am not going to do it. Bishop Gaskell and I are going to have to meet one another. We are going to have to converse with one another and work this thing through'....I didn't realize all that I was getting into with that, but I don't regret doing it. It was the right decision for me...." Powell did Clinical Pastoral Education in Milwaukee so that she could meet her new bishop and get a sense of what was happening in the diocese. The morning of her meeting with Gaskell, retired Bishop Daniel Corrigan and his wife invited Powell to their home to share communion with them and then breakfast. She reflects, "That was the most moving thing that he could have done. He knew enough about Bishop Gaskell and his

[Gaskell's] position and the opposition that I was against. He was the most compassionate and loving individual, he and his wife. I will never forget that....It was a precious moment. So in a lot of ways, I met people that I would have never had the opportunity to meet if I had not had to go through this experience....Even at the Louisville Convention...O. C. Edwards, who taught New Testament at Nashotah House...came and sat next to me and we conversed....It was the right decision for me because I am a stronger person today having gone through that and clearer about my vocation than I could have ever been."[17]

Victoria Hatch, like most younger siblings, spent many of her early years doing whatever her older sister, Nancy Hatch Wittig, did not; but there was no escaping the fact that, as she reflects, "throughout our lives the Church was always front and center."[18] Victoria Hatch finished her final three semesters of college at American University where the Episcopal community always sent a delegate to the diocesan convention of the Diocese of Washington. She was a little older than her fellow students and was asked to attend convention as their delegate. She recalls, "I went to the diocesan convention which was really my first experience of the Church on the political side, and that in itself was a phenomenal experience: seeing the Church with all of its muddiness...and there were some things going on internally in terms of [asking myself] 'What is God saying to me?' In the midst of that, I ran to be the first woman vestry member at St. James, Leesburg. I was told several times about what women's roles were and that that was not one of them.... The gnawing became more and more persistent. So finally in the summer of 1971, I went and talked to Phil Smith who had been chaplain at Virginia and now was Suffragan

---

[16] Ibid.
[17] Ibid.
[18] Interview with Victoria T. Hatch, May 18, 2010.

of Virginia. He encouraged me to consider and apply....I then talked to Sid Saunders....So after those conversations, I finally went ahead and said, 'O.K. God. I will apply to seminary, but I am not going to do anything else.'" While her bargaining with God continued, Victoria Hatch's mentors had expanded her horizons; and though she entered seminary without postulancy the Fall of 1972, she soon was a postulant from Virginia.

Victoria Hatch

Thus, as the seminary faculties of the Church began to publish contributions to the debate over women's ordination, Virginia Seminary had women students of every persuasion: those who experienced life-changing episodes, those to whom came slow revelations, and those who had doors opened to them by mentors.

The files of Cecil Woods indicate a September 21, 1972, statement by the Faculty of Philadelphia Divinity School was received on October 17 and contained in part the following: "The Christian priesthood is Christ's, and through him it is his people's. The ordained priest shares in Christ's priesthood and represents the priestly body, the Church. If women are full members of the priestly body, then they cannot but have the basic qualification for ordination to the Church's priesthood." By the time the Special Meeting of the Faculty was held on October 26 and 27, 1972, the Faculties of the Episcopal Consortium for Theological Education in the North East had adopted the entirety of the PDS statement and had sent their endorsements to the House of Bishops which was to meet the following Monday. The Special Meeting of the Faculty was called immediately after Chapel on October 26 to consider endorsing the statement by the other seminaries. Classes intervened before any action could be taken. The meeting reconvened after chapel October 27 without reaching any conclusion. A third session was held during lunch the same day. Intercommunion with churches which did not permit women's ordination was apparently the issue which slowed the process. Dr. Mollegen suggested a compromise which allowed the faculty to endorse the PDS statement and which read in part, "Neither ordination of women nor restriction of ordination to men is of the esse of the Church. Concurrence with the statement of the Episcopal Theological Consortium of the Northeast does not intend to coerce any autonomous or relatively autonomous Anglican authority into compliance with its position." The final paragraph of the minutes of this meeting reads, "It was requested that we vote by secret ballot and the vote was taken. The motion passed 18 'yes', 2 'no' and 2 abstentions. It was agreed by the faculty that in addition to sending our statement, we should report to the House of Bishops the actual vote of the faculty."[19]

At the regular Faculty Meeting on November 1, the Dean thanked the faculty for their willingness to meet several times the previous week at the Special Meeting to deal with the statement about ordination of women. He announced the vote of 18 for, 2 against and 2 abstentions by which the resolution passed; and he informed the faculty that he had sent a letter to the House of Bishops through the Presiding Bishop, reporting the faculty's con-

[19] Faculty Minutes, October 26, 27, 1972, passim, RGV4 Faculty, Virginia Theological Seminary Archives, Bishop Payne Library, Alexandria, VA.

currence in the statement of the other faculties and also "expressing our particular concerns."[20]

On November 29, 1972, the following appears in the Faculty Minutes: "Letter from Women Students re: Ordination of Women The Dean read a letter from the women students at the Seminary, thanking the faculty for their time and consideration of the question of ordaining women. (A copy of the letter is attached.) It was noted that the letter requests some opportunity for discussion with members of the faculty. Some questions were raised as to how we might most appropriately engage in such discussion and the secretary was instructed to reply to the letter and express the faculty's thanks and also to offer the possibility of entering into discussion."[21] This letter was signed by 13 women as "The Women of VTS," among them Victoria T. Hatch (at that time in the M.T.S. program but who would transfer to the M.Div. program on Sept 19, 1973)[22] and Patricia Merchant Park.

Clearly, tension was building toward the October Louisville General Convention. Booty writes that "[i]n March 1973 it was reported that the Student Body supported the ordination of women by a vote in proportion of three to one."[23] A conference for Episcopal Woman Seminarians, "The Ministry of Women in the Episcopal Church – Present and Future," was held at VTS March 30-31, 1973.

Marion Kelleran, meanwhile, retired as Professor and Chair of the Department of Pastoral Theology in June of 1973 and went on to become Chair of the Anglican Consultative Council. During her years on the faculty, and after, she was an outspoken proponent of women's ordination. Her departure meant there were no women on the faculty of Virginia Theological Seminary.

The media were eager to keep the controversy in the Episcopal Church in the news. On August 19, 1973, the "Washington Star-News" listed 300 women out of 40,000 ministers in the Methodist church; 242 out of 9,000 UCC; and 91 out of 13,000 Presbyterian ministers. Swedish Lutherans had ordained women to the priesthood since the '50s. American Lutherans had ordained seven women priests in the past three years, the first in the Western Hemisphere being Elizabeth Platz in the Lutheran Church in American in November, 1970.

There were numerous additional publications that disseminated information about women's ministries, including a book entitled "Our Call." Underwritten and edited by Frances Trott, this book, published by the Episcopal Women's Caucus of the Diocese of Newark, collected the stories of seventeen deacons, candidates, and postulants who described their responses to the call of God. Among the VTS contributors were Peggy Bosmyer [d. 2008], Nancy Hatch Wittig, Patricia Merchant Park, and Victoria T. Hatch. "Our Call" was distributed August 23, 1973, to every General Convention deputy and every bishop and was accompanied by two letters: one from Margaret E. Gilman, ECW President – Diocese of Newark; and one from the Rev. William L. Rawson (VTS '67), Rector of St. Andrew's Episcopal Church, Lincoln Park, New Jersey. Of the seventeen contributors, two would proceed to irregular ordination in Philadelphia after the '73 Convention [Nancy Hatch Wittig and Carter Heyward] and one in Washington D.C. [Lee McGee].

Then it was time for the 64th General Convention, opening in Louisville on September 29, 1973.

---

[20] p. 1. It should be noted that Professor James F. Ross was ordained in the United Church of Christ and always abstained from voting on matters of Episcopal polity.
[21] p. 1.
[22] p. 2 of Sept. 19, 1973 Faculty Minutes.
[23] Board Minutes, 1972-1977 (March 19, 1973), Executive Committee. See (May 12, 1973), full Board.

Patricia Park

Patricia Park, president of the senior class, was elected by the student body of VTS to be one of two students (the other being Joe Reynolds) financially sponsored by the Board for Theological Education to attend. Carlyle Gill (VTS '76), Victoria Hatch (VTS '75), and Peggy Bosmyer (VTS '74) as well as Nancy Hatch Wittig (VTS '72) were among others present. Betty Works (VTS '75) also attended and remembers a conversation that echoed the issues with which Mary Belfry had struggled: "I was standing there talking to some of the seminarians, and somebody was congratulating me on getting engaged; and one of the original [what would later be called] Philadelphia eleven came up to me and said, 'Why would you want to mess up your life and get married?'"[24] Nancy Hatch Wittig recalls, "[In the writing of 'Our Call'] is where some of us tried to be very lady-like, but some of the things that were said by some of the men [at General Convention in response] just blew our minds that this is what this had opened up in some of them. There was a lot of pretty misogynistic stuff: [For example,] we were accused of 'cosmic lesbianism.' Most of it, thankfully, has gone from memory. Amnesia works." These conversations vividly illustrate that the lid had been lifted on the

Nancy Hatch Wittig

Pandora's box of sexuality.

The Rev. Dr. Albert T. Mollegen, Professor of New Testament Language and Literature at VTS, was a deputy to General Convention from the Diocese of Virginia; and the Rev. Richard J. Jones (VTS '72, later to become Professor of Missions and World Religions) was a deputy from the Diocese of Ecuador. Jones relates, "I was there as a deputy only because the Diocese of Ecuador didn't have that many people who could cope with the English language and being a deputy at General Convention. So I was sent even though I was a very green, new priest, ordained to the priesthood in Ecuador. I do not remember all the propositions that came before General Convention on the subject [of women's ordination], but what loomed larger in my memory of that General Convention was the changing of the canon on remarriage. I vividly remember Robert Farrar Capon getting up and leading the report from the committee to the House of Deputies about how it was time to take a pastoral approach and not a punitive legal approach. This is what we are going to do: Take it away from being primarily a bishop's judicial tradition and make it a pastoral judgment of the priest who actually knew the parties. The bishop would be informed and consent, but we were making great strides forward. Then a year later, he got divorced. That loomed larger in my mind, in my memory, than legislation which was attempted and did not pass. The only thing I remember about changing the ordinal was that one version/one resolution came before the deputies, failed, and then some of the back room people who knew how General Convention worked wanted to get a revote, wanted to bring it back up for reconsideration. They had to get somebody who had voted with the majority to ask for the reconsideration. Albert Mollegen and somebody else, I think Henry Rightor, found me amongst the list of

[24] Interview with Betty Works Fuller, May 6, 2010.

innocents who were deputies who had that privilege; and they arranged for me to get the speakers, the Presidents of the House, and be recognized at the microphone. So my one speech to the House of Deputies, Louisville, Kentucky, 1973, was to say, 'I misunderstood my vote yesterday, and I request an opportunity to vote again.' It failed the second time, too. I guess they had lined up two more votes and had hoped it would change the outcome, but it didn't; so I was a parliamentary pawn in the larger strategy, but I was pretty innocent. I knew Henry Rightor was working hard, drawing on his state legislator of Arkansas experience, to work things through the processes of General Convention. I knew that Marion Kelleran, known to

Richard Jones, 1972-73

us as 'Ma,' was both a mentor and friend to women students, as to all students, and that she and Henry were allies in opening the cause of ordained ministry to women. But I never knew much about her role in relation to General Convention and the Episcopal Church. I was more aware of her role chairing the newly formed Consultative Council....She made this joke about this high-sounding position of Chairman with the Anglican Consultative Council: She said, 'Yes, chairman of the universe.'"[25]

Even the "chairman of the universe" who had painfully witnessed the decades-long struggle to seat women as lay deputies could not convince General Convention that the true Chairman of the Universe was calling women to be ordained to the priesthood and episcopacy.

"The proposed canon change on ordination of women failed, 50-43 in the clergy order, with 20 divided votes. In the lay order the vote was 49-37, with 26 divided votes."[26]

Critics of the decision would fault the archaic voting system whereby, for example, the Diocese of Ecuador [with 186 communicants] and the Diocese of Los Angeles [with 93,493 communicants] each had the same representation; but the voting system was even more complicated than that: A split vote in a delegation was counted as negative. Moreover, the loss could not be blamed solely on the voting system. The women of the East Coast were oblivious to how deeply rooted women's secondary status was and is in the rest of the country.

While Bishop Phil Smith (VTS '49) recalled a life filled with people who were the means of grace, refocusing his perceptions, such was not the case everywhere. Smith's predecessor as Bishop of New Hampshire, Todd Hall, had for twenty-five years changed the Church through pastoral care. Smith commented, "When I became the Bishop [in 1973], I didn't have anything to clean up. I just had to be true to what was going on and not muck it up!" In other words, the Church in New Hampshire was already moving to new understandings: Church School Committees consisted of men *and* women. The Woman's Auxiliary demanded and received Commission, not auxiliary, status. Studies on homosexuality began in 1973. Women deacons were raised up out of the life of individual congregations and the life of the diocese. Grace was in motion. Or as Bishop Smith said, "We meet the Spirit of God and of individuals first, before any other members of the Trinity."[27] But New Hampshire was only representative of the northeast corridor of the country.

Heather Huyck's research into the events of 1973

[25] Interview with Richard J. Jones, April 7, 2010.
[26] Journal of General Convention, 1973.
[27] Interview with the Rt. Rev. Philip A. Smith, March 24, 2010.

convinced her that the women and their supporters who favored women's ordination "confused their own intense familiarity with the issue for concern throughout the Episcopal Church. Woman's [sic] ordination lacked breadth—it was still primarily an East Coast effort—and depth—too few people not themselves seeking ordination cared about it passionately....Both the women seeking priesthood and the issue itself needed greater exposure throughout the church."[28]

But it was not just a "familiarity" issue. While there were no statistics available to be compiled at that time because ordained women in leadership was a brand new phenomenon, certainly no one was polling people on their deep psychological fears of women in 1973. Unfortunately, "greater exposure" would not solve the problem. That assessment was far too simplistic. Patriarchy and paternalism are deeply engrained in the psyches of men and women. Or as the Very Rev. Canon Charles A. Perry (VTS '61), Provost of the Washington National Cathedral, put it, "The issue of women's ordination is as much a psychological issue as a theological issue."[29]

The Office of Women's Ministries of the Episcopal Church, in updating the "Reaching Toward Wholeness" study prepared for the General Convention of 1988, found the following statistics to be true as late as the 21st Century: "In 2002 as compared with 1987 fewer people at all levels of the church are aware that barriers to women's full participation in the church continue to exist. In general, acceptance of women in leadership positions is greatest at the national level and steadily decreases at the diocesan and congregational levels....In 2002 at all levels of the church, ordaining ethnic minorities is a higher priority among both men and women than ordaining

women. In the dioceses the larger the membership of the congregation, the less willing respondents are personally to have a woman as their rector....Diocesan level respondents from the Northeast are more likely to endorse women's ministry as church leaders, than those from the South. **Congregational characteristics are not randomly distributed among regions.** The **Northeast** congregations have more women in leadership positions (more women rectors and a larger proportion of women on the vestry) compared to those responding from the other three regions <u>combined</u>. The **South**, in contrast, stands out in being more likely to have members responding who are in larger congregations, which are significantly less likely to currently have a woman as rector or a woman in any other clergy position (e.g. assistant or associate minister, vicar, interim) than the other three regions <u>combined</u>. Congregations in the South, as well, have the fewest women on the vestry as compared to the other three regions. The **Northcentral** stands out from the other regions in having congregations, which are significantly more likely to be located in urban and suburban areas than congregations in the other three regions <u>combined</u>." [emphases theirs]

Obviously, assumptions about what is normative vary from one part of this country to another, but regional customs ignore the fact that they have one thing in common: European American male experiences are exclusive. They do not constitute the whole of reality. When white male authority is privileged, particularities of social context and history are often disregarded; and the experiences of the marginalized, discounted. Why some parts of this country, some parts of this world, are more conservative than others is a question beyond the scope of this

---

[28] Huyck, p. 80.
[29] Minutes of the meeting of the National Committee of Episcopal Clergy and Laity for the Ordination of Women to the Priesthood, Washington D.C., June 18, 1973, p. 2.

study. Perhaps it is enough to say, "The *pneuma* blows where it wills/wishes, and you hear the sound of it, but you do not know where it comes from and where it is going; so it is with everyone who is born of the Spirit."[30]

On a Sunday morning after General Convention at St. Patrick's Parish in D.C., a black quartet was singing "We Shall Overcome"; and Blanche Lee Powell stopped in the middle of leading the service, conscious of the fact that when the language of the prayer book after Louisville said "men," it clearly meant "men." She relates, "I couldn't say it. I just thought 'No, I am not going to use that language.' It seemed like an eternity to me. It was probably just a few seconds, but I changed the language on the spot....After the service...Kit pulled me aside and said, 'Blanche, what were you thinking? What were you doing?' And I said, 'Kit, I couldn't use that language. I had some choices: I could change the language like I did; I could leave a blank space and not say anything there....' I said, 'No, I did what I had to do.' And the next Sunday, he changed the language. The very next Sunday. But he had been in the Civil Rights marches and that kind of thing, so that is where he was....He was there for me. There were a lot of people who were supportive in spite of all the resistance we had to go through. There was support, and I guess that is how we got through it all....If I had known, I probably would have still been teaching PE. If I had not been so naïve and known the kind of resistance you would meet [pause] but I didn't know. But I don't regret any of it. I know I am a different person because of it."[31]

In November of 1973, Alison Cheek (VTS '69), Carlyle Gill (VTS '76), and others participated in a debriefing session at VTS of the women who had worked for women's ordination at the Louisville Convention and their supporters. Those in attendance were deeply depressed and bitter. Cheek pondered, "As I listened to it all, it became clear to me that there was no way to go politically, that the structure of the voting system was such that we were stuck....I was beginning to feel that I couldn't stand up Sunday after Sunday and do my deacon's work at the altar as if it were O.K. that that was as much as a woman could do. It wasn't O.K. with me, and I was feeling that I was losing my integrity."

As for Carlyle Gill, once a student at the Seminary, involvement in the movement for the ordination of women came quickly. She reflects, "The canon had been changed to ordain women as deacons in 1970, but most women couldn't really put that sentence together in their head[s] and make much sense of that, I think....When I actually got here and started in the Fall of 1973, it was very clear to me that this was 'it,' and that I really did feel called to ordained ministry, and it was a match....

Carlyle Gill

We did what we could do, how we could do it....There were no models. It was making it up yourself....You not only were making it up yourself, but one had to make it up in such a way as somebody had to be sure about it.... Some people may not like it or understand or whatever, and, well, that just was; but it didn't shake my conviction about it all."[32] Though she had come to seminary without a sponsoring parish or diocese, Gill obviously "made it up" in such a way that Immanuel-on-the-Hill became sure

[30] John 3:8, Revised Standard Version.
[31] Interview with Blanche Lee Powell, July 10, 2010.
[32] Interview with Carlyle Gill, May 19, 2010.

about it: That parish soon sponsored her for ordination in the Diocese of Virginia.

Faculty Minutes of December 5, 1973: "The Alumni Association is planning a conference here on the subject of the ordination of women. A copy of the letter sent to alumni by the Rev. John C. Harris (VTS '55), Chairman of the Executive Committee of the Alumni Association, is attached. A few faculty and a few students will be invited to join members of the Alumni Association at this meeting....

"Patricia Park Pat has expressed some concern about the faculty's response to ordination of women and to recommendations for them. A copy of her letter is attached.

"There was a considerable discussion as to how we should appropriately respond to her letter. Some members of the faculty thought we ought to offer a very strong resolution supporting ordination of women and engage in a course of education for the Church on this subject. It was finally moved by Dr. Allison and seconded by Dr. Rightor that this faculty respond to Patricia Park's letter asking us to 'risk the unknown of a perpetual diaconate' by assuring her that we have heartily and unanimously endorsed her for candidacy and in doing so anticipate our recommendation not to the 'perpetual diaconate' but to the 'diaconate.' Whereas we are grateful for her willingness to minister in whatever state of life it shall please God to call her, the vast majority of this faculty have committed themselves to making it canonically pos-

Patricia Park

sible for the vocation of further ordination for all qualified women, including Patricia Park. To this end the Seminary, in cooperation with the alumni, are planning strategy sessions next month and regardless of the outcome, we assure her that we stand with her in what we feel is an authentic vocation to ministry.

This motion carried."[33]

On Dec. 15, 1973, at the Cathedral of St. John the Divine in New York City, Carol Anderson, Emily Hewitt, Carter Heyward, Barbara Schlachter, and Julia Sibley, all New York deacons, presented themselves to Bishop Paul Moore for ordination to the priesthood.[34] Moore allowed them and their presenters to participate in the entire service leading up to the laying on of hands but refrained at that point from laying hands on the heads of the female deacons. Half the congregation walked out in support of the women.

Thus, 1973 ended in frustration but also with new images in play. Women wanted and want to be recognized as part of the mainstream of the Church, as part of the body of Christ. They could not and cannot afford to be identified as radicals lest they lose the capacity to be heard. Time and again, how to convert from within is the challenge for a sacramental Church. Women's ordination represents an outward sign, a symbol, an icon of the fullness of God. How do ordained women, the symbolic feminine, dare to help the Church think theologically? Ultimately the first women ordained would find that they could not change people's minds. They could only change people's experiences; and, thereby, the people themselves changed their minds.

Outward and visible signs of grace were available. Making them inward realities was yet to come; but, as always, the initiative was God's.

[33] p. 3.
[34] Marie Moorefield had planned to join in presenting herself for ordination but was ill.

GRACE
in Motion
CHAPTER FOUR

"I do not want you to be unaware, brothers and sisters, that our ancestors were all under the cloud, and all passed through the sea, and all were baptized into Moses in the cloud and in the sea, and all ate the same spiritual food, and all drank the same spiritual drink. For they drank from the spiritual rock that followed them, and the rock was Christ."

1 Corinthians 10:1-4
New Revised Standard Version

If women were to be visible signs of something new, signs that were recognizable by others, how was that to happen? A sign is not a stand-in or a substitute for a thing [*res*]. A sign has a future referent. It points to that of which it is a part and by which it is shaped. Just as the rock from which the Israelites drank in the wilderness pointed to Christ, so the Israelites were sustained and shaped by that rock. Grounded in the testimony given to them by God, they witnessed new life.

The women who were signs of new life could only witness to the insight God had given them. They were shaped by the vision they had been given. True, that understanding was different for each of them. Some did indeed think that the basic issue for which they were struggling was justice. Others found something else motivating them. But to a woman, they were molded by an image of what the future could hold. They could not testify, for only God gives true testimony: Only God knows fully. But they could witness to what they saw.

The term *martyria* is variously translated "witness or testimony," as if these two words were interchangeable. But in the book, *Conversations with Scripture: 2 Isaiah*, author Stephen Cook notes that God gives Israel a *testimony* on Mount Sinai. At Exodus 25:16 *martyria* is a technical term for "written solemn duties [or] official commands" of God. Such testimony, in this case referring to the tables of the Decalogue, produces awe, as Cook writes, "a consuming desire to embrace God's wondrousness and to place our everyday, ordinary lives before God as an offering."[1] Just as the theological meaning of the covenant between God and humanity is nothing like a contract between two equally bound beings, so testimony comes from God to us like the voice of thunder, forcing us to our knees.

How piteous the common understanding of testimony as a statement of personal relationship with Jesus, an altar call whose subject is me and Jesus, domesticating rather than revering the Holy. Such statements shine a light on one individual and leave no room for the listener who has not encountered such an event, leaving that listener to wonder, "What's wrong with me that I have never found God in this way on my own?" This emphasis on a personal and private quality of relationship is not generative of authority: Such evidence of intercourse does not author identity and values in those who listen to such statements. What's more, when one's personal experience becomes the focus of "testimony," there is no opportunity for discussion, reflection, or deliberation on the part of the community of faith.

Some would claim that testimony is a confession of faith. But what is the theological warrant for that confession? Is its purpose to establish a relationship with the hearer by being vulnerable and revealing oneself? If so, such a confession is a private arrangement, not a sign or symbol or icon that helps the Church think theologically. An emphasis on ethos, the character of the speaker, forecloses deliberation and discussion. Perhaps the better claim to make is a profession of faith rather than a confession of faith, a declaration which better fits the category of proclamation as, for example, when we profess our faith as we recite the creeds.

Witness, on the other hand, is shared experience, an evocation of contexts to which listeners can relate in order to reflect, contemplate, and deliberate. How to think theologically about what we see at work in the world requires meaningful reflection and evaluation on the part of a community.

---

[1] Stephen L. Cook, *Conversations with Scripture: 2 Isaiah* (New York: Morehouse Publishing, 2008), 26.

How can we differentiate theologically between testimony, witness, and proclamation? Let us begin with a chart of first principles or grounds:

	Testimony	Witness	Proclamation
Purpose:	the revelation of God	witness to revelation	- declarative assertion - a mirror of something more than simply our own experience
Aspect	done by God	in the Holy Spirit, the community contains the truth; shared experience	- teach the life to which Scripture witnesses
Theological Warrant	God's longing & God's delight	ecclesiology: not the institution but the catholic body of Christ	- we don't preach ABOUT Jesus. We preach Jesus & His message

The first women ordained were witnesses, contemplating, weighing, and judging the reasonable, dealing their listeners the options and inviting them to think about a vision of the future, bidding them share in reflection on the grace initiated by God. Thus they witnessed to and proclaimed a Life by reflective, reasoned deliberation within a community, a community that is always becoming something more than we can know. Participating in that deliberation, the Church preaches not herself but Jesus Christ as Lord[2] and witnesses to grace in motion.

[2] II Corinthians 4:5.

The new year opened with concrete steps being taken to correct the fact that for seven months there had been no woman on the faculty of Virginia Theological Seminary. Dr. Marianne H. Micks had entered Windham House for graduate study in 1946. Because women were not permitted to sit in regular classes at General Theological Seminary, Micks attended evening sessions at Windham House and was awarded an M.A. in Religious Education by Columbia University in conjunction with Union Theological Seminary in 1948. In 1957 she was one of the first two women to earn a B.D. degree from an Episcopal seminary, in this case, Church Divinity School of the Pacific. Although Yale College still did not admit women, Micks was subsequently able to enter Yale Divinity School with one other woman and was awarded a Ph.D. in religion in 1960.

The minutes of the Faculty Meeting of Feb. 6, 1974, record the following:

"I. <u>MARIANNE MICKS</u> The Dean reported that he had polled the Board and that Dr. Micks had been elected as professor of Biblical and Historical Theology. He said he thought that we had a good possibility of her accepting and that he would notify the faculty as soon as he hears her response.

"II. <u>WOMEN STUDENTS</u> The Dean reported that the women students who had originally planned to come to the faculty meeting today asked to defer this meeting for a couple of weeks until after some of them have talked with the new presiding bishop. [The February 8-9 meeting with John Allin included the first post-Louisville meeting of the Episcopal Women's Caucus Steering Committee. Allin remained adamantly opposed to the ordination of women.] They thought it would be

Marianne Micks

more useful to have a conversation with us after this meeting.

"It was moved by Dr. Rightor and seconded that we invite the women students to come to the faculty meeting on February 20 and that all departmental presentations be moved forward one meeting. This motion carried.

"The Dean said that the women wanted us to know some of the concerns which they would like to discuss with us on the 20th. He listed them as follows:

(1) The need for women on the faculty;

(2) The possibility of a woman assistant at the Center for Continuing Education;

(3) Their impression that some members of this community are ignoring this issue;

(4) The need to take into account the material written on the subject of ordination of women;

(5) Possibility of having women clergy take part in special services here;

(6) The small role given to the women at the ecumenical service on Friday, January 25."[3]

The March 1974 *Journal* reported: "On February 13, the Very Rev. Cecil Woods, Dean…, announced that Dr. Marianne Micks will join the faculty of the Seminary in the fall of 1974." Marianne Micks not only became a strong advocate for women's ordination but a leader in feminist thinking, sensitizing women to covert discrimi-

[3] pp. 1-2.

nation of which they had been previously unconscious.

Faculty Meeting, February 20, 1974, VIII.

"Consultation With Women Students At their request the women students were invited to meet with the faculty to discuss questions of concern to them, particularly the ordination of women. The following students came to the Faculty Meeting: Gill, Thompson, Park, Randall, Works, Bosmyer, Suriner, Shoberg, Nease, Powell.

"The Dean welcomed the women to the meeting and apologized for the fact that we had been unable to schedule the meeting any earlier. He invited them to express their concerns to the faculty. The following notes are not an attempt to reproduce the entire discussion, which lasted for about an hour and a half, but simply to suggest the areas touched on and to summarize the conclusions.

"(a) The women were concerned about educating the Church on the subject of women's ordination. What can and should this faculty do and how does it relate to what other seminary faculties are doing? Blanche Powell pointed out that Bishop Allin is going to appoint a committee to set up a committee [sic] to study this issue. She thought that Dr. Mollegen would be one of the people consulted.

"(b) Concern was expressed about the need for a theological statement on the subject of ordination of women, particularly one which went into the question of the positive reasons for such ordination.

"(c) There was considerable discussion of the question of whether an individual bishop should ordain a woman without the consent of the whole Church.

"(d) There was discussion of the role which deacons have in the Church.

"(e) The question of our relationship with other churches was raised, particularly the fact that there are many other churches which already ordain women.

"The discussion reached the conclusion that it would be good to prepare several position papers on the question of ordination of women and the meaning of sexuality and have them distributed to parishes and generally throughout the Church. It was suggested that it would be very desirable that these position papers represent not simply the position of this faculty or this Seminary but be cooperative ventures involving the faculties of other Episcopal seminaries.

"It was agreed that the Dean will appoint a planning committee to begin work toward this goal."[4]

That there was discussion of the question of whether an individual bishop should ordain a woman without the consent of the whole Church (item "c" above) reflects the fact that the Episcopal Women's Caucus had decided at their February meeting to split into three groups which would pursue different strategies: education, political organizing, and symbolic/dramatic action. The politically oriented group would become the National Coalition; the third, more radical group, Women's Ordination Now. It was W.O.N. that would press for action by individual bishops without the consent of the whole Church.

On April 30, a letter was issued by Dean Cecil Woods forming the Committee on Women's Ordination. Both men and women were invited to serve on this committee. Betty Works, Noreen Suriner, and Carlyle Gill were among the students who accepted the invitation. The Faculty Minutes of May 1 reflect the following membership: "Committee on the Concerns of Women Students The Dean reminded the faculty that when we had our consultation with the women students, we had agreed that a committee would be appointed to discuss and consider the concerns they have about ordination and the place of women in the Church. The Dean appointed

[4] pp. 3-4.

the following committee: Mr. Sanders, Chairman, Dr[s.] Fuller, Price, Rightor, Micks, Mr. Powell, Miss Suriner, Miss Works, [Miss Gill,] Mr. Rich, Mr. Ward. The committee will have its first meeting at lunch in the small dining room on Wednesday."[5]

In the meantime, the Alumni Association of VTS organized and widely publicized a Symposium on Women for the Ordained Ministry, sponsored by the Executive Committee of the Alumni Association, and held at VTS on May 22, 1974. Participants included the Rev. John C. Harris (VTS '55), Pres. VTS Alumni Asso. & Board Trustee; and co-chairs Deacon Nancy Wittig (VTS '72) [Managing Editor "The Newark Churchman"] and the Rev. William Dols, (VTS '58) Rector Immanuel on the Hill and Board Trustee. Pat Park, President of the Class of '74; the Rev. William. Swing (VTS '61), co-chair of the Task Force on Women, Diocese of WA and Rector, St. Columba's; the Rev. Professor Henry Rightor (VTS '48); and the Rev. Dr. Charles Price (VTS '49) led symposia. Ninety-two people representing several seminaries attended, a number and constituency far exceeding the "few faculty and a few students" to be invited to join the Alumni Association as originally envisioned in the minutes of December 5, 1973. Booty reports that the conference "was also a meeting to devise strategies to achieve General Convention's approval of the ordination of women to the priesthood

Nancy Hatch Wittig

and to the episcopate."[6]

Early in July of 1974, Alison Cheek answered a telephone call from Nancy Wittig: "I said, 'Hello, Nancy. Are you at the [Leesburg] farm?' And she said, 'No, I'm not. I have got something to tell you, but I have to tell you under the seal of the confessional.' I said to myself, 'What's Nancy done! And why is she talking about it on the telephone?' Then she said, 'Three bishops are going to ordain some women deacons to be priests in Philadelphia at the end of the month.' I said, 'Wow!' And she said, 'I am calling to see if you want to come on board.' It was the first time in my life that I was aware of three things happening at once: It was like my heart started up and said, 'yes,' my head started calculating the risks, and my body was sort of having symptoms of panic. I told her, "Yes, I think I do, but I want to talk to my bishop and rector about it.' She said, 'Yes, but talk to them in confidence because the bishops who are ordaining are elderly men, and they will make it public before they do it; but they will have to go through a lot of stress beforehand....' [My husband] Bruce and I had been drinking coffee in the living room, and I told him what Nancy had said. Then I said, 'If I go to this ordination, I will be deposed. Then I will be deported because I will be working illegally on [your] diplomatic visa that only allows me to do church work....' Bruce said, 'If you have to go, I will go with you' which was one of the most touching moments in my marriage. I went and talked to my rector; and he said, 'I don't know how I feel about the way you are going to do it; but if I had had a call to the priesthood and a bishop had offered to ordain me, I know what I would do.' And then I went to see the Bishop; and he said, 'As Bob Hall I will support you all I can, but as the Bishop of Virginia I might have to depose you....' A long time into

[5] pp. 1-2.
[6] Booty, 310.

the struggle a reporter asked [Bishop Hall] why he hadn't deposed me; and he said, 'Because I wanted to save the vocation of a priest.'"

That Spring Nancy Wittig (VTS '72) had been in contact with community organizer and deacon, Suzanne Hiatt, who believed there were a handful of bishops who would be willing to ordain. Wittig recounts, "One of the things that we felt very strongly about was the need for there to be more than one bishop and more than one woman....Phyllis Edwards had taken such abuse; and because of that example, I was convinced that if we did the ordination of women, it could not just be one. It had to be as many as we could pull together because only that way could we withstand the craziness that went on. And it was true....[Sue] called me in June or end of May in '74 and said there was a possibility, and it might cost us everything. Probably be excommunicated, etc. So I thought about it and called her back and said, 'I'm in because it has got to happen. So then in later June there was a whole group of us who said we would come to Philadelphia and talk with each other....There were two meetings in Philadelphia before the ordination. One was prep: Can we really do this? We met over several days. It was at that meeting we started to go over the list of all the women deacons [who had been ordained for six months]....We each called some of the people that we knew and basically said, 'This is what we think is going to happen. Would you be prepared to sacrifice everything and be a part of this? There were no guarantees, and so people said "yes" or "nay." [Phyllis Edwards declined because she was the sole support of her mother.] Then there was another meeting, and I think by that point the handful of bishops had trickled down to four or five....The night before the ordination we met at Bishop DeWitt's place. Bishop Wells wasn't sure if he was going to go through with this...so we went home not knowing if he was going to show up the next day....Bishop Corrigan was going to be a part....Each

one of us had all the paperwork that was required except one thing....Basically, the plan was that we needed to speak to our bishops and tell them what was going to happen and ask them to keep the seal on it; and they all did. The only one who didn't was Ogilby."

The files of Cecil Woods contain a copy of the July 23, 1974, letter from Dr. Reginald Fuller to the Rt. Rev. Robert L. DeWitt, resigned Bishop of Pennsylvania, noting that the whole Church has the authority and power to ordain, not individual bishops, and citing the Acts of the Apostles and Ephesians 5:2 to support his argument. Fuller urged DeWitt NOT to ordain.

Did DeWitt take Fuller's argument to mean that he could act with and for the Church to ordain? Or did he, perhaps, recognize the age-old theological question: Is the Church formed by Christ or by the community? Did Christ intend to form a governing body? Is the community represented by Canons or by the emerging Church? Once again, power was the issue.

On Monday, July 29, 1974, the Feasts of Sts. Mary and Martha, DeWitt, joining with the Rt. Rev. Daniel Corrigan, retired Suffragan Bishop of Colorado and the Rt. Rev. Edward R. Welles II, retired Bishop of West Missouri did lay hands on

A new priest, Nancy Hatch Wittig, July 29, 1974

eleven women: Jeannette Piccard (age 79, the first woman to be ordained priest in the Episcopal Church), Alison Cheek (VTS '69), Nancy Hatch Wittig (VTS '72), Merrill Bittner, Alla Bozarth-Campbell, Emily Hewitt, Carter Heyward, Suzanne Hiatt, Marie Moorefield Fleischer, Betty Bone Schiess, and Katrina Welles Swanson (daughter of the ordaining bishop). The Rt. Rev. Antonio Ramos, Bishop of Costa Rica, participated in the service but remained in the sanctuary during the laying-on-of-hands. The service took place at the Church of the Advocate, Philadelphia, a predominantly black church dependent on the diocese for

David Booth Beers

its survival. The senior warden, Barbara Harris, had not believed women should be priests until her mind was changed by Suzanne Hiatt's ministry as deacon in that congregation.[7] Harris was crucifer for the ordination service; and Patricia Merchant Park (VTS '74), deacon. The preacher was Harvard professor Charles V. Willie, the first black man elected vice-president of the House of Deputies.

Alison Cheek was invited to celebrate the Eucharist at St. Stephen and the Incarnation, Washington, D.C., the Sunday following the Philadelphia ordinations. David Booth Beers,[8] Professor Albert T. Mollegen, and A. Katherine Grieb (VTS '83) were in the congregation that day. At that point in the service when the Sursum Corda begins, a letter of inhibition from the Rt. Rev. William Creighton, Bishop of Washington, was read; and the rector, the Rev. William A. Wendt stated, "Because Alison is inhibited today, I will inhibit myself. For the first time in thirty years, I will not say the Mass today."[9] He seized the sacred vessels and walked down the aisle with them.[10] There was no absolution pronounced and no communion celebrated; however, the congregants in the gallery began to sing "We Shall Overcome," at which point the Revs. Bill Wendt and Loren Mead lifted Cheek to their shoulders and carried her through the congregation.

---

[7] Conversation with Alison Cheek, May, 2010. Harris later became the first female bishop in the Episcopal Church, consecrated Suffragan Bishop of Massachusetts on Feb. 11, 1989, with Florence Li Tim Oi and Carter Heyward as concelebrants.

[8] In 1973 vestryman David Booth Beers was elected to the Standing Committee of the Diocese of Washington from St. Patrick's parish. He subsequently resigned to become Chancellor of the Diocese under Bishop John Walker. He was a deputy to General Convention for five conventions and chair of the deputation from Washington in 1985, the same year he was elected to the Board of VTS. He was elected to Executive Council in 1988 and 1991 and, half-way through Edmund Browning's twelve-year term as Presiding Bishop, became Browning's Chancellor and legal counsel. At that point Beers resigned from all other Church responsibilities except his membership on the Board of the Seminary. He has been Chancellor of the Episcopal Church USA and Board member of VTS since that time.

[9] Interview with Alison Cheek, May 13-16, 2010.

[10] Interview with David Booth Beers, June 10, 2010.

Grieb describes the event in these words: "Alison…was invited to celebrate the Eucharist. I was there for the Sunday when they got all the way up to the actual Prayer of Consecration and stopped, and there was no Eucharist that day; and we all lived into the pain of the fact that women couldn't do that, that her ministry wasn't recognized. So, she was carried on the shoulders of the men around the chancel that day, and it's one of the days I will probably always remember my whole life."[11]

Meanwhile, the newly-elected Presiding Bishop called an emergency meeting of the House of Bishops for August 14-15, at a hotel near O'Hare International Airport, Chicago. The atmosphere was tense. The movable walls of the meeting room were set up so that there was just enough space to seat the House of Bishops with one row around the outside for the press. The proceedings were piped into the adjoining room. Most of the Philadelphia Eleven attended, but very few of the Bishops would speak to them. Nancy Wittig recalls "mean and nasty things" said by various bishops: "I think that the meeting in Chicago was horrendous, and Charles Willie resigned as vice-president of the House of Deputies because of that."

Bishop Phil Smith and Alison Cheek did have a conversation during the Chicago meeting. Smith had known Cheek since his days as professor and chaplain at

LEFT TO RIGHT: *Loren Mead, Alison Cheek & Bill Wendt on Sunday, August 4, 1974.*

© WASHINGTON POST – GETTY IMAGES

VTS during which time she was a student. He had a long relationship with her and her family. He recalled, "I remember listening to her in that first sermon that she preached here [at VTS]; and I thought to myself, 'Oh, wow! This is a different kind of sermon.' So I thought 'Boy, what an example' because her preaching was so pastorally oriented and right on target for the people...." With good-natured laughter he remembered their encounter in the tense atmosphere of Chicago: "We had an argument over this whole business of the women's ordination in Philadelphia....I was getting very irritated with her because she had now a new edge to her that I didn't cotton to, and we were really heated. I said, 'Alison, you have a messianic complex!' And she said, 'Well, and you have the mind of the Sanhedrin!'"[12]

Confusion reigned: The Bishop of West Missouri, Arthur Vogel, had quoted a Roman Catholic theologian from Boston who later repudiated how his work had been used, saying the women were priests and should be put to work. The vote by the Bishops on the question of whether or not necessary conditions for a valid ordination were present in Philadelphia was so complicated in phraseology that many of the bishops found themselves voting in opposition to their own opinions.

A scathing Sept. 3, 1974, assessment by Deans

[11] Interview with A. Katherine Grieb, May 25, 2010.
[12] Interview with the Rt. Rev. Philip Smith, March 24, 2010.

Harvey Guthrie, Edward Harris, and Hays Rockwell reported on the Chicago action of the House of Bishops: "Episcopal and priestly ministries [are] ministries of Christ to the Church and not simply ministries arising from the Church with the consent of the Church....They are sectarian, congregational and Donatist otherwise.... There are implications of the Gospel for the question of the ordination of women to the priesthood and the episcopate....[We are] disturbed both at the content of what was done [at O'Hare] and the process leading to the final action....Procedurally it was a painful thing to see the bishops of our branch of the Anglican Communion judging the implications for faith and order of the Philadelphia ordination on the basis of no adequately prepared report of their theology committee....Theologically a simplistic answer was given to an extremely complicated question....The Bishop of West Missouri…led the bishops to adopt the position taken by the Donatists in the fourth century to the effect that sacramental acts done by clergy who had under pressure recanted the faith were invalid.... To follow out the logic of the Donatists and of the action of our bishops is to deny that aspect of Holy Orders which holds Episcopal and priestly ministries to be ministries of Christ to the Church and not simply ministries arising from the Church with the consent of the Church....Morally the action of the bishops avoided the real issue."

Meanwhile, the bishops of the eleven women sent out directives to their dioceses warning of consequences if the women were invited to celebrate in their churches. Alison Cheek and Bishop Hall had agreed to keep one another apprised of intended actions. The Sunday following the Chicago meeting, Cheek announced to the rector of St. Albans that she would not wear her stole as a deacon.

John Frizzell responded, "Well, neither of us will wear stoles." However, at the time for the sermon that morning and without warning, Frizzell announced that a letter from the Diocese of Virginia directed that Cheek be regarded as a deacon, not a priest. Cheek had not received a copy of this letter from Bishop Hall and was "thunderstruck." Though she sang lustily during the service, the congregation was weeping; and when she reached her car afterward, she too began to cry and was unable to stop. She drove to the Seminary where Henry Rightor "patched [her] back together again." Not long afterward, Frizzell wrote her a letter outlining what he wanted her to do as a deacon; but her response was, "I can't be a deacon anymore," and Bishop Hall released her from St. Albans into limbo.

The female students of VTS had returned to seminary that Fall of 1974 with mixed feelings. Victoria Hatch, Betty Works (now Mrs. Frank Fuller), Blanche Lee Powell, and Mary Belfry were among the seniors; Carlyle Gill and Georgia Shoberg, middlers. Betty Works Fuller, for her part, was furious with her own father for having gone to the Philadelphia service. She did not think it was a good thing. The night of July 29 she had "landed up in Dr. Mollegen's living room—his wife is my godmother—and I just was hysterical....I felt like it wasn't helping the whole movement, and I was just really upset."[13] Similarly, Mary Belfry's reaction was "I didn't like it. They weren't being good little girls. *I* was a good little girl, and it was working for *me*. I was very obedient."[14]

Victoria Hatch remembers the first sermon of the academic year after the Philadelphia ordinations delivered, as is customary, by Dean and President Cecil Woods: "The sermon was entirely a slam on what had happened in Philadelphia, and I sat there gritting my teeth. I re-

[13] Interview with Betty Works Fuller, May 6, 2010.
[14] *Journal* 1986, p. 5.

member flying out of the sacristy after I had done my duties in the sacristy and bursting into tears and going to Henry Rightor ranting my rage. He said, 'You know it is going to be a rough year for the women because of what has happened, but it needed to happen. You are O.K. Don't worry about it.'"[15] Carlyle Gill also remembers, "Cecil [Woods] and Dick Reid could barely deal with the [changes in the] prayer book and the ordination of women."[16] Yet, both Victoria Hatch and Carlyle Gill speak warmly of the support they observed on the part of Trotter, Woods, and Reid for women's ordination and the encouragement they personally received from these professors. The reflections of a student who entered in 1976, A. Katherine Grieb, shed light on the seeming contradictions in the remembrances of Hatch and Gill: "It was the Bible and Theology Departments that were shaping the discussion about women in creative ways....The Bible people were fantastic: Frank Van Develder, Jim Ross, and Murray Newman were all convicted about this and Dick Reid, Reginald Fuller....Cecil Woods struggled, I think, with women's issues....It was not a good time for him...."[17]

Henry Rightor

There are no documents in the seminary archives to support what Trotter, Woods, and Reid's interior struggles may have been. Booty reports his impressions—"The faculty found itself seriously divided over the irregular ordination in Philadelphia on July 29, 1974, of women to the priesthood"[18]—without attribution. Records of meetings attended by supporters of women's ordination, faculty resolutions passed, and letters sent all evidence the backing of and assistance to the movement of women's ordination on the part of the majority of professors of VTS. Personal letters between Cecil Woods and Alison Cheek during these critical years may be found in the archived student files of Alison Cheek. They evidence tender concern on the part of Woods and Cheek for one another. One thing seems clear: Faculty *and* students were dealing with conflict between duty imposed from without versus feelings of personal obligation to convictions held within. Cheap grace it was not.

On Sept 15, 1974, at Immanuel on the Hill, a group of 45 lay and ordained men and women organized themselves into committees to address the crisis in the Church: a Diocesan Standing Committee, an Education Committee, a Mexico meeting [of the House of Bishops] Committee, and a Support of the 11 women Committee. Their assignments were as follows:

Diocesan Standing Committee group – set up a meeting with Bishop Hall to explore his openness to ordaining a woman if approved by the Diocesan Standing Committee; see to the election of delegates to the 1976 General Convention who are favorably inclined toward the ordination of women; work to enable regularizing Alison Cheek's ordination; propose a meeting for Cheek with

[15] Interview with Victoria T. Hatch, May 18, 2010.
[16] Interview with Carlyle Gill, May 19, 2010.
[17] Interview with A. Katherine Grieb, May 25, 2010.
[18] Booty, 310.

the Standing Committee.

Education – Organize material available and facilitate distribution of that material; work with Province 3 ECW's and Bishops; make up a new brochure; ask Bishops for money to support this work and get help from the Evangelical Education Society.

Mexico Meeting – ask Bishop Creighton to convene Bishops of Province 3 to deal with the ordination of women issue and to go to Mexico with a united stand; urge progressive Bishops to caucus at the beginning of the Mexico meeting with a united stand to reconsider Chicago decision, urge a special convention, and consider ordaining women now; support the Cambridge meeting; "prayer-in" possibilities.

Support of the 11 women – in individual dioceses, bring pressure to bear on Bishops to change the Chicago action; work on Bishops through Clergy Associations; encourage women; raise money to support women in national appearances; send women in teams so as not to put one on the line; form male clergy groups to work on supporting women.

Attendees included Blanche Powell (VTS '75), Churchill Gibson (VTS '56), Vienna Cobb Anderson (VTS adjunct instructor), William Wendt, Carlyle Gill (VTS '76), William (VTS '58) and Shirley Dols, Cecil Woods (VTS '53), Victoria Hatch (VTS '75), Albert Mollegen (VTS '31), Charles Price (VTS '45), Pat Park (VTS '74), Cynthia Wedel (VTS '79H), Henry Rightor (VTS '48), Bettie Lacy, Bob Kevin (VTS '51), Ted (VTS '53) and Sarah Eastman, Reginald Fuller (VTS '84H), James M. Green (VTS '63), Edgar Romig (VTS '69H), John Frizzell (VTS '54), Pam Chinnis (VTS '83H), Charles Perry (VTS '61), Alison Cheek (VTS '69), and Mary Page

Rollins (VTS '78H).[19]

The Faculty Minutes of Sept. 16, 1974, demonstrate the concern over the crisis by this notation: "Special General Convention Mr. Estill proposed that the faculty adopt a resolution urging the Presiding Bishop to hold a special general convention to deal with the question of the ordination of women. The faculty seemed to favor this idea. There were a number of questions about the practical wisdom of such a move. Would there be enough new deputies to change the outcome, and what would be the effect of having it closer to the events of this past summer? It seemed in general to be wise to suggest this move, and IT WAS MOVED BY MR. ESTILL, SECONDED BY MR. ALBRITTON, THAT WE AGREE IN PRINCIPLE TO REQUEST THE PRESIDING BISHOP AND THE HOUSE OF BISHOPS TO CALL A SPECIAL CONVENTION TO DEAL WITH THE QUESTION OF THE ORDINATION OF WOMEN TO THE PRIESTHOOD AND THAT WE ASK THE COMMITTEE TO PRESENT A DRAFT RESOLUTION TO THIS EFFECT STATING ALSO OUR REASONS FOR MAKING THE REQUEST. THE MOTION CARRIED. The Dean appointed Mr. Estill as chairman and Dr. Rodgers and Dr. Price to draft the resolution."[20] [capitalization theirs]

The VTS resolution calling for a Special General Convention was dated Sept. 23, 1974. A cover letter of Sept 24 to House of Bishops was signed by Dick Reid. Other seminary deans were notified of this action by Cecil Woods on Oct. 1:

---

[19] From the files of Cecil Woods.
[20] pp. 1-2.

THE PROTESTANT EPISCOPAL THEOLOGICAL SEMINARY
IN VIRGINIA
ALEXANDRIA, VIRGINIA 22304

September 24, 1974

To our Right Reverend Fathers in God and Brothers in Christ,

Greetings:

The Faculty of the Protestant Episcopal Theological Seminary in Virginia at its meeting on September 23, 1974, voted unanimously to request the Presiding Bishop and the House of Bishops to call a special meeting of the General Convention in order to act upon the matter of ordaining women to the Priesthood. A copy of that resolution is enclosed.

We do this in awareness of the cost involved in such a meeting but aware too of the heavier cost involved if this matter is not dealt with until the regularly scheduled Convention in 1976.

Our many women students from a number of dioceses throughout the Church reflect what we see to be a general sense of frustration and confusion in the Church.

Surely an issue of this magnitude deserves the immediate and concentrated attention of our elected leaders, and we earnestly request your action upon this resolution.

Faithfully yours,

Richard Reid.

Richard Reid
Secretary of the Faculty[21]

Enclosure: Copy of Resolution

[21] Letter from Richard Reid to the House of Bishops, September 24, 1974, Faculty Minutes, RG V4, 1973-1975, Folder #40, Virginia Theological Seminary Archives, Bishop Payne Library, Alexandria, Virginia.

THE PROTESTANT EPISCOPAL THEOLOGICAL SEMINARY
IN VIRGINIA
ALEXANDRIA, VIRGINIA 22304

A Resolution of the Faculty
The Protestant Episcopal Theological Seminary
In Virginia
September 23, 1974

Whereas the actions of the 1973 General Convention failed to clarify the mind of the Church on the issue of the ordination of women to the Priesthood; and

Whereas widespread confusion and controversy remain throughout the Church over this issue; and

Whereas there are numbers of women in the Diaconate and in our seminaries desiring ordination to the Priesthood; and

Whereas the present plan for considering this matter in 1976 prolongs unnecessarily the agony of indecision and the divisiveness of the issue; now, therefore, be it

RESOLVED: The Faculty of the Protestant Episcopal Theological Seminary in Virginia requests the Presiding Bishop and the House of Bishops of the Episcopal Church to call a special General Convention expressly to deal with the matter of the ordination of women to the Priesthood.

That Fall the Episcopal Divinity School distributed to all seminary faculties a paper entitled "The Meaning of Ordination with respect to Philadelphia and Chicago" and asked for support of this paper from other seminaries. The thesis of the paper was that "…the Philadelphia ordinations met all of the conditions necessary for a 'valid' ordination in terms of traditional Anglican and catholic criteria, but that these ordinations were 'irregular' because of the non-fulfillment of certain canons." The paper cited *Doctrine in the Church of England* to support its position. However, a dissection of the paper and *DCE* by VTS professor of homiletics Milton Crum concluded that *DCE* supported the position of the House of Bishops in Chicago, rather than the statement of EDS. The faculty of VTS were persuaded by Crum's reasoning and on October 8 voted no support for the EDS argument. It took Cecil Woods until November 26, 1974, to send a letter to EDS declining to endorse their statement and stating that, contrary to what EDS claimed, *Doctrine in the Church of England* did not support their position.

The House of Bishops formed a Committee on Theology at Oaxtepec, Mexico, on October 13-18, 1974. On October 19 Suffragan Bishop John Walker of Washington brought a resolution to the Oaxtepec meeting calling for a special General Convention. Standing committees of WA and central NY had officially called for a special convention, just as a special convention had been called on the issue of racism years before. But such a resolution required two-thirds of the signatures of the 220-member House of Bishops, and only 150 attended the meeting in Mexico. Presiding Bishop Allin was not in favor of a special convention. The Faculty Minutes of November 4, 1974, record the following: "Bishop Burt – The Dean reported that he had received a letter from Bishop

Burt [chairman of the Committee on Theology] thanking us for our statement calling for a special meeting of the General Convention on the ordination of women. He said that the bishops had decided not to hold such a convention but that a special committee of the House of Bishops had been appointed."[22]

On October 24, 1974, the *Washington Post* reported that the Standing Committee of the Diocese of Missouri had approved ordination to the priesthood of all qualified candidates, regardless of gender. Its Bishop, George L. Cadigan, refused to proceed, citing collegiality of the House of Bishops.

On Reformation Sunday, October 27, Alison Cheek joined Jeanette Piccard and Carter Heyward in celebrating communion at a packed ecumenical service held in Riverside Church, New York City. All three notified their bishops of their intentions several weeks prior to the celebration. Jeanette Piccard had engraved invitations made and sent to every Episcopal Bishop. The service was an Episcopal liturgy and was Cheek's first public celebration as a priest. She recalls, "My husband was away on a bank mission, and I was trying to put some things in a suitcase to go down the night before to stay the night with Carter. All of a sudden, I was paralyzed with this awful dread. I felt that I was like a South Sea islander who was gong to break some strict taboo, and I was finding it hard to get my act together and get off. Frank Durkie, who was one of the associate priests at St. Stephen and the Incarnation, called me on the phone to see how I was going to New York; and I said that I had a plane ticket and was flying. He had been going by train or bus or some other way. He could hear in my voice that something wasn't right, so he changed his arrangements and traveled with me. I don't know if I actually talked to him about what was happening, but I know that he took me through it. Once

---

[22] p.1.

I got to New York and was with my sisters, this completely disappeared; and when we actually did the service, it just felt right and good, and I wasn't nervous at all."

Grace had come into play in a tangible way. Cheek reflects, "Everything that you could feel in an experience I think we felt. But quite a bit of it was really painful and hurtful. So it wasn't at the time that it felt like grace; but afterwards, looking back and seeing where it led me, I really am extremely grateful for that ordination, for the rejection of me by the Church after that ordination. I remember one release in particular: I had grown up trained to be a people pleaser, and I really wanted everyone to love me. I went to see Bishop Walker and tried to make peace with him. He said, 'Well, Alison, a million people hate you and will oppose your regularization.' I was a little bit shocked and stunned when he said that to me; but afterwards I realized that the people who are important to me are still there loving me just the same and that my life was going on just the same, and it really didn't matter if a million people hated me. That was a tremendous release. That I think was a gift of grace from John Walker."

On November 1, 1974, the *Washington Post* reported that Nancy Hatch Wittig had resigned as curate of St. Peter's Church in Morristown, NJ because "'there is a significant lack of confidence in me as a person worthy of the Christian ministry.' Her action came after the parish vestry refused to affirm her priesthood." The rector of St. Peter's had asked her to wear her stole as a deacon until the controversy around the Philadelphia ordinations had been sorted out. She refused. She then attended two vestry meetings at which she was lectured about how Jackie Robinson[23] was quiet and so she should be quiet. Wittig comments, "Really what they did was beat up on

the rector; and I realized that he had, out of the goodness of his heart and a sense of the right thing, hired me but was totally blown over by the negatives. I then found myself pregnant and thought it a good time to step aside for awhile."[24]

On Sunday, Nov. 10, 1974, Alison Cheek celebrated at St. Stephen and the Incarnation, Washington, D.C., defying—along with rector William Wendt—orders of Bishop Hall, who had inhibited her in VA and Bishop Creighton, who had asked Father Wendt to cancel Mrs. Cheek's participation. A *Washington Post* article the next day called General Convention's voting by unit [i.e., two votes "yes" and two votes "no" means one vote "no"] a "technicality." The Rev. L. A. Paul Rose filed charges with Creighton against Wendt on November 15. Wendt was to be brought to ecclesiastical trial April 30-May 2, 1975.

In the files of Cecil Woods is an internal memo dated December 3, 1974 from Charles Price to Dean Woods, Sid Sanders, Reg Fuller, and Henry Rightor reporting on a lunch meeting of the Committee on Women's Ordination: "Mixie suggested, and we all agreed, that its scope should become the place of women before God and in the Church, of which the topic of ordination to the priesthood would be a part." Betty Works Fuller, Noreen Suriner, and Carlyle Gill were among the students [both male and female] on the committee. This committee was formed, before the Philadelphia Eleven were ordained, by Woods' letter of April 30, 1974.

On December 8, at the invitation of rector Peter Beebe and the people of Christ Church, Alison Cheek and Carter Heyward celebrated at Oberlin, Ohio, beginning a long relationship with that parish.

After the Philadelphia ordinations, at St. Patrick's Parish, Washington, D.C., seminarian Blanche Powell had

---

[23] Jackie Robinson was the first black man to play on an American professional baseball team.

[24] The magazine "The Christian Challenge" then published debates about whether or not the Wittig fetus had been ordained as well.

invited parishioner David Booth Beers, delegate to General Convention and member of the Diocese of Washington Standing Committee, to meet with Alison Cheek and a small group of other parishioners to talk about the ordination of women to the priesthood. Among those in attendance was Jane Holmes Dixon, a member of the diocesan Task Force on Education. Dixon recalls, "Blanche was persuading David that the Standing Committee and the General Convention really needed to move, and that women should [be] passed by the Standing Committee for ordination to the priesthood so that they would be ready....They need to be there to put it sort of in the bishop's face that the Standing committee has said, 'Yes' to these women so Bishop Creighton cannot say, 'Well, the Standing Committee hasn't acted'... and David was sort of, 'Well, we've done this and we've done'....[Blanche] said, 'When are you going to get down here in the mud with us and really slog this out?' And the Standing committee did do it. They voted."[25]

A *Washington Post* article on December 15, 1974, reported that the Standing Committee of the Diocese of Washington approved ordination of qualified candidates for the priesthood "without regard to gender." Bishop Creighton refused to proceed without prior approval from General Convention: "I am responsible for ministry to the whole church and not just to the diocese," he is quoted as having said. What the article did not say was that in a very unusual move, the Standing Committee had held an open hearing at St. Alban's Parish and had spent a day listening to witnesses speak out on whether or not the Diocese of Washington should move forward. At the close of the hearing, the Committee voted seven to one to present to the bishop three women for ordination: Lee McGee, Alison Palmer, and Betty Rosenberg. Creighton re-

sponded that he would wait to ordain until after the 1976 General Convention; but in the meantime, he would not ordain anyone, male or female. Furthermore, Creighton announced to the Standing Committee that if he could be persuaded that he had the authority to ordain a woman in 1977 if the Minneapolis Convention did not adopt a change in the canon, he would ordain a woman regardless of the outcome of that Convention. David Booth Beers was commissioned to research this possibility and was given a monograph by the most recent Anglican Consultative Council to study. The thrust of the paper he presented to Creighton was that the same language appears in the ordinal for all three orders and that the General Convention had already explicitly authorized ordination of women to the diaconate, thereby construing the word "he" to mean "he" or "she." Creighton's response to the paper was, "Great"; and he pledged to ordain women in 1977 even if the delegates voted in 1976 to bar women from the priesthood. He was the only bishop to make such a pledge.[26]

In the files of Cecil Woods are letters of December 31, 1974, to Urban Holmes and Fred Borsch seeking contributions to be included in the Reginald Fuller/ Charles Price faculty-student collection of position papers supporting the ordination of women. Positive responses were received from both about the necessity for such action.

Thus a critical year ended, a year spent under a cloud and through the sea, guided by grace.

[25] Interview with Jane Holmes Dixon, June 8, 2010.
[26] Interview with David Booth Beers, June 10, 2010.

Grace
in Motion

"For by grace you have been saved through faith, and this is not your own doing; it is the gift of God...."

Ephesians 2:8
New Revised Standard Version

Just as testimony comes to human beings from God and witness by human beings follows, so grace comes to humans from God and faith by humans follows. Faith is not our own doing. Grace comes first, enabling faith. But the events through which we pass and through which grace works are not always without pain. The participants in the events of the decade of the seventies often experienced tortured reasoning, anguished decisions, and sorrowful consequences. As Alison Cheek observed, "A lot of hurtful things were necessary ingredients for grace."

One could well ask why such pain is necessary, and one answer might be that nothing worth having is easy. But of one thing we can be certain: "We know that all things work together for good for those who love God, who are called according to his purpose."[1] Thus, it would prove true over the years that grace is possible even in confrontation. And as Nancy Hatch Wittig reflected, "I think the Episcopal Church has continued to grow and stretch…and I am very proud of the Church because it means the faith is getting through, that the institution which is a human construct can change and can review again 'are we living the life we are called to live?' Periodically from different generations the Church forgot what it was supposed to be about, and it will always need to have that reminder. There will always be people that the Holy Spirit puts in our midst who will chal-

lenge us to step out of our comfort zones, and you never know when that is going to happen."

– 1975 –

The *Virginia Seminary Journal* of January 1975 is, with the exception of the book review section, devoted entirely to women's ordination. Pictured on the cover are Professor John Woolverton and nineteen unidentified women. Articles include "Ordination of Women in Theological Perspective" by the Rev. Charles P. Price, professor at VTS; "The Deployment of Clergy Who Happen to be Women" by the Rev. Roddey Reid, Executive Director of the Clergy Deployment Office; "Journey to Philadelphia-

Uncut photo of twenty women and John Woolverton

[1] Romans 8:28, New Revised Standard Version.

the City of Brotherly Love" by the Rev. Alison Cheek; "Pastoral Letters" from the Rt. Rev. John H. Burt and the Rt. Rev. H. Coleman McGehee; "Bishop White and the Philadelphia Ordinations" by the Rev. Henry H. Rightor, professor at VTS; "A Special Parish" by the Rev. William C. Bridgforth and Mrs. Dorrie Dolby of Pine Bluff, Arkansas; "She Lifts our Hearts" by the Rev. John B. Coburn; "Sorting it Out" by the Rev. Patricia M. Park; and "The Diocese of Washington: Task Force on Women in the Church" by Mrs. Marion Henry. Price argues that "ordained persons represent the Church to itself and before God [as well as] represent God to the Church, or Christ to the Church...[and] that women are able to bear the representative function today as they were not in time past."[2] Reid points out that "if a man and a woman apply for the same job, the man will be hired even if the woman is equally or better qualified,"[3] a statistic that remains true today. Burt [Chairman of the Committee on Theology of the House of Bishops] holds that the Philadelphia "ordinations" were invalid, the position taken by the House of Bishops at Chicago, rather than irregular; McGehee takes the "irregular" position. Rightor asserts "General Convention has compromised its own authority and integrity by consistently refusing to provide the Church with representative government"[4] and "[t]he canonical authorities of the individual dioceses can restore order to the Church now, by regularizing the Philadelphia ordinations and proceeding with the ordination of other women to the priesthood."[5] Through its publications, it appeared that the Seminary's posture was in favor of the ordination of women even as a few faculty withheld endorsement.

A summary article in the *Washington Post* of February 21 noted that the board of inquiry into whether four bishops would be brought to trial for ordaining the eleven women in Philadelphia on July 29 would be held that day; that Washington Bishop William F. Creighton would also be formally told that day that the diocesan Board of Presenters unanimously approved bringing Wendt to trial; that similar charges were being brought against the Rev. Peter Beebe, rector of Christ Church, Oberlin, Ohio; that several new organizations were being formed to support women priests; and that Episcopal Bishop John H. Burt of Ohio announced that he will resign as "an act of conscience" if the national church's convention fails to vote for ordaining women. Here again is ample evidence of the conflict between duty and conscience, a conflict faced by many.

For example, the debate on campus continued: Betty Works Fuller recalls, "Several of the Philadelphia Eleven and [what were to be] the Washington Five came to campus and wanted us to form a support group. But what it turned into was that they wanted us to support them and their struggles, but there was no reciprocity in terms of helping us. I guess they were not in a place where they could be mentors for the next generation. I went to a couple of the sessions, and I was angry. Keeping in mind, I was still in my early twenties; and so I think maybe there was a sense of separation between...[pause]. I would love to be in a conversation now with some of the ladies who went through that, to see what was going on; because when you look at it, very few of them ended up in parochial situations....It would be interesting to see again over the generations...."[6]

In April of her senior year, Blanche Powell en-

[2] *Virginia Seminary Journal*, January 1975, pp. 3-4.
[3] Ibid., p. 9.
[4] Ibid., p. 14.
[5] Ibid., p. 16.
[6] Interview.

countered on campus a priest from her diocese, Murray Trelease, who was doing continuing education at VTS. He said to her, "Blanche, they are going to nail the coffin on you. They are not going to ordain a woman in the diocese of Milwaukee. You have got to get out of that diocese if you are gong to be ordained." This news was confirmed by another priest of that diocese who took a straw ballot of the Commission on Ministry/Standing Committee. In response Cecil Woods, Sid Saunders, and Milton Crum arranged to send a copy of a sermon Blanche Powell had preached at VTS to Bishop Gaskell. It was a sermon whose thesis was "You can't go home again," and Carlyle Gill had had to talk Powell through it the night before delivery because Powell was "a wreck." Powell recalls, "I cried through that sermon. I thought I wasn't going to get through it, but Milton Crum waited on me to pull myself back together....Apparently [Gaskell] listened to it. And when I had to meet with him, he did share some really intimate things with me. I saw a tear in his eyes....I saw him as a human being."[7] Powell was able to get out of the Diocese of Milwaukee and into the Diocese of Virginia. She reflects, "It was the support of people like that faculty at VTS. There were a couple of faculty members who didn't support our being ordained, maybe two or three. They didn't let on. At one point I remember Dean Woods talking to [one]...saying, 'If you don't support our women here, what are you doing here?'...kind of that, not the same words: 'If you can't support our women being ordained then maybe you shouldn't be here.' So Cecil was good. I liked him. I thought a lot of him. We had a good faculty, and that's really where I found the support of VTS [because] we had some classmates who couldn't deal with us, especially if we were involved with the Caucus. There were some women who wouldn't involve themselves with a caucus. They kind of rode our skirt tails: We were the

ones who walked the front lines, and some others wouldn't come to the Caucus; but I know it made me a better priest, made me a stronger person, clear about my vocation. I would not wish that experience on anybody, but I am grateful in so many ways because of the people I met along the way and what I learned about me along the way....It made me more willing to speak up and to take on a position like that. Sometimes I think I knew the experience of crucifixion and needed to know that experience of resurrection." Grace had manifested itself in confrontation.

Blanche Powell

On Saturday, April 5, 1975, the *Washington Post* published an article in anticipation of the trial of the Rev. William A. Wendt in which the work of the local chapter of Women's Ordination Now was prominently mentioned and the efforts of Carlyle Gill, highlighted: "Before his unusual and emotionally-charged ordeal begins, local members of Women's Ordination Now (WON) hope to see funds for his defense grow to at least $5,000 to meet lawyer's expenses and witnesses' travel....A communicant of Alexandria's Emmanuel Church is a spearheader of the local effort. Leading the campaign with her are Carlyle Gill, a Virginia Theological Seminary student and field worker at Immanuel Church on the Hill there....Both the Rt. Rev. John M. Allin, presiding bishop of the U.S. Episcopal Church, and his predecessor, Bishop John Hines, have been subpoenaed to testify....Allin did little to endear himself to the growing number of women, graduated

[7] Interview with Blanche Lee Powell, July 10, 2010.

from seminary and elevated to the deaconate [sic], waiting to become priests. He observed during a press conference if there was no theological reason not to let women be priests he was still waiting to hear a good reason to let them be....Hines [declared the Philadelphia eleven] priesthoods were valid."

On April 30 at St. Columba's Church, Washington, D.C., the Rev. William A. Wendt was brought to trial for disobeying the godly admonition of his bishop. In her senior year in law school, Katherine Grieb attended both the trial and the appeal because "other sorts of disciplinary trials are not so rare, but a trial about theological principle is rare." Grieb continues, "The whole life of the parish [St. Stephen's and the Incarnation] was consumed with the trial because the parish had wanted to be tried along with Bill. Canon law doesn't hold the parish responsible. The rector is held responsible. But this parish was so strongly committed to lay leadership that we tried to get the vestry and the senior wardens and the parish as a whole tried along with Bill Wendt. It didn't happen. It was an important attempt, I think, looking back on it now."[8]

Among the witnesses called were Alison Cheek and Marion Kelleran. When asked if she had publicly celebrated Holy Communion at the Church of St. Stephen and the Incarnation on November 10, 1974, Cheek replied, "Yes. I presided at the Eucharist. We all celebrated."[9] When pressed about the fact that she had not waited to exercise her priesthood, she responded, "Sun shines, rain falls, wind blows, and priests preside at Eucharists."[10]

Marion Kelleran's testimony began as follows:
"Q. Give us a brief statement, Doctor, regarding your opinion of the Defendant's character.

"A. Well, sir, if I can use a term which I heard used yesterday, the word 'character' is indeed a word of art, and I would have to go into a long philosophical discussion.

"I do not hold the definition of the word 'character' that I would have held, say, in 1965. I think there is a vast change in our understanding of this.

"It would be generally agreed, I think, that Father Wendt is a 'character.'

(Laughter)

"I do not mean this in anything except to say that he has a unique quality, and Father Wendt would be the first one to say that his unique quality and my unique quality are not necessarily easily compatible.

Marion Kelleran

"We march to very different drums. I am a conservative, law and order, get our card in on time, say you are coming to the meeting, be prompt person. And Bill Wendt is an available, open, human, non-organization type.

"It has been my fate to be a bureaucrat, and on the whole, that's been a very happy fate. But the result is that my first memory of dealing with him was extraordinarily difficult, because we undertook a program at his request, and then he hired someone to run a program who didn't want the program that we had spent a good deal of time and energy on.

---

[8] Interview with A. Katherine Grieb, May 25, 2010.
[9] Ecclesiastical Court of the Diocese of Washington the Board of Presenters v. The Rev. William A. Wendt April 30, 1975-May 2, 1975, p. 196.
[10] Ibid., p. 197.

"But I learned from this experience to appreciate a quality in Bill Wendt which, I think, is relevant here, and that is, he is always way ahead of me in seeing the importance and the depth of human experience, and he responds to that more than he does to organizational structure. That's my experience of him, and I learned to appreciate this.

"I sometimes describe myself as 'Emmaus Road Christian.' I do not always, like the men on the Emmaus Road, know when I am walking with Christ.

"The next day, I say, did not my heart burn within me, and Bill Wendt seems to know when he is walking with Christ, and he has helped me and taught me to have a much more acute conscience than I have either been given or have managed to suppress over the years, in the interest of being a bureaucrat.

"I hope that is clear. At any rate, the acuteness of his conscience and his ability to walk in other people's shoes and to know how they feel has been one of the great learning experiences of what has been a very lovely relationship; not always an easy one. I'm told the saints were difficult, and I'm difficult and not a saint.

"But my affection for him and my admiration are equal, and I owe him a great debt in stirring up my conscience.

"(Mr. Bou): Thank you.

"(Chief Judge Thomas): Any questions from the Church Advocate?

"(Mr. Stirling): I wouldn't dare ask her a question. (Laughter.)"[11]

Here was a woman not only able to work within the structures of the institutional Church but also able to reflect theologically upon the implications of the actions of its members, the epitome of grace in motion.

Though the matter of conscience was an underlying thread running through the three-day trial, the issue defense attorney William Stringfellow argued was that of the validity of the ordination of Alison Cheek as against the church advocate/prosecutor's position that the issue was whether or not Wendt had disobeyed the godly admonition of his bishop. The *Washington Post* reported that as Wendt "headed for the witness stand, the final witness in his own defense, some 50 persons, most of them members of his Church of St. Stephen and the Incarnation, rose in silent tribute to him. It was the nearest thing to a demonstration that took place in the decorous court."[12] The decision of the court was that the question at hand was not the ordination of women, per se, but that Wendt had violated the godly admonition of his bishop.

The appeal to the Standing Committee, the reviewing court, was a difficult period. There were three women on the Standing Committee, among them Sally Bucklee and Verna Dozier. The four men were David Booth Beers, the Rev. Ed Romig, the Rev. Bill Swing, and the Rev. Almus Thorpe, substituting for the Rev. Ted Eastman who had a conflict. The women voted to reverse and set aside the conviction. The men sustained the conviction. Beers wrote the opinion which argued that when one is accused of something and one breaks the rule, even because of conscience, one still breaks the rule and takes the consequences. The consequences in this case were that Bishop Creighton took Wendt to one of the lower chapels at the Cathedral and issued the following sentence, "Bill, please don't do this again."[13]

Alison Cheek elaborates on this scene: "[It was] a public reproof which was given in a chapel in the Wash-

[11] Ibid., pp. 232-235.
[12] *Washington Post,* Saturday, May 3, 1975, A6.
[13] Interview with David Booth Beers, June 10, 2010.

ington Cathedral, and of course it was a small chapel which I think the Bishop chose deliberately because they didn't want a huge 'to do.' It was packed of course, including press. Lee McGee, who was then a deacon at St. Stephen and the Incarnation, and I decided that we would stand one each side of Bill when he had to stand up before the Bishop, to say 'Hey, this is not just Bill Wendt.' So when the time did come, we did get up and stand each side of him."[14]

The newspapers continued to keep the Episcopal Church's turmoil in the news: The *Washington Post* reported on May 3 that Presiding Bishop John M. Allin had been cited for contempt of the ecclesiastical court for failing to appear to testify in Wendt's trial.

On June 20, the Rev. Peter Beebe of Christ Church, Oberlin, Ohio, was brought to trial. Officials in Ohio had attended William Wendt's ecclesiastical trial and seen that it was dangerous to allow testimony as to the validity of the orders of the Philadelphia Eleven. They, therefore, ruled in Ohio that no testimony as to validity would be given or taken. Moreover, witnesses were not allowed to listen to the testimony but were shut up in the witness room. Alison Cheek, one of the witnesses, recalls of this trial, "It did not have any of the tone that the Washington trial did. It was pretty awful. He was found guilty by five priest judges; and before they gave their verdict, they praised him for living out the gospel! It was so odd; it was a very odd trial. But I think it was at that trial I realized that this wasn't just a community with a difference of opinion that was trying to resolve it. This was war. I had always told Bishop Hall what I was going to do before I did it so that he wouldn't be surprised by a newspaper landing on his doorstep. After that trial, I called him

and told him I wouldn't be telling him anymore what I would be doing....All of a sudden [telling him] felt silly, two-faced or something. There was something about that trial in Ohio that had a stark impact on me. I stopped thinking that people could be persuaded and simply responded to invitations to act as priest when they made sense for me....That was painful." The *Washington Star* reported on June 23 that the Rev. Peter Beebe, in open defiance of his bishop's order to desist, had allowed Alison Cheek and Carter Heyward to celebrate communion in his parish for the eighth time.

On August 6, 1975, the *New York Times* reported that the Rt. Rev. John E. Craine had vowed not to ordain anyone, male or female, until the 1976 General Convention, that the Rt. Rev. William Creighton of Washington had said he would ordain women after the 1976 Convention even if the delegates voted to bar women from the priesthood, and that the Rt. Rev. John Burt (VTS '43) of Ohio had threatened to resign if the convention barred women from the priesthood.

On Sunday, September 7, 1975, at St. Stephen and the Incarnation, the Rt. Rev. George W. Barrett, resigned bishop of Rochester, who in 1965 had headed the Presiding Bishop's Committee to Study the Proper Place of Women in the Ministry of the Church, ordained Lee McGee (a member of the parish), Alison Palmer, Diane Tickell, and Dr. Elizabeth (Betty) Powell Rosenberg (VTS '72)[15] to the priesthood. The Rev. Alison Cheek, the Rev. Peter Beebe, and the Rt. Rev. Robert DeWitt participated in the service. Another member of St. Stephen and the Incarnation made a special effort to attend: Katherine Grieb was waiting tables that night to put herself through law school. She had to carry a change of clothes to work and

---

[14] Interview with Alison Cheek, May 13-16, 2010.
[15] After her graduation from VTS, Rosenberg earned a Doctor of Ministry degree from Bexley Hall.

ride the bus to be present; but as she says, "I really wanted to be there…somehow you get to the things that you really want to get to."[16]

Betty Powell reflects on the Washington Four ordinations: "The way you move those in power is you create enough chaos that they have to change. They have to move. So it became clear that there had to be another ordination to prove that this [the Philadelphia Eleven ordination] wasn't just a one-time thing. It wasn't going to stop. We were serious. This had to happen. It was time."

Bishop Creighton had issued a pastoral letter, read that Sunday morning in churches throughout his diocese, asking Episcopalians to stay away from the rite. As a result, half the members of the Diocesan Task Force on Education attended; and half did not, among them Jane Dixon. She comments, "One of the women being ordained had asked me to read the Epistle. I decided not to go. I was a good girl." Here again is an example of the self-image of a woman raised in a conservative part of the country [Mississippi]. Being a "good girl" was her *modus operandum*: "I was used to doing basically what I was told."

On September 12, 1975, a *Washington Post* article quoted Henry Rightor as saying that the bishops who refuse to ordain "are defying their church's canons and constitution more than are the 15 women who have been irregularly ordained."

Meeting from September 19-26, 1975, in Portland, ME, the House of Bishops issued "A New Statement by the Committee on Theology on the Ordination of Women…there is an immediate and formal correlation between the powers of the ordained ministry and the community within which that power is exercised. To say a correlation is found between community and the sacramental power of the ministry is to say that each refers to the other in order to be itself; neither is itself in isolation from the other….A bishop can legitimately function and be himself only within community for community, although his ministry derives from Christ in ordination, not from the community." This statement sought to bolster the bishops' Chicago statement that the ordinations of the fifteen women were invalid versus the carefully reasoned arguments of Rochester theologians Professors Richard Norris, Eugene Fairweather, J. E. Griffiss, and Albert T. Mollegen calling the ordinations sacramentally valid though canonically irregular, so no re-ordination would be necessary.

Henry Rightor

On September 24, the *Washington Post* reported the censure of the ordaining bishops: Presentment charges against the four ordaining bishops were presented to Allin by thirteen bishops. Bishops Corrigan, Welles, and DeWitt were censured. The action of the Rt. Rev. George W. Barrett was decried. The article concluded with this announcement: "In other actions, the bishops approved a resolution, introduced by the Rt. Rev. William F. Creighton of Washington, calling for study of 'steps to be followed, *either on approval or rejection of the ordination of women*' at the church's General Convention next year with 'special attention' to the plan voted earlier this year by the Anglican Church of Canada. The Canadian plan gives *the head of each diocese* the option of deciding whether or not to or-

---

[16] Interview with A. Katherine Grieb, May 25, 2010.

dain women priests or to license those already ordained." [emphases mine]

The Faculty Minutes of November 3, 1975 contain the attachment of a letter dated Oct. 29, 1975, from the rector of St.Paul's Haymarket, the Rev. Robert H. Crewdson: "Finally we are concerned over the way controversial issues are handled by some professors. We are referring specifically to the reported appearance of Allison [sic] Cheek to teach in Dr. Rightor's class on one or more occasions last year. There was no report that the other side of the issue was represented. We in the Diocese of Virginia are aware of Dr. Rightor's strong desire to have women ordained. We believe that to have someone come to a class and teach one side of the issue without having a qualified person present the other side is of questionable integrity."

Some women from Virginia Seminary continued to feel pulled by both sides of the debate: Deacon Mary Hansley was on the staff of the Cathedral in Minneapolis where there was a politically active group working for women's ordination to pass at the 1976 General Convention to be held in Minneapolis. She comments, "It was a wonderful group of both men and women, but two of the eleven ordained [the Rev. Alla Bozarth-Campbell and the Rev. Jeannette Piccard] were leaders of this committee. They were from my diocese, and I thought, 'Maybe I have a responsibility.' I was invited to join the group, and I went to the first meeting. It was the group's assumption that the Philadelphia ordinations were the only way to go. I didn't understand it well enough to really know what I thought about it. I made a statement saying so. I'm surprised I was still alive when I came out of that meeting. I didn't speak out *against*. I just said I didn't know….They just ate me alive. Came down on me. It was awful. I can

understand now, because I feel that way sometimes about people who don't understand. *I* didn't understand. I went to two meetings and couldn't stand it. I was having enough trouble trying to figure out why I was there anyway. Convention came and I was in Minneapolis. There was all this wonderful noble language, and yet I thought, it really doesn't matter if it passes or not. Women can minister anyway. I was so myopic, so into my own personal stuff. Here was such an historic event, and I didn't understand a thing. That's what is sad."[17]

– 1976 –

The February 23, 1976, Faculty Minutes include the following notation: "<u>Georgia Shoberg</u> (VTS '76) Dr. Reid announced that Georgia will be teaching the introductory Greek and Hebrew course in the fall. This arrangement was made in order to free Dr. Reid for the extra duties in connection with the Dean's sabbatical."[18]

The files of Cecil Woods contain a letter dated March 2, 1976, from the National Coalition for Women's Ordination to the Priesthood and Episcopacy. The letter was sent in an Immanuel-on-the-Hill envelope and its letterhead lists the following individuals: Chairperson Rev. George F. Regas, All Saints, Pasadena; Rev. Patricia Merchant Park, Vice-Chair, Seminary P. O., Alexandria; Policy Board members Pam Chinnis, Marion Kelleran, Henry Rightor, Bishop John Walker and others. It mentions Pat Park's traveling since the previous June "to Diocesan Conventions, church pulpits, conferences and panels" for political and educational action purposes. Carlyle Gill clarifies the distinction between this Caucus and others by noting that the National Coalition was most helpful politically, getting deputies to vote and organize. Gill herself was part

---

[17] *Virginia Seminary Journal*, January 1986, p. 5.
[18] Faculty Minutes, p. 1.

of Women's Ordination Now, what she and others recognized as the radical arm of the movement.

At the May 1976 Commencement, Georgia Shoberg and Jule Carlyle Gill were among the graduates to receive a Master in Divinity degree. Gill believes she obtained her first job out of seminary largely due to Cecil Woods: She was called to be Assistant University Chaplain at the University of the South in Sewanee, Tennessee, a college which had just recently become co-educational. She notes, "There were a lot of very conservative students here [at VTS], many of whom were from Sewanee, and they were horrified that I was going to go there to be the chaplain to the college." None of the St. Luke Seminary faculty was a woman, and Gill was the only woman in the college administration. She recalls, "I remember when I first was ordained a priest, the big news in Sewanee was my ordination…but also every week something called the *Sewanee Purple*

LEFT TO RIGHT: Carlyle Gill & Georgia Shoberg

comes out with a list of who's preaching and who's celebrating. People would come when I preached and stayed away when I celebrated. Or if they hadn't read the *Purple* and saw me coming in last in line as celebrant, people would leave in droves. By the time I left—I was only there three years—that was over."[19]

On June 1, 1976, the faculty were informed of the following decision: "The Dean announced to the faculty that Georgia [Shoberg] will attend faculty meetings next year since she will be serving as an instructor in bibli-

LEFT TO RIGHT: Georgia Shoberg, Charles Price, Churchill Gibson

cal languages."[20] The *Virginia Seminary Journal*, Summer 1976, contained a broader account: "*The Rev. Georgia H. Shoberg*, a member of the Class of 1976 receiving the Master in Divinity cum laude, has been appointed Instructor in Biblical Languages for 1976-77. Miss Shoberg who was ordained deacon in June is spending the summer as a member of the staff of Christ Church, Grosse Pointe, Michigan. She holds B.A. (with High Distinction) and M.L.S. degrees from the University of Michigan (1968), is a member of the Cathedral Church of St. Paul, Detroit and was active as a lay teacher and counselor before entering Virginia Seminary….The Rev. Miss Shoberg will be the second woman on the faculty for next year. She joins Dr. Marianne Micks, Ph.D., Professor of Biblical and Historical Theology."[21] Georgia Shoberg is pictured in the 1976-1977 *Catalogue* as instructor in Biblical Languages. Alison Cheek can be seen in the December 1967 *Seminary Journal* in a photograph entitled "Virginia Seminary Faculty 1967-68"; and she was pictured in the 1968-69 *Catalogue* among the list of faculty. Cheek, however, had not been invited to attend faculty meetings, presumably because

[19] Interview with Carlyle Gill, May 19, 2010.
[20] Faculty Minutes, p. 1.
[21] *Journal*, p. 3.

she was still a student when she held the title "instructor in Biblical Languages."

Correspondence had been received[22] from the Rt. Rev. John H. Burt, Bishop of Ohio and Chairman of the Theology Committee of the House of Bishops, actively seeking responses from seminaries to the interpretation of the Doctrine of the Church cited in his committee's report. A faculty committee consisting of Micks, Price, Fuller, Rodgers, and Rightor proposed a response on June 2, 1976, to which Dr. Reid and Dr. Micks voted no and Drs. Whitney, VanDevelder and Ross abstained.[23] The vote recorded on the revision notes that Goodwin, Ross, Whitney, VanDevelder, and Reid abstained.[24] The motion to "distribute a copy of this statement to our own graduates who were ordained in Philadelphia or WA" carried with Goodwin, Whitney, Reid, and Ross abstaining. On June 15, 1976, a letter on behalf of the faculty to Bishop Burt recommended "necessary canonical action to remedy deficiencies" ["(a) The ordinands were not canonically certified by their respective Standing Committees and Bishops. [and] (b) The Bishops were not acting with juris- diction or canonical authorization.] "be taken retroactively by Bishops and Standing Committees." Five members of the faculty abstained.

Meanwhile, the book for which Cecil Woods had sought contributions from scholars of the Church was published. Entitled *Toward a New Theology of Ordination: Essays on the Ordination of Women*, it was edited by Marianne H. Micks and Charles P. Price. The forward by John M. Krumm, Bishop of Southern Ohio, asked readers to come to the essays "with a readiness to have the Spirit of Wisdom speak through them to your mind and heart."

Contributors included Reginald H. Fuller, Professor of New Testament at VTS; Frederick H. Borsch, Dean of CDSP; Lloyd G. Patterson, Professor of Historical Theology at EDS; Arthur A. Vogel, Bishop of West Missouri; Urban T. Holmes, Dean of the School of Theology at the University of the South; James E. Griffiss, Professor and Sub-Dean at Nashotah House; Ruth Tiffany Barnhouse, Clinical Assistant in Psychiatry, Harvard University; Frans Jozeph van Beeck, S.J., Professor of Theology at Boston College; and Henry H. Rightor, Professor of Pastoral Care at VTS. These essays put forward carefully reasoned, in-depth arguments which considered all aspects of the arguments for and against the ordination of women. The essay of Ruth Tiffany Barnhouse, the only female contributor, would continue to provide guidance for the church debates of the twenty-first century. All the essays concluded in favor of the ordination of women.

Thus, a chorus of witnesses was assembling: Bishops who would refuse to ordain men until women could be ordained; bishops who threatened resignation in the event women's ordination did not pass the 1976 Convention; bishops who sought to work through channels to validate local option; bishops who vowed to begin ordaining women in 1977, regardless of the outcome of General Convention; caucuses of men and women, lay and ordained, who worked political channels behind the scenes and others who worked to support those already irregularly ordained; theologians and scholars who published supportive essays; and male deacons such as the Rev. Robert W. Prichard [later Arthur Lee Kinsolving Professor of Christianity in America and Instructor in Liturgy at VTS] who refused

---

[22] On Feb. 18, 1976.
[23] Faculty Minutes, June 2, 1976, p. 2.
[24] Ibid., p. 4.

to proceed with his own ordination to the priesthood for two and one-half years, until women could be ordained priests.[25] Grace was in motion in confrontation.

The *Journal* of Summer 1976 reported on the progress of a graduate from the previous year: "Featured in a recent article in the Torrence, CA "Daily Breeze" was VTS graduate Victoria Hatch ('75)…'despite the controversy within the Episcopal denomination over women entering the ordained ministry, Miss Hatch has 100% acceptance from the St. Cross congregation.' Miss Hatch is employed in Hermosa Beach, CA, the first ordained woman deacon in the Diocese of Los Angeles."[26]

Victoria Hatch

The *Journal* of Fall 1976 pictures on the cover the incoming class: A. Katherine Grieb was among 12 other women shown as well as the first married couple admitted *together*, David and Henrietta Williams, he only recently having accepted the idea of women priests and she seeking the permanent diaconate.[27]

Also entering that Fall was Patricia Thomas.

Patricia Thomas

Thomas had been the second female Senior Warden at St. Andrew's, State College, Pennsylvania, the first having served during World War II. She was very active in her parish, functioning as lay reader, chalice bearer, and Sunday School teacher. As Carlyle Gill had similarly observed, for Thomas, when the Church first began to talk about the ordination of women, "it just didn't seem real."[28] But in 1974 she started attending a Diocesan School of Christian Studies and gradually began giving herself permission to admit that she really wanted a seminary education. This possibility she negotiated with her husband and two children; and leaving them to develop new family coping mechanisms, she commuted between her dormitory room at VTS and the family home in State College, beginning in the Fall of 1976.

On September 16, 1976, at the General Convention in Minneapolis, legislation permitting the ordination of women to the priesthood and episcopacy passed. It was not a grace-full process. Heather Huyck summarized as follows: "The [National] Coalition [for Women's Ordination to the Priesthood and Episcopacy] played off the [irregularly ordained] women priests and W.O.N. [the more radical Women's Ordination Now caucus] with its leadership of Pat Park, Helen Havens, and S. Columba Gillis,

---

[25] Huyck, p. 51, notes that "The National Coalition had seven bishops on its Policy and Advisory Boards. One of these, the Rt. Reverend Richard Trelease, attended most of the Coalition meetings and was invaluable as a member. The extent of Episcopal support for the National Coalition is best illustrated by the fact that 47 percent of their contributions came from bishops."

[26] *Journal*, p. 36.

[27] The *Journal* editor's designation of the Williams' as a "first" is somewhat misleading. In fact, two other couples had attended VTS at the same time: Stephen R. Park (VTS '73) and Patricia Merchant Park (VTS '74) as well as Frank Fuller (VTS '74) and Betty Works Fuller (VTS '75). The Williams' were simply the first couple to enter in the same class.

[28] Interview with Patricia Thomas, May 11, 2010.

all women deacons. It could assure the institutional church that not all women who sought ordination to the priesthood were rebels....[29] The women, particularly Pat Park, were often angry at the mentality and techniques used in such politics. But they realized that the men they were cooperating with had skills to teach them if they wanted to work within the institutional church. Each women [sic] had to decide if winning the vote was important enough to her to accept the methods involved. Most did decide the vote was that important....[30] By focusing on the right of women to enter the church's clergy rather than the necessity of women to change the church, the Coalition reassured the church....The Coalition focused on the legalistic 'right' of women to be ordained; W.O.N., on the symbolic 'necessity' of women to answer God's calls to the priesthood. The one approach was rational and intellectual; the other, more affective."[31]

Thus, something was gained and something was lost: The vision of wholeness, the idea that women priests could move the Church to deeper levels of mystical, theological understanding was subordinated to an Enlightenment stance based on human rights and human equality. As a matter of expediency, female clergy were promoted as "professionals" rather than symbols. Basically, the Church did not change: She simply retrenched. Perhaps it was too much to expect that confrontation with the lesser gods of human nature could be beneficial, that people could come to recognize that sacrifice does indeed make holy. In any case, struggle with unconscious attitudes was avoided. Through tortured reasoning, anguished decisions, and sorrowful consequences, the institutional Church was kept on life-support; and grace slipped into the shadows.

Patricia Merchant (Pat Merchant Park at the time) recalls, "I left the Convention exhausted and went home to my two and a half year-old daughter Laura. On Monday of the General Convention with only three days remaining, the House of Bishops voted to require the 'irregularly' ordained women to be ordained again, something they said they would never do. When I was reached by phone and told of the decision, I was furious. This action was a betrayal of the good work that had been done by the Coalition. I sent my bishop, Bishop Hall of Virginia, a telegram. I told him that I would not be ordained and other women deacons would join me if the bishops did not rescind this vindictive action. To my amazement, Bishop Hall read my telegram on the floor of the House of Bishops; and this action was changed. Women priests would be 'received' into the priesthood by their Bishops."[32]

Members of the Triennial Meeting of the Episcopal Church women also chided the House of Bishops, calling their decision to require reordination "mean-spirited." Writing of this event, Suzanne Hiatt repeated observations she had made years before: "It was small wonder, then, that the 1976 General Convention voted that women could be ordained to all orders of ministry (including the episcopate). The events of the intervening years had reversed the conventional wisdom of the 1973 Convention that it would be more trouble to ordain women than not. By 1976 it was clear that the more divisive course for the church would be to continue to deny ordination to women. At the 1976 General Convention, the bishops approved measures to admit the fifteen

---

[29] Huyck, p. 204.
[30] Ibid., pp. 217-8.
[31] Ibid., pp. 251-2.
[32] Written reflections received from Pat Merchant April 30, 2011.

women priests to regular standing without reordination. Despite that, the House of Bishops has never revised its 1974 and 1975 opinions that no ordinations took place in Washington and Philadelphia."[33]

The *Seminary Journal* published subsequently to General Convention says nothing about the passage of legislation in favor of women's ordination. Then junior seminarian Katherine Grieb recalls, "There was a reception [on September 16] at Dick Reid's house, a party. Word went through the dorms and we were invited to come to the Reid's house for a celebration, and somebody rang the chapel bells. I remember [a male faculty member] saying to me, 'There are people here who are hurting. Don't you think you can NOT ring the chapel bell?' I actually didn't ring the chapel bell, but somebody had, and I was in favor of it. I thought it was a time of liberation and celebration, and his thought was that we should be very quiet about it, and that was hard. That was very hard."[34]

Mary Belfry's reaction was ridden with angst: "When women's ordination passed, I was just dumbfounded. The parish set my ordination date without even asking me. They were more excited than I was, saying, 'We're going to do it in January! The bishop called and talked to me about wanting to ordain me at the same time he regularized Alla Bozarth-Campbell and Jeannette Piccard, and what a wonderful healing thing this would be. And I said, 'Hold it. Wait a minute. I don't know if I want to be ordained. I don't mind waiting until April. Why are you all forcing this?' Meanwhile, the parish was going ahead. The dean said, 'Don't be silly, of course you're going to be ordained. Everyone was doing it for

me."[35] Belfry goes on to say why she declined to be ordained with the other two: "I refused. I wouldn't have anything to do with them. You see, they were naughty and I was good. If they had put us together, I would have had to be responsible for those naughty ones, and my parish wouldn't have liked that. They didn't want their good little girl tainted by those naughty women! So I was ordained by myself a week or so after they were regularized."[36]

On October 4, 1976, the Faculty Minutes record the following: Ordination of Women "Dr. Reid expressed surprise at the amount of negative reaction among the men students concerning the admission of women to the priesthood. He spoke of the protest action which occurred the morning after Dr. Trotter had preached and of the poor attitude of some of the students generally. Dr. Trotter thought that the immaturity and cowardice of this form of reaction was [sic] disturbing. Mr. Pregnall reported that there was deep feeling among the women in not being free to express their joy at the vote in the General Convention. Dr. Whitney mentioned that elsewhere in the church there are various meetings to heal this divisiveness. In Pennsylvania there was a conference for clergy and their wives called 'Heal and Deal.' A similar conference was held in Arlington, Va. Dr. Fuller asked if there might be some opportunity outside the regular worship services to celebrate the occasion of women being admitted to the priesthood. Dr. Micks said such a proposal is forthcoming. The matter is to be brought before the faculty Worship Committee soon."[37]

The Winter 1976 *Journal* records "Congratula-

---

[33] *Religious Institutions and Women's Leadership: New Roles Inside the Mainstream,* ed. Catherine Wessinger (Columbia, South Carolina: University of South Carolina Press, 1996), 217.

[34] The bell calling people to chapel is located in the tower of Aspinwall.

[35] *Journal*, pp. 5-6.

[36] Ibid., p. 6.

[37] p. 3.

tions to Alison Cheek (VTS '69) chosen by TIME Magazine as one of the twelve 'Women of the Year.' Mrs. Cheek was cited as a symbol of 'the new consciousness of women' and noted as having been the first woman to celebrate Communion at a U.S. Episcopal Church. She is employed as a priest at Washington's church of St. Stephen and the Incarnation."[38]

If grace in motion bestows the ability to negotiate the byways of the institutional Church while still maintaining theological integrity, then faith in what is not yet seen is absolutely necessary. Sometimes it is confrontation that is required to take the Church to a new level of understanding, but always it is grace that enables faith and is available in that confrontation. What was not yet seen in 1976, the image of wholeness, was still to be experienced. But by the grace of God, women began to raise the outline of that image before the face of the Church; and in that revealing there would be benediction for all.

[38] Detractors would note that it took twelve women to equal one man as person of the year in *Time Magazine*.

GRACE
in Motion
CHAPTER SIX

"I once had a dream. I dreamt that even though a man, I was pregnant, pregnant and filled with nothingness, like a woman who is with child, and out of the nothingness, God was born."

Meister Eckhart

"Nothingness" in our driven world has the pejorative connotation of emptiness or oblivion. But there is another way to think about nothingness. Nothingness denotes space, a *tabula rasa,* a new horizon. Might it be that the holy Wisdom of God, the *hagia Sophia,* requires our facing the unexamined side of our supposedly objective, carefully ordered lives, turning to the kingdom of God within to encounter an unanticipated Subject and new life?

It is a fact that in Western educational systems, women are taught to think like men: in linear, non-discursive patterns of logic. One argument for linear logic, an objective appraisal of life limited to human parameters, is found in the German philosopher Heidegger's assertion that language precedes experience. An aspect of that claim is that language orders our lives. By ordering our thoughts in certain ways, we understand our experiences in certain ways. But ordering limits, and labeling constricts. Moreover, such judgments rely only on conscious reasoning and make no allowance for intuitive or instinctual understanding.

God does not fit into our neatly circumscribed categories. God's awe-full grace quite often is bestowed drop by drop through the metaphoric, inventive kingdom within human nature. God creates *ex nihilo.*

– The Unfolding of the Wisdom Within –

In 1833, Oberlin had become the first co-educational college in the United States. In the 1850's, several mid-west and western state universities became co-ed. But women's colleges, which began to appear in the mid-nineteenth century, afforded students the opportunity to model themselves after both men and women's leadership

Katherine Grieb

because women's institutions gradually began to hire equal numbers of men and women faculty. By attending the women's college Hollins, Katherine Grieb was not only able to see women in leadership but also to exercise leadership, such as being president of the Action for Peace group. Thus, when after college she attended law school and started hearing about things that women could and couldn't do, she knew better because she had seen women class presidents and vice presidents. In law school she became interested in how people change from within. In her own words, "I got interested in conversion."

– 1977 –

The ordination of Pat Park on Jan. 2, 1977, marked the beginning of grace-filled celebrations attended by hundreds who had already been converted to the possibility of new life for the Church. Park's was the first ordination of a woman to the priesthood in Virginia and the second regular such ordination in the United States. The *Washington Post* summarized the service as follows:

Patricia Laura Merchant Park last night became the first woman in the Washington area ordained an Episcopal priest with the full blessing of her church.

The two-hour ordination rite, held in the field house of the

Episcopal High School in Alexandria, was marked by an atmosphere of joy and celebration and was meant to signal the beginning of a new era in the Episcopal Church, which for centuries has restricted its priesthood to males.

Nearly 100 persons—many of them members of Immanuel Church-on-the-Hill where Mrs. Park had served as a deacon for 2 ½ years—watched the colorful ceremony, conducted by Episcopal Bishop Robert Hall of Virginia. Those present included many who had fought for women priests in the Episcopal church….

Although none of the irregularly ordained women has had her priesthood formally recognized by the church, two of them—the Rev. Alison Cheek and the Rev. Lee McGee—helped distribute Communion during yesterday's service.

Last night, the congregation joyfully shouted the Amens, the "Thanks Be to God" and other responses indicated in the ordination ceremony previously reserved for men. They joined prayerfully in the Communion service presided over by the new priest. Afterward they gathered at the far end of the field house for a stand up pot-luck supper and more rejoicing.

Nearly 100 clergymen and women in ecclesiastical robes—most of them Episcopalian but some from other denominations as well—marched in the processional at the beginning of the service. At Bishop Hall's invitation during the ordination ceremony most of the clergy—including one Roman priest—trooped forward for the traditional laying on of hands on the head of the new priest. Many added a hug and a kiss as well.

Then on signal from a beaming Bishop Hall, the entire place erupted into a cacophony of bells of every kind brought by the church members to meet their new priest.

Some opponents of women priests had reportedly sought, unsuccessfully, to secure the use of facilities at Virginia Theological Seminary a few blocks away for protest services….

Dr. Marian [sic] Kelleran, retired Virginia Seminary professor and the first woman to head the world-wide Anglican Consultantive [sic] Council, took note of the landmark nature of Mrs. Park's ordination in her sermon. She took as her text "fear not," the first two words of the Christmas Angel: "Fear not, I bring you tidings of great joy…"

The words "fear not" in the Bible, she noted, "nearly always indicate a new and therefore confusing message" to those being forewarned. By the same token, she went on, the words "fear not" are appropriate words for the church as it is today, and they are appropriate for the bishop of this diocese "who," she predicted, "would be struggling with calls from irate people who had read about this ordination this morning."

The words "fear not" are also appropriate "for Pat," who Dr. Kelleran said is "entering an order where there are few other women."

Dr. Kelleran emphasized that the ordination of Mrs. Park will not mark the beginning of "parallel priesthood of men and women in this or any other church…there is only one priesthood of the risen Christ."[1]

The February 1977 *Virginia Churchman* contained a touching photo of Pat Park recessing from her ordination with daughter Laura, not quite three years of age, holding her hand.[2] Also pictured was Blanche Lee Powell being presented for ordination, flanked by the Rev. Dr. Albert T. Mollegen and the Rev. Dr. Charles Price, at St. David's, Manassas, in the Ben Lomond Community Center on January 8.

On Feb. 12, 1977, in a brief ceremony at St. Paul's Memorial Church in Charlottesville at the beginning of the service of ordination of Constance Chandler Ward to the priesthood, the Rt. Rev. Robert B. Hall officially recognized Alison Cheek's ordination to the priest-

[1] Marjorie Hyer, *The Washington Post*, Jan. 3, 1977.
[2] Laura was born in late January of 1974, information provided by the Rev. Dr. Robert Prichard who was master of ceremonies/bishop's chaplain at Pat Park's ordination.

hood. Cheek recalls, "All Bishop Hall said to me was 'Alison, you were ordained a priest in 1974 in Philadelphia, and the Bishop and Standing Committee of this diocese welcome you as a priest of this diocese.' He really wanted me to do it because then everybody would know that I was free to be invited to any parish in the diocese; so I did it, and of course never a soul invited me to do anything in the diocese."

The Winter 1977 *Journal* reports, "At this writing five women graduates of the Virginia Seminary have been ordained to the priesthood of the Episcopal Church: **The Rev. Mary S. Belfry** (VTS '75), Diocese of Minnesota, **The Rev. Peggy S. Bosmyer** (VTS '74), Diocese of Arkansas, **The Rev. Victoria T. Hatch** (VTS '75), Diocese of Los Angeles, **The Rev. Patricia M. Park** (VTS '74), and **The Rev. Blanche L. Powell** (VTS '75), Diocese of Virginia. Three women graduates' ordinations have thus far been regularized: **The Rev. Alison M. Cheek** (VTS '69), Diocese of Washington, **The Rev. Dr. Elizabeth P. Rosenberg** (VTS '72), Diocese of Washington, and **The Rev. Nancy H. Wittig** (VTS '72), Diocese of Newark. VTS students **The Rev. Elizabeth W. Myers**, Diocese of Central Pennsylvania, and **The Rev. Pauli Murray**, Diocese of Massachusetts, have been ordained to the Episcopal priesthood;[3] former student **The Rev. Jeanne E. Clark** was ordained to the Gospel Ministry of the United Presbyterian Church in the U.S.A., and graduate **The Rev. Phyllis K. Ingram** (VTS '66) is an ordained minister in the United Church of Christ."[4] This edition of the *Journal* must have gone to press in late February of 1977. For Belfry, Bosmyer, V.T. Hatch, Park, and Powell were priested in January; Shoberg, in March; and Gill, in April.

The Faculty Minutes of March 21, 1977, contain the draft of a petition to the Standing Liturgical Commission stating that the faculty "requests that you complete the task of removing from the Proposed Book of Common Prayer all of the generic uses of male nouns and pronouns…we believe that the effort should be made since so many women find it difficult if not impossible to worship when this kind of language is used." Likewise the Faculty Minutes of May 31, 1977, reflect a similar effort: "Commission on Church Music Mr. Albritton reported that the Commission on Church Music had acted favorably on our request. We will be receiving a letter from them informing us that we have been authorized as a trial use site for new hymns."[5]

These attempts by the faculty were well-intentioned, but the unexamined undercurrents still at work against acceptance of women as reflections of the wholeness of God complementary to men had not and have not been dealt with. It is difficult to know whether the offense taken, and given, by the author of the following letter was predicated on the symbology of language or a latent misogyny. In either case, a scurrilous response to the faculty's request from the Standing Liturgical Commission was received via a letter of July 5, written on letterhead of The Standing Liturgical Commission of the Episcopal Church, Office of the Coordinator for Prayer Book Revision:

[3] Anna Pauline "Pauli" Murray was the first African American woman enrolled in a VTS degree program; however, her M.Div. degree was conferred by The General Theological Seminary. Norma Lee Blackwell (VTS '82) was the first African American woman graduate of VTS, information provided by Julia Randle, archivist of VTS.

[4] *Journal*, p. 22.

[5] p. 1.

5 July 1977

Dear Dr. Reid,

I acknowledge receipt of your letter of 21 June, transmitting the view of a majority of the members of the faculty of the Protestant Episcopal Theological Seminary in Virginia to the effect that it would be better to delay the adoption of the proposed Book of Common Prayer by another three years after 1979, than to allow masculine nouns and pronouns to remain in the Book of Common Prayer. There is a proverb, Greek in origin I believe, that the best is the enemy of the good. The course your faculty suggests would, in my humble opinion, ensure the rejection of the Proposed Book and the retention for an indefinite period of the 1928 BCP.

However, this is only one man's opinion (Pardon the sexism of the colloquial phrase). I am sure that Dr. Charles Price would be far more effective in persuading the Standing Liturgical Commission to adopt the course he advocates, than I possibly could be in opposing it. I am also convinced that the outstanding scholarship of Dr. Reginald Fuller would carry far more authority than my own inadequate knowledge of Greek, in persuading biblical scholars that the phrase "firstborn among many brethren" is an inappropriate translation; or that the story of the Prodigal Son would be more persuasive as the story of the Prodigal Sibling.

All I can venture to put forth is my own experience of 20 years in the United Nations, several of them spent in working with Dr. Ralph Bunche, the only American Black of any standing for a long time; and two years of them spent, inter alia as Secretary of the Committee on the Reorganization of the Secretariat, where the present formulae for national and geographical quotas in the composition of the Secretariat were worked out; as well as my more recent experience as priest-in-charge of a predominantly Black congregation in a predominantly Black neighborhood (the controversial Andrew Jackson High School is within a few blocks of my Church) – all these experiences, plus my own previous career as a foreign-born member of a predominantly Anglo-Saxon diplomatic service, and now that of a priest in an "Anglican" Church – all these experiences have made me not unacquainted with the phenomenon known as tokenism. I can smell it a mile off.

Of the 19 signatories of your letter, 17 would appear to be male and 2 female – a ratio of eight and a half to one. Perhaps the ratio of female students more than makes up for this glaring imbalance. I don't know. But may I in all Christian siblinghood suggest to you that the fig leaf of verbal and pronominal euphemism is not an adequate cover for the predominately male composition of the faculty.

It may be, of course, that all the male signatories have already tendered their resignations with a view to being replaced by female scholars. On the other hand, you may wish to call in a consultant, at an appropriate fee per diem, to help you adjust the imbalances referred to. In that case I humbly offer my experience, briefly outlined above, as suitable qualification to assist you in this task.

As the tenor of this letter suggests, I promise you that, should your offer be attractive enough, there will be no pussy-footing on my part in working out a formula for an adequate student admissions policy, and for faculty promotions and tenure procedures, with primary regard to race, sex, and national origin.

The immediate objective of the exercise would be, to use the vocabulary of today, to maximize the credibility of your collective stance in this matter.

Yours faithfully,
The Rev. Leo Malania
Coordinator for Prayer Book Revision

c: All members of the Standing Liturgical Commission[6]

The faculty debated for two meetings how to respond to this letter, finally deciding to do nothing.

The first week of May, the faculty had received word of the sudden death of Alison Cheek's husband, Bruce. Cheek remembers, "Cecil [Woods] came to my husband's funeral. Bill Wendt had asked me what were [Bruce's] favorite hymns, and one of his favorite hymns was *The Battle Hymn of the Republic*. We sang it at his service; and Cecil said to Dick [Reid], 'Don't you ever tell anybody I sang that.' [Cecil] was a Southerner....The first time I officiated as a priest in the Diocese of Virginia was to say the Requiem Mass at Bruce's funeral. That was the first time I did that in Virginia and my own parish church. John Frizzell was very good: He stood at my side;

[6] Letter from Leo Malania to Richard Reid, July 5, 1977, Faculty Minutes, RG V4, 01/19/1976-12/18/1978, Folder # 08/31/1977, Virginia Theological Seminary Archives, Bishop Payne Library, Alexandria, Virginia.

and we had an agreement [that] if I broke down, then he would just carry on. But once I got into the liturgy, that was all right. It isn't you anymore, and I just felt that was the last gift I could give my husband....It was very healing, very healing."

The Summer 1977 *Journal* contained a long article on the deployment of clergy women. The author, Sally Hamilton, was a Master's degree candidate in Women's Studies at George Washington University and wife of 1955 VTS graduate Michael Hamilton. She writes, "The Seminary office does not see a greater problem in the placing of women students than men students in assistant jobs, but it does foresee an enigma when these women desire to be rectors....[But then, in seeming contradiction:] Two-thirds of the rectors who made their pilgrimage to VTS to interview students as prospective curates did not talk to the women students...the ambiance at the Seminary confirmed and stroked the women as they were when they arrived as incoming students: dependent, accommodating and perhaps naïve. Incubation is valid if it is an agent for maturation, but an unrealistic support system may have rendered a disservice to the women students....The VTS Alumni Association provides a rich exchange of job information within the church, but some of the women graduates feel they do not have access to the interchange of the 'locker room' milieu which characterizes many male dominated associations."[7] She concludes, "There is a tendency throughout our whole society to take women's issues less seriously than those of men, which testifies to the almost child-like status women have occupied in the western world. The Task Force on Women in the Diocese of Washington, D.C., reported: 'Consciousness raising has taught us that the unconscious factors surrounding women are in such turmoil that there is a prevailing reluctance to take seriously women in the church.'"[8]

"I had never really had people take me seriously," reflects Jane Holmes Dixon; but the mentoring she received from Verna Dozier and the Rev. Jim Anderson (VTS '61) challenged her. She comments, "It goes back, to me, to being taken seriously, which I consider to be the beginning of doing justice. That for me as a female person who grew up in a very privileged world, who had all the opportunities that one could want, to be taken seriously was something that happened to me when I was about thirty-five years old; and it was such a powerful experience that I believe that respecting the dignity of every human being, that's what that means." Dixon remembers walking through the nave and out the door of St. Patrick's Church the night of the meeting with Blanche Powell and David Beers concerning the ordination of women and saying to the two women with her, "You know, this will never happen for me, but I have a daughter, and maybe she might want this. We have to support this." But by the Fall of 1977, she had met with Bishop Walker who said, "I think you ought to go to seminary for a year to see whether you do feel this call." So she enrolled in the M.T.S. program for an exploratory year.

Likewise, in Minneapolis Mary Hansley continued her ministry, now as a priest. On a few occasions people would refuse to take communion from her, but there were no violent public displays as was the case with other

---

[7] pp. 14-15.
[8] p. 18.

early female priests.[9] Hansley reflects, "I was third on the staff of the cathedral. There were other people the public could go to. Nobody had to take me seriously."

Meanwhile, the faculty status of Georgia Shoberg changed. The Faculty Minutes of August 31, 1977, contain the following announcement: "The Dean reported to the faculty that Georgia had been appointed as Assistant Chaplain on a half-time basis. He noted that the Alumni Executive Committee had urged that there be an ordained woman on the faculty as part-time chaplain and that they had made available some money to help with the salary. After the last faculty meeting in the spring, it became clear that there would be the opportunity to offer this job to Georgia since the parish [Immanuel Church-on-the-Hill] was interested in having her as a half-time assistant. The Dean said he had consulted with those members of the faculty who were available and had decided to make the appointment."[10] This fact is further elaborated in the minutes of the Executive Committee Meeting of the Board of Trustees, September 26, 1977: "Assistant Chaplain As the Dean had informed the

Georgia Shoberg

members of the Board by letter, he had appointed the Rev. Georgia H. Shoberg as a part-time assistant chaplain for a two-year term. This was a special arrangement suggested by the Alumni Association whereby Ms. Shoberg would work half-time at the Seminary and half-time at Immanuel Church-on-the-Hill. The Seminary and Immanuel are sharing equally the cash salary and perquisites, although the Seminary's half is partially offset by a contribution from the Alumni Association of $2,000 a year."[11] Also included in the Board minutes are these details: "Report of the Associate Dean for Student Affairs and Chaplain Mr. Gibson reported that one of the dormitories, Sparrow, had been closed this year, but that the others were all full....Mr. Gibson also stated that the arrangement with Ms. Shoberg was working out very well. He said that while Ms. Shoberg had been chosen to be a viable role model for the women preparing for ordination in this seminary, her ministry as chaplain is not limited to the women students."[12] It is unclear whether "not limited to the women students" means Shoberg was accepted in her role by the male students or whether her on-campus ministry as assistant chaplain included women students as well as wives of the male students. An article in the November 1977 *Journal* describes a meeting assistant chaplain Shoberg and chaplain Churchill Gibson held with VTS women students and wives, a group called "Coterie," "to share personal religious journeys and discuss 'Growing As A Christian.' After her talk Ms. Shoberg responded to

---

[9] Deacon Carter Heyward's hand had been intentionally scratched by a man to whom she administered the chalice until she bled. He is quoted in Darling (p. 125) as saying, "I hope you rot in hell." CDSP graduate Lois Hoy was bitten at the altar rail and tripped in procession at Grace Cathedral. In an e-mail on October 1, 2010, she notes, "The feelings, both hostile and pathological, that were expressed during services in those days were, unfortunately, fairly common." The pathology continues to this day: rape, stabbing, death threats, stalking, and hate mail. There are also reports of domestic violence committed against women clergy who would lose their jobs if they were to divorce. For statistics of harassment against young clergy women see: http://www.youngclergywomen.org/the_young_clergy_women_pr/2008/05/by-susan-olson.html

[10] Faculty Minutes, p. 2.
[11] Board Minutes, p. 2.
[12] Ibid., p. 3.

questions from members of the Coterie group and expressed an understanding of the women's individual time schedules and family life pressures....[The president of Coterie] noted Georgia's busy schedule and added personal appreciation for the guidance she had offered to the group."[13]

Georgia Shoberg & Churchill Gibson

On September 30, 1977, Presiding Bishop Allin issued a statement to the House of Bishops saying that despite the decision of General Convention, he was "unable to accept" women priests. On October 3, at the behest of Dr. Rightor, the faculty expressed their continuing support of the many women who had been ordered deacons and priests and those preparing to be and distributed a unanimous resolution to all alumni/ae and the deans of all Episcopal seminaries and the VTS Board.[14] At the next faculty meeting on November 1, some objections were raised regarding "Faculty Resolutions Designed to Influence Church Decision-Making."[15] On Nov. 21, 1977, the minutes reflect that "The Board passed a resolution very similar to that passed by the faculty supporting the ordination of women."[16] The Council of Seminary Deans passed a comparable resolution on December. 2, 1977. Presiding Bishop Allin remained unconvinced. By the end of 1977, over one hundred women had been ordained to the priesthood in the Episcopal Church U.S.A.[17]

The Faculty Minutes of March 21, 1978, contain the following: "Women Students' Concern about Interviews Serious concern has been expressed by some of the women seniors about the fact that clergy coming to interview applicants are not willing to consider a woman. In some cases this has led to very embarrassing situations. Interviews with women have been scheduled and then when the man arrives he makes it clear that he will not consider a woman. It was proposed that we might have a rule or norm that anyone who comes here to interview students must be willing to interview women as well as men. After some discussion it was agreed that the Dean and Dr. Reid would bring to a future meeting a draft of a letter which might go with the names of seniors seeking jobs encouraging clergy to interview all applicants."[18] Their draft was rejected on April 10 as having too much emphasis on justice and being demeaning to women. Micks, Shoberg, Carr, and Blood were asked to draft a new letter to be sent out next year. It was approved May 8, 1978.[19]

Meanwhile, Marianne Micks and Frank Van Develder, as faculty representatives to the Board of Trustees, reported to the May 1978 Board meeting that "women continue to experience overt discrimination in job inter-

---

[13] *Journal,* p. 3.

[14] Faculty Minutes, p. 4.

[15] Quote taken from "Agenda, November 1, 1977."

[16] Faculty Minutes, p. 2.

[17] The Anglican Church of Canada had begun ordaining women to the priesthood Nov. 30, 1976. TEC (the Episcopal Church) began ordaining women to the priesthood on Jan. 1, 1977.

[18] Faculty Minutes, p. 3.

[19] Ibid., p. 4.

views and in more subtle ways."[20]

The Faculty Minutes of April 2, 1979, record the following: "The Dean read a letter from the Rev. Jack Iker of Sarasota, Fla. The letter registered a strong complaint concerning the statement, enclosed with the lists of graduates seeking jobs, which requests that job interviews be conducted without regard to a student's race, sex, age or other such personal considerations. There was general agreement that the letter represented a minority view and that there has been good cooperation from most interviewers. Dr. Parrent will respond to Mr. Iker, explaining the reasons for the Seminary's position."[21] Dr. Parrent did so on April 25.

However, finding suitable employment continues to be a problem for ordained women. University programs in Women's Studies have introduced our society to volumes of literature on the unconscious factors involved in women's leadership, and one tangible dynamic at work once women's ordination became a reality has been unique difficulty in deployment: There were and are bishops in every area of the country who will not allow the names of women to be submitted to search committees looking for a rector. There were and are rectors who will not consider a woman as a candidate for assistant. Women often take the jobs men refuse to take in small towns and part-time positions; and married women clergy, upon becoming pregnant, have lost jobs that had been previously secure. Contexts unfold but the people in them are not always converted.

Nationally, 9.7% of rectors are women, while 17.7% of vicars are women. 43% of women, versus 15% of men, report frequent problems in the ordination process. The average compensation package for men is $64,400; for women, $56,100. VTS professor David Gortner summarizes the Lilly-funded national research study, *Toward a Higher Quality of Christian Ministry*, conducted by him and by John Dreibelbis from 1999-2004 as follows:

"1) clergy leadership skills, work dispositions, and overall spiritual/theological orientation to ministry did not differ significantly by gender.

"2) there were marked gender differences in how clergy were treated in the ordination process, their church locations and sizes, and other matters such as compensation, hours worked, and duration of call at churches (all related to size).

"3) despite these differences in institutional employment (an enduring problem in TEC [The Episcopal Church] institutionally), there were no notable differences between men and women in terms of the effect of their leadership (positive, neutral, or negative) on church growth and vitality. and [sic], neither men nor women were better than the other gender in effecting change in congregations."[22]

Notwithstanding obstacles, women have walked in grace and known it: Alison Cheek recalls, "One time we were sitting in [Peter Beebe's] study, and he said, 'Alison, you are a born parish priest. How do you bear not to

[20] Report of Faculty Representatives to the Board of Trustees, April 1978 in VTS Board Book, 1978, RG Vol Board of Trustees, Virginia Theological Seminary Archives, Bishop Payne Library, Alexandria, VA.

[21] p. 1.

[22] E-mail from David Gortner to Judith McDaniel, July 11, 2010. In May of 2006, the Church Pension Group's FYI Research body published statistics for those ordained from 2003 through 2005, page 9, which note, "the highest-earning group in the exhibit are women under age 35, although the median compensation level for women ordinands overall is slightly lower than for men." A higher salary for women under 35 can be explained by the fact that multi-staff parishes which call younger women have budgets disproportionately larger than the average parish.

be one?' And to my very great surprise I felt tears prickling in the back of my eyes. Because I knew I couldn't be, having taken the acts that I had taken, I didn't know that I really wanted to be....At some time after I had been recognized by my diocese, the Washington Cathedral advertised a position. They wanted somebody to do pastoral counseling for the staff at the Cathedral and for people who wandered in off the street. Because I was very well qualified to do that, I put in my application. I was told afterwards that someone on the committee said, 'What's this one from Alison Cheek? A joke?' And I realized that at least in Washington, Virginia, and Maryland, I was *persona non-grata* and wouldn't get a church job. But after Bruce died, I did leave my practice and take a job in Philadelphia [1980-1982]. Two women had dreamed it up. It was back in the days when the Episcopal Church had Venture in Mission money, and two women had gotten the diocese to back them to start a center for women to drop into....I was hired to be the priest director and a Roman Catholic woman who had come out of a convent about eleven years earlier was hired as the co-director....So I suppose I got pushed, or I chose, to exist at the margins of the church because after the ordination I got really connected with a lot of marginalized groups, like with the gay movement and the black movement and women in poverty. That ordination was a gift to me and the church rejecting me was a gift to me."

Nancy Wittig reflects, "Initially when the ordination of women passed in 1976, it was not a permissive thing but it was part of the canons: Women could be ordained. I feel very fortunate that I was able to be in parish ministry for close to 35 years, and I loved the parish. I worked in two small, poor parishes....The one in North Jersey has not only continued but has expanded its ministry in the community. The one in Philadelphia lost itself for awhile but is now continuing. It is the only food bank in the whole north east part of Philadelphia now. There's

some good things I can look back on. And the people, they were tough. People underestimate small parish lay leadership, but they were faithful. Somebody did a very good job of being a missionary for the Episcopal Church in urban and rural areas. Most of those churches are still small, but they are healthy and faithful. But that I could be part of that was really very important for me and be present, too, as representing the Church. I was very involved in the diocese of PA in putting together the first regulations in terms of conduct and misconduct and

Nancy Wittig

worked with people from Washington, D.C. and other places to put together that first manual and then to take the heat when the men were very angry. They just kept saying, 'The insurance company is making us do this.' I said, 'Yes, but we wouldn't have done it if they hadn't'....The Bishops' Pastoral Committee who I worked with a lot really didn't want to deal with most of that....One of the things I did was I was available to people to help hear them through and then to run interference with a bishop to try to get a bishop to sit down and listen to the story and to let them know that that was wrong and be willing to invite people to try to expose that in various places so that other people could be released from the bondage that they had been under....I went across the country with [someone] to a bishop who would listen to help with the healing process....That is all that people wanted was for the Church to listen; and so I think women had a tremendous impact on that around the country, and that is something I feel has made the Church better and stronger. I think that is part of the fact that we were daughters of the Church. We weren't out to destroy the Church. We were out to help the Church be what it was called to be, and that means taking risks. That means standing with those who didn't have a voice, and that is certainly the kind of parish where I have been—those who didn't have a voice." Nancy Wittig was named honorary Canon of the Diocese of Newark in 1981.[23]

Meanwhile, Betty Works Fuller remained a deacon for 17 ½ years, principally because of her husband Frank's reservations about the ordination of women. During those years, she was licensed after her husband was ordained priest. "I assisted Frank at services, and you did whatever you needed to do to get a little church up and running. I taught Sunday school and found out there were no materials that were appropriate. After the first year, we started getting a few young families in. So having gotten 'C's' in Christian Education in seminary, I wrote a curriculum....I got a UTO [United Thank Offering] grant and an Episcopal Church Foundation grant that actually paid for all four years of the curriculum called 'Seedlings.' I started writing it in 1978 and finished the four years of the Sunday school cycle....Then we put together a non-profit corporation. I am still doing it, very small scale, because I don't have the time to do more; but at one point there were about 400-500 churches a year using it....There was, is, and probably ever will be a lack of attention to the churches who have a handful of children. And I always felt like I don't care if there is one kid. They deserve to have as good a Christian education as someone at a cathedral that has all the resources in the world. So over the years a lot of my ministry has not only been designing, writing, and training, but just talking on the phone to your rector or your city school teacher. I still get a few

calls from people asking, 'What do I do?' and just being a caring person. So I got to combine my love of pastoral care and my passion for designing Christian education."

Ordained deacon at the Church of the Resurrection, Alexandria, VA, on June 5, 1975, because the rector of her home parish in Leesburg did not believe women could be priests, Victoria Hatch was invited to preach occasionally in the Dioceses of Delaware and Virginia until she was hired sight unseen by St. Cross, Hermosa Beach, CA. She recalls, "I was the first ordained woman in the diocese and that was a challenge because it was extremely Anglo-Catholic, quite conservative. I arrived in January [1976] and at the diocesan convention in February there were demonstrations that I was there, a lot of hostility. I was put on show, if you will, as a deacon of honor and given this chalice which was about three and a half feet high; but I made it through all of that." She was ordained priest in January of 1977, and the following Fall began twenty-seven years of service as vicar of St. Agnes, Banning.

Victoria Hatch baptizing

Three months after ordination to the diaconate, Blanche Lee Powell was appointed by Bishop Hall as vicar of St. David's, a mission in Manassas that rented space in the Ben Lomond Community Center. Everything needed each Sunday had to be carried in and out: the sign, books, altar guild materials, vestments, coffee hour and nursery equipment. The man in charge of deacons was livid, and

[23] Louis Crew, p. 4.

Victoria Hatch presiding at a wedding

the priest who had started the mission said, "What do you think you are going to do? You're a woman!" Powell served as vicar of St. David's from 1975-1981, but the mission ultimately closed for lack of funds. After three years working at Montgomery Ward, selling furniture, she became rector of Christ Church, Pearisburg, VA, where she served for ten years. "I loved Manassas, too, but Christ Church....I love the community and had more support than I had ever known throughout my whole ministry. The support came from every direction: the community, the parish, ecumenically. I was involved in a spiritual direction group and a support group for clergy. For me it was a very positive time in my ministry. Then finally I went to Delaware to serve four churches as part of a team....I was their so-called team leader; and for me it was a positive experience, a very different experience, but a positive experience, the first time working with other clergy on a team." She retired in 2002.

After graduation from VTS as President of the Senior class, Pat Thomas became the chaplain at the Pennsylvania State University working "with" the Episcopal Chaplain who had been there quite a long time. They were never in the office at the same time. After a year, she was called to be priest in charge of a parish in Huntington, PA, the first woman in charge of a parish in that diocese. The president of the local college, his wife and daughter were members of that parish but did not come to church once while Thomas was there. She reflects, "In those early years, probably what was the hardest was not really knowing how other people were perceiving me. You didn't know who was 'fer' it, and who was 'agin' it. So I think that probably led me to walk on eggshells sometimes, trying not to offend people, trying not to be in your face with people." After Huntington she was called as assistant at St. Columba's, Washington, D.C. While at St. Columba's Thomas taught liturgics practica at VTS. She was also on the Alumni Association Executive Committee for several years and represented the AAEC on the Board of Trustees for five years. After serving St. Columba's for eight years, she was called to serve as Canon to the Ordinary for the Bishop of Washington. She was on the staff of the diocesan office for three years and a priest at Washington National Cathedral. After Canon Bruce Jenneker left the Cathedral, Dean Baxter offered her the position of Canon Precentor which she accepted. She left that position to become rector of Christ Episcopal Church in New Bern, North Carolina. She recounts, "As I reflect on that decision now, I would say that was a mistake.

Pat Thomas

Charles Perry & Pat Thomas

However, I felt like I was ready to be the one in charge of a large parish. I knew I was in charge of a big program at Washington National Cathedral in terms of liturgy, but I guess in some ways I was missing some of the pastoral work, too, with the people. She was at New Bern for three years. She is presently a VTS steward for the Class of 1979 and continues to do supply work every Sunday as the liturgy is central

Pat Thomas

to her ministry. "I think sometimes it's just those quiet conversations you have with people that are the genuine moments of grace. You know, going to the hospital late at night when you kind of drag yourself up there; and you think, 'I really don't want to be doing it because it's late,' but you have to. Then you get there, and you have the most wonderful connection with the person; and you just know that this is where you needed to be at that particular moment and that you have received a great gift from the other person. I think of the liturgical events, the baptisms, having the privilege of being able to baptize someone and being in some sense an instrument for the connection between this person and the Church, the Church at large. The weddings. And I think sometimes just sitting with people when they are in the process of dying, just being with them. I think those are the moments of grace....I have to think of those moments of ordination because they had taken so many years, and it had taken a firm sense of 'Yes, God, you are calling me to do this.' There were lots of people who affirmed that, but there were lots of people who did not; and so my experi-

ence was that I had to be able to affirm it no matter what, that what had to be the core for me was that God was with me—always...God was with me walking this walk, and the walk was to be an inclusive one. The walk was to be 'We are all in this together, come on, let's do what we are called to do.' So, I think that I receive the greatest joy in ministry when I am doing ministry with other people."

In 1977 while living in Switzerland, pregnant with twins, Elisa DesPortes Wheeler read on the front page of the *International Herald Tribune* the news that the Episcopal Church had voted to ordain women: "I broke into sobs and knew that I was to be ordained. I did not know how or when, but I was going to be a priest now that it was possible. In 1979 I received postulancy from the Diocese of Washington, and I reapplied to VTS to switch degrees and get an M.Div. I had an admissions interview with the Dean. He was furious at me for writing a disrespectful letter to the elder statesman six years before. The entire interview was his fury at me. I apologized and remained quiet as he berated me....

Elisa DesPortes Wheeler

"I had a daughter with a major birth defect of the trachea who needed constant nursing care. We had LPNs or RNs around the clock to help care for her. I was constantly torn between being at home and doing field work and seminary. At that time there were almost no women priests or seminarians who were married with small children. In the winter there was a week between semesters where there was a required course on music and singing. My daughter was having a lot of apnea and she needed an EEG to rule out seizures. It was scheduled on the morning of a choral class....I went to the acting Dean and explained what was happening and asked it I could miss the morning session to take her for this test. He came down very hard on me that I could not miss this class or I would not graduate....He was severe and adamant. I went to my car and wept and wept. I was weeping tears of frustration and despair and tears of being pushed to the limits of what I could do. I ended up having one of our wonderful nurses take her to the test, and I went to singing class.

Elisa DesPortes Wheeler

"I had no mentor those early years [1968-1970] at VTS, but I certainly did the final years of 1979-81. My parish priest, Edgar Romig (VTS '69H) at Epiphany Church in downtown, Washington, baptized my children, sponsored me for ordination, and became my field work supervisor....Edgar offered to create a position for me so I could be ordained. Fortunately, I found a position and did not need his help....I doubt there was any person in the Episcopal Church who did more for women than Edgar Romig....I spent twenty-four years as a parish priest and loved all of it."

The Fall of 1979 a classmate of Wheeler, Jane Holmes Dixon, returned to VTS to enter the Master in Divinity program with the endorsement of two discernment committees at her home parish, St. Patrick's, and the discernment committee of St. Dunstan's parish, Bethesda, MD, where she had completed an internship during the academic year 1978-1979. Entering the M.Div. program the Fall of 1979 for the first time were Anne Bonnyman and Margaret McNaughton. In the Fall of 1980 Martha Horne and Carolyn Irish entered VTS and, together with Jane Dixon, formed a close and lasting bond. This fact is significant in itself, for making and keeping networks was to become a source of strength for women.

Martha Horne

Carolyn Irish

The first women ordained had been largely alone. They were individuals who had pushed the boundaries and whose stories were isolated. Phyllis Edwards, the first woman deacon, had been brutalized by the experience of being the solitary ordained woman. Though Marion Kelleran had observed in 1971 that "the only thing to do was to unite," still, when the time came to batter down the doors that stood in their way in 1974, the Philadelphia Eleven were a disparate group of varying interests and motivations; and each followed her own path thereafter. They had no models. They had never seen a woman celebrate.

There was no one to talk with about such things as how one balanced this call with a husband's secular vocation; no one with whom to share stories of the pull of pastoral needs versus children at home who needed their mother; no one who knew how an unmarried woman might detect and prevent harassment as she entered into what had previously been a mystical, all-male preserve. Politically, ecclesially they were loners.

At a conference of women ordained in the early days, Alison Cheek observed, "These were women who had been *regularly* ordained in the pretty early days and worked really hard in a variety of parishes and in institutional parts and various things, and they just felt like they hit their heads on the ceiling. They were never going to be cardinal rectors. Should they try to become bishops? It was very interesting because they [had] come to the end of the road in that there was no where further to go that they thought they could go. I am not sure if they wanted to go or not." "Were they angry?" asked the interviewer. "No. That wasn't the prominent affect. They were more sad and couldn't figure out where they were or what they wanted. Yes, of course, they were angry, but they weren't acting out their anger. A lot of the young women priests now think everything is fine and dandy: 'What are these old people stuck in the past and harping about?' You feel sorry for them because they won't take their history seriously. They tend to repeat it, and they will hit their heads. It is no good saying, 'That's over; that's done.' I used to think back in the early days that there are a lot of men in particular who got there in their heads, but they certainly weren't there in their gut."

Women are still second-class citizens, if they are considered citizens at all, in countries around God's world. But in God's Church? Is the Church truly "in the world but not of it" in the way she recognizes the gifts women bring to an appreciation of the image of God? Or is she not impacted by cultural context. The early women could not be the creators of a new symbol because symbols arise not from individuals but from the community. They were, instead, midwives for the Church of an icon of the fullness of God. They ushered in the symbolic feminine in order to change people's experiences of God. It was left to the community to change its mind and allow God's wisdom to unfold within.

GRACE
in Motion

CHAPTER SEVEN

"Come to him, to that living stone, rejected by men but in God's sight chosen and precious; and like living stones be yourselves built into a spiritual house, to be a holy priesthood, to offer spiritual sacrifices acceptable to God through Jesus Christ."

1 Peter 2:4-5
Revised Standard Version

In the late 1970's and early 1980's, the mystical aura surrounding the Eucharist which the Episcopal Church retained from its Roman Catholic roots was still a powerful stone of stumbling in the minds of some of the Episcopal Church's members, impeding the presidency of women at the altar. David Booth Beers recalls, "Often the only places [women] could get jobs were the Morning Prayer, Protestant parishes....The Protestant churches embraced them while the eucharistically-centered churches often did not....Ann [Brewster Jones, VTS '77] told me the story that they were at a clergy conference, and a couple of the 'black suits' turned their backs on a woman priest. It wasn't Ann. It was another woman, a priest in the diocese. And [Bishop] John [Walker] asked the male priests to come see him in the corner. He said, 'You know, you may not believe that anything happens at the altar when they report to celebrate communion, but there's one thing you cannot dispute. They have been elected and ordained as presbyters in this Church; and as presbyters and professional colleagues, they are entitled to your respect.'"

Like a stone mason who sees within a block of marble a form yet to be realized, the community modeled the work God had given it to do; and the conversion of the Church from within slowly came forth, emerging from that stone of stumbling. Thus, the Church began to sculpt new perceptions and new ways of being, molding new layers of comprehension; and as she did so, she looked back and saw grace materializing.

– The early 1980's –

By the time Marge McNaughton was ready to enter seminary in the Fall of 1979, it was possible for the community to recognize a female symbol at the altar: "A key factor that influenced my decision to enter ordained

Marge McNaughton

ministry was that the Assistant Rector at Christ Church was a woman, the Rev. Nancy Sargent," says McNaughton. "Through her ministry I realized that it was possible for a woman to be a priest, which meant that perhaps I could consider that path. If she hadn't been there, I don't know if it would have occurred to me to explore the vocation to priesthood. In that way she was an icon for me."

McNaughton was a cradle Episcopalian but did not attend church until after college when she became active at Christ Church, Detroit. Both the rector, Samuel Johnston (VTS '36), and the Assistant Rector, Nancy Sargent, were important mentors to McNaughton. As she describes them, "They saw life and ministry from entirely different perspectives, which helped to shape my understanding of the breadth of thought and theology in Christianity."[1] Shortly after joining Christ Church, Marge had two tangible experiences of the Spirit: At her first Christmas eve service, she experienced for a moment Jesus' joy and presence. In her own words, "[t]he second experience was God's giving me the gift of forgiving a person who had hurt me for a very long period of time. And at the very same moment of receiving that gift of forgiveness, God forgave me for the anger and indifference that I felt for the same person. Through that experience I was free in a way I had never experienced before. The history of the hurt didn't change, but the unforgiveness that had corroded my spirit was lifted. I never could have forced myself to forgive; it was only through God's grace that it was possible. That experience sealed my faith and inspired my desire to study and to learn as much as I could about God

---

[1] Interview with Marge McNaughton, April 9, 2010.

and the Christian life. A couple of years after joining Christ Church, I made my way to seminary. At that time in the diocese of Michigan, with the Rt. Rev. Coleman McGehee (VTS '57) as diocesan bishop, the ordination of women was well supported. The postulancy process was fair to women and mercifully short, so I was able to attend seminary after a nine-month process. I knew, by that privilege, that I was standing on the shoulders of the Philadelphia Eleven, ordained in 1974, who paved my way to seminary at a very great cost to themselves. They endured far more hostility and abuse than I have in twenty-eight years of ordained ministry. I will always be grateful for their courage and steadfastness in pressing on for those of us who came after them."

McNaughton entered VTS at the age of twenty-four, with very little knowledge of philosophy or theology. She recounts, "The voices of women theologians were silent in the curriculum, with the exception of the theology and teaching of Dr. Marianne Micks, known as 'Mixy.' She was the only woman on the faculty and a lifeline for the women students. She was a very creative theologian and a wonderful teacher. She opened the doors to a wider view of theology that included different voices. She opened my eyes to see the exclusion of women in theology and society, and my ears to hear exclusive language and know how significantly it influenced thought. I believe she was the guiding force that sensitized the VTS community to the importance of using inclusive language. The men on the faculty were definitely supporters of the ordination of

Marianne Micks

women and were conscious of using inclusive language. Sexism at VTS, however, was still alive and well.... [W]hen we were rising seniors, the VTS community was surprised when not only a woman was elected student body president but...two more of us were elected to the remaining key positions of student body leadership. I remember that after the election, one of our male classmates put up a large sign that read 'The Year of the Woman.' We were hopeful about the future for women at VTS....Before we graduated from VTS and were actively pursuing jobs in our senior year, we knew that there were code questions that would be asked of the single women (not the men) in almost every interview: One was, 'do you think you will get married?' which meant 'are you a lesbian?' The general assumption in the Church at the time seemed to be that if women wanted to enter a 'man's' profession, then they must be lesbians. Another code question was 'do you intend to have children?' which meant, 'we don't want you to take time away from the church to raise a family,' or it meant, 'how can a woman be pregnant and serve at the altar?' Or 'a mother shouldn't be in ordained ministry while she is raising children.'

Marge McNaughton seated next to Jim Ross

"After ordination, almost all of the clergywomen I knew had people walk out during services while preaching or celebrating. At other times we dealt with being laughed at, dismissed, demeaned, insulted and harassed. I remember that one woman had someone spit on her hand while she was giving communion. A number of people over time have walked out on me while I was celebrating or preaching. On the first occasion, I tried to think positively, 'Well, gee, everybody else stayed. So that's good,'

Marge McNaughton

though it still stung. What happened after that particular service, however, was very surprising and full of the grace of God. The men who were serving with me on the altar that morning also noticed the obvious exodus, and they were more incensed than I was. The men couldn't believe what had happened and saw for the first time that there was real hostility towards women in ministry, even in the Church.

"In parish ministry, I really enjoyed being a priest and building relationship with parishioners. They taught me a great deal about priesthood simply by being who they were. At the same time those first few years in ministry were isolating and difficult….One of the factors was the location of my first parish….It was in a small town/almost rural situation, far from any women assistants (there were no women rectors at the time). In addition there were no women who had been in ordained ministry long enough for me to find a mentor or a role model. It was not at all easy to meet with young clergy, not only because of the long distances to travel from my location but also because of not knowing if it was 'ok' to take time away from work to do something that I mistakenly thought was just for myself and not also [for] the church. Eventually, I joined a colleague group, found friends outside the parish, and felt steadier as I grew in faith and priesthood.

"Four years after I had been ordained, I was in an interview for a position as an associate rector. I stated to the rector that I hoped to have children one day and asked if there would be accommodation for that, maternity leave for instance. I'll never forget the first line of his response. He said, 'Look, this is a real job.' There it was again.

"Another obstacle encountered in ministry was harassment. There were no resources in the Church at the time to warn you to be on guard about it. There was nothing to draw on to know how to even identify it let alone deal with it once it was right in front of you. It was a risk to report it since most likely one wouldn't be believed. It was better to keep quiet and manage the situations on our own. As classmates we called each other, but we didn't know anyone in our dioceses who would really understand the dynamics of the situation or who had the authority to help deal with it.

Marge McNaughton

"I think sexism was one of the biggest obstacles for me, and even now that demon is everywhere. If it is not blatant, it lies right below the surface….What grieves me for the graduates who are young women is that they will run into sexism as well as harassment or sexual harassment. Young women clergy, and perhaps young men just starting out and trying to understand the life of ordained ministry, are often more easily pushed around, treated dismissively, or not taken seriously. That's the part I can't stand. They leave the VTS community with strength and enthusiasm, and then many of them have to go out and face those kinds of evil alone."[2]

McNaughton's classmate, Anne Bonnyman, had pursued a Master's degree at Villanova in order to either teach at a Roman Catholic high school or run a Catholic Christian education program. She remembers, "I fell in love with the academic study of the Bible and of theology. It just blossomed, intellectually. And also, in the course of studying theology in the Bible in graduate school, I was very drawn to Protestant theology and figured out that I was really in the wrong church. I became very interested in Reformation theology and so eventually found my way to the Episcopal Church….I was in graduate school at Villanova at the time the Philadelphia Eleven were being ordained. I had no sense of personal connection to it, consciously, but I was riveted by the story. Just riveted. So I do think there was something really primal in that for me as well. I joined the Episcopal Church, in Tennessee actually, right as the canons were changing to permit the ordination of women….I worked in a church as a Christian Education leader and really saw that I was in the wrong place, that my place was going to be at the altar and in the pulpit….I—call it grace or call it luck, probably both—was in a diocese where—unusual in the South—as soon as the canons changed, the Bishop of Tennessee, Bill Sanders, was ready to have women go through the process. That was very rare in the South. The reality was the canons changed, but you had to find a bishop who would follow them. And you had to find a diocese that would begin to let women through the process. The obstacles put up were very creative of ways of getting around the canons based on appropriateness or fitness. There was that ruse that you can't be ordained unless you have a job, and of course women needed help finding

jobs. I was spared some of that. I had a supportive bishop, and I became a postulant in 1977 and entered VTS in 1979 with my bishop's full support.

"VTS was a good experience. It was a supportive place. The classroom experience was wonderful…stimulating, challenging, the most exciting place in the world. The curriculum was so good at honoring spiritual integration at the same time as we were doing the intellectual work. I had wonderful teachers. I felt like my preparation was excellent. The hard part for me was that I was thirty years old. I had lived on my

Anne Bonnyman

own, and it was really hard to be part of dormitory life. It was a conservative community in those days, and I chaffed in the living situation; but I felt well prepared. I know there is a lot of pressure on seminaries to teach practical things. My sense of that now, these many years later, is that the practical things are always changing; and what I got was a really fabulous theological education. One of my challenges now is to teach leaders in congregations to think theologically in an increasingly secular environment. I learned that at VTS. I think my education was stellar. The reality is that we lead a different Church from when we were ordained. It's a different world. There's no way in 1982 you could have anticipated all this. So keep teaching the really hard courses. It really matters…."

Once out of seminary, the beginnings of networking became important: McNaughton and Bonnyman had female classmates, fellow priests upon whom they

[2] See the book by Nancy C. James (VTS '84), *Standing in the Whirlwind* (Cleveland: Pilgrim Press, 2005), which documents harassment, property damage, and attempts to arrange her "accidental" death.

could call when the going got rough. But they were still isolated geographically: "Mentors were few and far between for women clergy. We had each other, but there was nobody out there in front of us who could tell us how this was going to work, or encourage us. We really were the front wave, and I longed for a woman in my life who had done this before, to help me. We really were out there doing it by ourselves." This reality is demonstrated in the fact that Bonnyman has been the first woman in each of the parishes she has served in her ministry: "I was the first woman in 1985 in east Tennessee when the bishop put me in charge of a brand new congregation. I had been the first woman in my diaconal parish. I was the first woman to be in charge of a large congregation when I went back as interim rector of my diaconal parish, the largest church in the diocese. And that shocked people, that a woman

Anne Bonnyman & Ron Abrams

was put in there even as an interim. By the mid-nineties, I was looking to move on to the next thing. I found that in the South that just wasn't going to happen: All I could find were entry-level positions. Then I was called to be the first woman rector of a historic church in Delaware; and in 2006 I was called to be rector of Trinity Church in Boston, another historic church.

"Here is what I've learned: Congregations go through a huge transition in adapting to a woman as their leader, as their rector. It doesn't matter how many assistant rectors, associate rectors they've had. It [a woman rector] is a new dynamic. It's difficult. Because our congregations tend to be well-educated people, it's not something that anybody wants to own up to; and it gets acted out in a lot of different ways. Sequential time, historic time does not make any difference. It's the time in the life of the community. So now in the Episcopal Church there are only a handful of us who are rectors of very large parishes. We are experiencing in our ministries what we experienced twenty and thirty years ago in the smaller churches where we started out, the same dynamic. So oftentimes, here in Boston, I thought, 'This reminds me of east Tennessee in 1985. This reminds me of Delaware in 1995.' I've spoken with other women in my position….This dynamic is a huge transition and creates conflict in the life of a church. It also can be lived through and come out of on the other side. You have to be good at conflict management and good at tenacity, as well. In providing a different kind of model, the issue is how women's leadership looks and feels different. I've encountered that in every place I've ever served. In time people say, 'We get it. We're buying into this.' But it does look and feel different. Our church still has such hierarchical leadership models. We are slow to follow the secular world which moved to more collaborative leadership models twenty-five years ago. It comes out, I think, around issues in women's leadership.

"We can never live up to people's expectations or our own. Learning to live peaceably with that, to make my peace with that, is hard. This is very privileged work. The best thing is that miracles happen in congregational life, that untenable situations are redeemed when we least expect it. We learn from each other. There is God's presence in community. That is profound and always surprising. We are invited into people's lives at a level that is just extraordinary, and that is a real privilege and a real blessing."[3]

For Christians being in community is not an option: One cannot be a Christian alone. One of the roles of community is to give individuals identity; an-

Anne Bonnyman

other is to create symbols. How that happens is a mystery; but, as Phyllis Tickle has observed,[4] the church of mystery has always trumped the church of rules: Community takes precedence over the institution. Through hard-earned experience, Anne Bonnyman had learned that the spiritual life of communities moves at different paces in different places; but at all times and in all places, there *is* God's presence in true community.

As these awakenings were happening, it had become apparent that if Georgia Shoberg were to remain on the faculty of VTS, she needed to obtain higher qualifications. The Faculty Minutes of Oct. 27, 1980, record that "[i]t was moved…and seconded…that we nominate

March 22, 1983.[8] Shoberg completed her Ph.D. but never taught after that.

The May 11, 1981, Faculty Minutes reflect that "the Dean spoke to the faculty about the need for an ordained woman on the faculty. He noted the importance of having an ordained woman in the light of the large number of women students who are preparing for

Georgia Shoberg for an Episcopal Church Foundation Fellowship for graduate study. The motion carried unanimously."[5] On April 27, 1981, one reads that "[t]he Dean announced that there would be a farewell party for… Georgia Shoberg at his home on Tuesday, May 19."[6] Subsequent financial support for her continuing education was recorded in the Faculty Minutes of May 4, 1981,[7] and

Georgia Shoberg

---

[3] Interview with Anne Bonnyman, August 31, 2010.
[4] Convocation Lecture delivered October 5, 2010.
[5] Faculty Minutes, p. 1.
[6] Ibid., p. 1.
[7] Ibid., p. 1.
[8] Ibid., p. 3.

ordination, but also because it is important to represent in the faculty the role of ordained women in the church….It was moved…and seconded…that the faculty endorse the Dean's nomination of Mary Belfry as associate chaplain and director of alumni/ae affairs after the Board [makes a] decision to create such a position."[9] Minutes of the May Board meeting read as follows: "Associate Chaplain and Director of Alumni/ae Affairs The Rev. Georgia H. Shoberg, who has been Assistant Chaplain for several years, has resigned to pursue advanced study in New Testament. For the last year she has been working full time at the Seminary since her contract for half-time work at Immanuel Church-on-the-Hill had expired. The Dean proposed that a new position be created for her replacement, namely, Associate Chaplain and Director of Alumni/ae Affairs….The Dean then nominated the Rev. Canon Mary S. Belfry, an ordained alumna of this Seminary who has demonstrated the skills required. She was highly recommended by her Bishop and the Dean of the Cathedral Church of St. Mark where she has worked as Canon since January 1977….an initial three-year appointment after which she would be eligible for re-election to serve at the pleasure of the Board. The motion passed unanimously."[10]

Jane Dixon graduated with a Master in Divinity degree at Commencement 1981. Despite her credentials,[11] she interviewed for sixteen different positions before David Jones (VTS '68) offered her a job at Good Shepherd, Burke, VA. She notes, "It was the grace of God that I went to work with David and had three wonderful years with him. Then Frank Wade (VTS '66) called me to work for him at St. Alban's for two years. Then I was called to be rector at St. Phillip's in Laurel as the second female rector in the Diocese of Washington."

Meanwhile, grace was calling Carlyle Gill elsewhere. "People were astounded that I would want to leave Sewanee….Jon Bruno's (VTS '77) wife Linda called me at Sewanee one night…and said, 'There's a fabulous parish out here that you would be perfect for. Can I put your name in?'….It was an associate position at a parish called St. Augustine by the Sea in Santa Monica, and I interviewed. Those were really great years in some ways for women. As hard as it was in some ways, in other ways it was really exciting because there were so few of us, and the places that really wanted to have a woman on staff were eager to get you. So finding a job was not hard at all for me. I was offered a job. Every time I looked for a job, I got a job. So very unlike now….There was a fair amount for me of welcome initially, but it was the experience I had of the glass ceiling which was I was never going to be a rector in Los Angeles, which at the time was a pretty conservative place, too. And I knew in order to be a rector, I had to get out of that diocese….So I came to Washington and was rector of St. Stephen and the Incarnation….When I came here to Washington, which was in 1987, there were still only—Jane Dixon was at St. Phillips, Laurel, and Vienna Anderson was at St. Margaret's and Karen Johnson was at St. Ann's, Damascus, and I was the fourth woman rector in the diocese….[my predecessor at St. Stephen's] was a member of what they

Jane Dixon

[9] Faculty Minutes, pp. 1-2.
[10] p. 2.
[11] Though she was to become the second female bishop in the Episcopal Church, she was the first to be a college and seminary graduate.

used to call themselves the Cardinal Rector Colleague Group….They were very clear. They did not want women in that group, which would have been a golden opportunity for them and for any women because that would have been a chance to really help women in, but they were very clear about it….I approached [a friend in the group] about it. I said, 'You know, I don't really get this. I mean,

LEFT TO RIGHT: *Verna Dozier, Jane Dixon, Carlyle Gill in 1987*

the guy who was the rector of St. Stephen's right before me was in this group. Why am I not in this group?' And [he] said—I think this is almost a verbatim quote—'We have agreed to remain all male.' They wanted to do that and intended to and did for years. I was finally a member of that group, but not until I was the interim rector at St. Alban's; and it's only because I really went after them that time. I really put up a big fight about it all and told them just what I thought about it….There were many, many grace-filled moments in that parish. One of the things that I did there that was very important and dangerous was—St. Stephen's at the time was in the middle of the crack cocaine drug market in Washington in the 1980's. They were all—this one gang, which was called the 'Newton Street Crew,' basically did their dealing, their business

on the front steps of St. Stephen's because churches are perfect because at night there's nobody there. It's dark, and they can work unimpeded. So what we decided to do, a group of us starting out very small, me and one other person at the beginning, was just to sit outside every night <u>with</u> them. It was very sort of nonviolent. We did nothing except sit there on folding chairs, and it grew. More and more parishioners came and sat. The choir began to rehearse out in front, you know. More neighbors started coming out and sitting. Bob Mondello, who works for NPR, lived across the street, came over, until we had a big gang of people every night, rain or shine, whatever, sitting outside with the drug dealers, some of whom we got to know and developed relationships with. But what we did, we interrupted their business; and they had to move. They didn't stop doing what they did, but they didn't do it at St. Stephen's anymore. It was a real—oh, it had some evangelism to it, but there was something about it that was very grace-filled. It was a very loving thing that we did and very loving for the block because kids started coming out to play. People felt safe. It was a reclamation of that little piece of Newton Street. [My mother] would have been horrified if she knew that I had been sitting outside with drug dealers who killed people, one of whom they killed on our steps. So there was grace in that, in that sort of, in some ways, naïve but still brave…." After St. Stephen's, Gill took a year's sabbatical. Then Frank Wade called her to be an interim associate which turned into a ten-year term as senior associate at St. Alban's, after which she served as interim rector when Frank retired. She now does spiritual direction.

Yet in 1981 the community, the Church, remained on the verge of new awareness. In some instances that recognition was instantaneous. In others, the recognition of grace took years. As Anne Bonnyman had observed, different people and places took different paces. That Fall Katherine Grieb had returned to VTS, joining

Katherine Grieb

Martha Horne and Carolyn Irish who were by then middlers.

Martha Horne had grown up in the Episcopal Church in North Carolina. She reflects, "I didn't want to be a Christian educator or missionary; those were the only vocations that I had experienced women working professionally in the Church. I don't think I would have been interested in ordination at the time if it had been a possibility because it was the study that I enjoyed the most and not the prospect of a vocation within the Church." Her undergraduate degree required that every freshman take a course in religion: "The religion course was the most intellectually engaging, so I took another religion course the next semester, which I found equally fascinating. I graduated with a major in religion from Duke, but no intent to use it professionally. I was also just three hours short of a psychology major and expected to enroll in graduate school in psychology." But after a year in a counseling psychology graduate program, she decided against psychology as a profession and took the Law boards: "I went down to the SMU [Southern Methodist University in Dallas] bookstore and looked at the legal books; and it was the dullest, driest literature I had ever seen....I thought, 'I can't spend three years reading these dull books!' I was discouraged and [my husband] Don said to me, 'Well, you know you always loved those religion courses at Duke.' So I started taking courses at Perkins School of Theology, a Methodist Seminary located on the campus of SMU, and I had the same experience as in college: I just loved the study and the intellectual engage-

ment. I was taking moral theology, Hebrew Bible and Church history. I loved all of it and was really encouraged to continue there and to begin doctoral work which I expected I would do."

Her husband's vocation moved them from Dallas to Alexandria in 1980, and Horne transferred her academic credits from Perkins into the M.Div. program at VTS. "We arrived in the summer and joined a parish in our neighborhood: St. Andrews, Burke. Our next door neighbor was the organist there and Randall Prior was the vicar [later, rector]....Randall arranged for me to talk with Bishop Hall and the chair of the Commission on Ministry....They were both very encouraging." She notes, "Again, my interest was primarily in an academic vocation, but I was strongly encouraged to consider ordination. The Bishop of Virginia, Robert Bruce Hall...agreed to waive the residence requirement, even though we were new in the diocese; and he was extremely encouraging and supportive, as were people here at VTS....The first time I had seen a woman celebrate the Eucharist was in 1979 when I visited VTS for the Conference on Ministry. There were no ordained women in Dallas, and I did not know any women priests....

"There was only one woman on the faculty when I came to VTS. That was Marianne Micks, of course. She also encouraged me—both to be ordained and to pursue doctoral studies and an academic vocation....I will never forget a class I took from her. I don't remember the name of the course, or what made me sign up for it; but it was a very interesting class. Mixy made us aware of the invisible nature of women in much of Church history. She cited a particularly well-known, definitive and often-assigned Church history text book....When I took the class in 1981, she told us that in the previous edition of this text...there was only one woman whose name appeared in the long index at the back of the book; and it was the Virgin Mary. Mixy was a real bridge between the past and the future in the Episcopal Church....It could not have been easy for Mixy here. My experience in the Council of Deans was just for five days a year, but Mixy was the only woman on the faculty for a considerable time. I remember once when she was on sabbatical (or it could have been after she retired and Barbara Hall was on sabbatical) that I was the only woman in faculty meetings for a whole semester, and that was very difficult. I think what it must have been like for Mixy during those years of being the only woman, but how much she did to create a place for women here, how she really worked to make this community a place ready to receive and welcome women.

"In the ordination process there weren't any obstacles, but there were frustrations....All spouses were always interviewed by the COM [Commission on Ministry]. I think it is a good thing to interview spouses during the ordination process, but the focus of the interview was only slightly on trying to assess whether Don was supportive of my ordination. Instead, there was a definite undertone of 'does she have your permission to do this?'

"The year I graduated I was asked to teach Greek as an adjunct [at VTS] the following year. Our children were still fairly young, and St. Andrew's [Burke, VA, where Horne had been the first woman seminarian] was at a point where they needed an assistant, but they couldn't really afford a full-time assistant. It was in our neighborhood, just a mile and a half from our house, so I made the decision that I would take a half-time position at St. Andrew's so that I could teach Greek here [at VTS] and have time with my children. After a few months, I was asked to work at Christ Church on my day off [from St. Andrew's] as well. When Bishop Hall waived the residency requirement for me, he said, 'But I want you to do field ed in Virginia' so I did it at St. Andrew's; and they wanted me to stay on after I was ordained. I didn't really ask the Seminary: It was just something Randall and I

worked out with the Bishop, and I think it served all of us well. As I think about the women in my class, Cally went to the Church of the Epiphany in Washington where she had done her field education...I think there was only one woman in our class who had difficulty with her first placement. Most of us came from dioceses that were already supporting the ordination of women. So it wasn't like the first few years after the 1976 General Convention decision. Placement of women was radically different in '83 than it had been in '79, for instance."

Horne was the first ordained woman at St. Andrew's and first ordained woman at Christ Church. "When I began work at Christ Church, it was on my day off from my position at St. Andrew's....I think the rector was under some pressure to have an ordained woman, but he was also really worried that there were a lot of people who were not ready or didn't want to have a woman on the clergy staff. So I started doing a woman's bible study on my day off, which was a wonderful experience, one of the most fulfilling things I have ever done....There was only one time that I was aware of [at St. Andrew's or Christ Church] when someone [a man] refused to take communion from me....

"There were other frustrations around compensation: When I went to Christ Church, I was not given a housing allowance; and after I had been there a little while, I realized that the other assistant was receiving a housing allowance of more than $1,000 of tax-exempt income per month. He and I were ordained to the diaconate together, in the same service, on the same day in Richmond....After our ordination we started work on the same day in our respective churches. We had exactly the same amount of experience as ordained clergy. I protested this one day after I had just found out about this. The rector came into my office, and I sort of exploded; and he said, 'But Martha, you have a house, you are already living in a house.' Well, we were living in a house in West Springfield, and I was commuting more than twenty-five miles per day through terrible traffic. Meanwhile, my male colleague was living in Old Town a block and a half from Christ Church in an historic, eighteenth-century house, receiving a $1,000 monthly tax-exempt housing allowance. And I said, 'You know my colleague also has a house and my colleague's wife…commands quite a nice salary.' 'Oh! well,' the rector replied, 'but she would really like to stay at home and have a baby.' So then I had to go to the vestry and request a housing allowance. It wasn't that the rector went to them and said, 'This is the right thing to do.' I had to go and make the case to the vestry, and the housing allowance I was given was not as much as my male colleague. Compensation issues have continued to be a big issue for or-

Richard Reid & Martha Horne

dained women. If you look at the statistics of the Church Pension Fund, they continue to be an issue for women. That problem is not just confined to women working in the Church, so I would put this in the category of a frustrating injustice, but not really an obstacle."

Horne had served two years at St. Andrew's and full time at Christ Church for approximately a year and a half when Dean Richard Reid invited her to be Assistant to the Dean at VTS in 1986: "I ended up leaving Christ Church sooner than I had intended or expected." [12]

Horne, Dixon, and Irish each speak of the importance of networking and of the bond of community the three of them developed which allowed them to be sounding-boards for one another as they made decisions in ministry. Carolyn Irish observed, "Martha and Jane were my support. We worked for each other for over fifteen years,

LEFT TO RIGHT: Jane Dixon, Martha Horne & Carolyn Irish

and we often went off for a weekend somewhere together or simply out to lunch just for time together to talk. We initially thought that nobody would hire us, but we were very close and still are very close friends to this day." [13]

Carolyn Irish had been brought up as a Mormon, but as an adult Irish became an active lay woman at Grace Church in Georgetown, Washington, D.C. The vicar at that time advertised it as "a church for bored Christians and interested pagans," and Irish considered herself both. Then she had a very powerful experience of call which she shared with very few people. She recalls, "At some point I did tell a psychiatrist, however. I said, 'I want to know if this is crazy?' I had never had a good Christian education in my life, so I really didn't know what was authentic and what wasn't, what was crazy and what wasn't. The psychiatrist said to me, 'You have asked a question which is outside the bounds of my technology. If you want to sit and

[12] Interview with Martha Horne, March 31, 2010.
[13] Interview with Carolyn Irish, May 12, 2010.

visit with me, I would be pleased; but I can't answer the question.' I respected him for that." She went before the vestry of her parish. "They were very warm and open about it. The rector was less so, but you know it was early days…1978. The whole pre-seminary part stretched out for two years in the Diocese of Washington. It was lengthy. I entered VTS in the Fall of 1980.

"My three years at seminary were really such a gift in my life. In maturing, I was not at home in the Mormon Church as I grew emotionally, intellectually, and in other ways. So I was very grateful when I found the Episcopal Church and felt, as so many of our people do and I confirm here, 'I have found my home.' Because I had a graduate degree in philosophy and I had taught, I had pretty good analytical skills and felt competent to apply those skills to theological study. I didn't know much about Church history from the LDS [Church of the Latter Day Saints, i.e. Mormon] point of view, nor did I know the Scriptures with the exception of a few stories which I could remember. It was no easy task to prepare me, but they did it with such grace. I think with great appreciation of my teachers and of my classmates as well. It was absolutely amazing. I do recall when I was going through the process for postulancy in the Diocese of Washington, members of the Commission on Ministry were very concerned about my having young children to look after. It was clear to me that care for my children was far more important to me than it could possibly be to any member of the Commission and that I would look after my children first and foremost. In fact, one of my children was hospitalized for a couple of weeks with a bad burn. I went everyday after seminary to the hospital to visit him before going home and attempting to do my homework. One evening, I decided to leave the seminary and start the next year again. The next day I went to seminary I forgot to resign. I became so engaged in what the classes were that day, I just continued on the next day as usual."

Irish found that her experience at VTS was a good one in terms of the relationship between the male and female students: "We were in the minority, but we held our own. I remember our pride at graduation [All four honors graduates were women: Grieb, Horne, Irish, and Sukie Curtis.] but also our dismay that the faculty reports on the women would include comments such as 'dresses appropriately' or 'is well groomed' or whatever, but failed to notice the dirty hair and dirt in their fingernails of our male peers. A bit one-sided here, we thought. I think they were nervous. I think everybody was nervous. It was a very big change for the Church and a challenge for women to be patient. Disappointments came often and early. It would take a long time for the Church to embrace this change. Today half of our clergy in Utah are women. This has not been intentional on my part, but it is a fact of which I am very proud.

"After I graduated I served the Church of the Epiphany in downtown Washington. At that point the rector was quite ill, so the vestry raised money for a half salary. I had been a seminarian there, so they knew me. They didn't want to go through searches or other process; so they just called me one night about 10:30 p.m. and said, 'Will you stay with us?' That was an amazing year and, at the same time, a broad experience of the church. I knew that when the six months were up and the rector was well, which he was, I would probably move elsewhere.…I went to Virginia to the Church of the Good Shepherd after Epiphany. David Jones was the rector, and his assistant was Jane Dixon who had just taken a position at St. Albans. So he called me up and said, 'I want you out here.' But I was there for only a year before moving to Michigan."

After her move to Michigan, Irish became the first woman among several archdeacons. She notes, "There were several women at Epiphany in Ann Arbor who had served there as seminarians with limited duties. In Michigan my area of responsibility covered a diocese with twice

Clergy women and men of Utah

the number of churches as my episcopacy covers in Utah. [Bishop] Coleman [McGehee] said, 'When there is a new vicar or rector, you are to install them. You go and do that piece rather than me.' For almost all of them it would have been the first time they would have a female at the altar, and several were not prepared; so we did the service or installation as part of Evening Prayer. The transition was difficult and gradual for many, so I tried to encourage women to be patient and tolerant of early rejections. It is difficult when people say 'no' to you and quite natural to take it person-

Carolyn Irish

ally, but I think I was very blessed along the way, perhaps for no other reason than being in a different situation."

After three years serving a congregation outside Ann Arbor, Michigan, and as one of McGehee's archdeacons, Irish returned to Washington, D.C. to serve on the staff of the Shalem Institute. She recalls, "My senior year in the seminary was when Shalem appeared on my horizon. I didn't know anything very much about prayer or the spiritual life. I felt confident in other ways that I would be a good teacher, a good pastor and administrator, but spiritual leadership was something I had never thought through, so I went to Tildon Edwards, an Episcopal priest who was the founder of Shalem. With great embarrassment I said, 'I think I have missed something, and I need your help.' So I began then to take prayer very seriously and to allow it to enrich all the other work I did, including my life now as a bishop....In 1993 I worked with Carol Crumley at the National Cathedral to establish a

Carolyn Irish

prayer center. Things seem to just unfold and happen. My life has always been that way. You see things happen and you say 'yes' to something…. I think it has been primarily about doors opening. But of course I could have said 'yes' or 'no.' I believed then and still believe that I was called by God to be a priest of the Church; I was called by the Church to be a bishop [in 1996]. I believe that the Holy Spirit works through the Church, and that same Spirit has been present in other bishop elections I have observed. I have had people ask me to coach them towards the episcopacy, which I think is really quite odd. It is the Church that calls and invites us to listen, pray, and discern."

Thus, upon graduation in 1983 Horne and Irish began their ministries with half-time positions in the parishes they had served as seminarians. John Woolverton, Professor of Church History at VTS, had just been called to be rector of Trinity parish in Portland, ME; and with no other jobs available in the Diocese of Washington, Katherine Grieb decided she wanted to work with Woolverton. There were, as she says, "only two problems: One was that the parish

Katherine Grieb

didn't want an assistant; and if they were going to have an assistant, they certainly weren't going to waste money on a woman." So she served in his parish for free. As she says, "I think this is often true for women: You learn how to do the thing you need to do in order to be able to do the thing you want to do." To earn money she went to work as a special assistant to the president of Bates College, Lewiston, ME, doing development. She notes, "I had no clue that I was going to be teaching. I thought I was headed for parish ministry, and I *was*. I was just trying to *get* there, but it seemed logical to me to work in an educational institution in order to get where I wanted to go in parish ministry. That seemed very sensible. So I am grateful for my time at Bates. I loved it. I was there about five years." When Woolverton left, Grieb was approached and asked if she would apply as rector. She turned them down because she was on her way to graduate school at Yale. The parish then proceeded to hire a woman rector. Grieb recalls, "I was the first woman in my two field education parishes—Transfiguration in Silver Spring and Holy Communion, Southeast—one suburban and one inner city parish. So I had had some experience being the first woman that they had seen, and you are basically doing a lot of calming. You don't do anything innovative, particularly. You just go in, and you are very solid; and after a while they wonder, 'What were we afraid of?'"

The Faculty Minutes of May 29, 1984, record that "Mrs. Hansley was reappointed to her position as Associate Chaplain and Director of Alumni/ae Affairs, to serve at the pleasure of the Board."[14]

Meanwhile, Rosemarie Sullivan had entered VTS. Sullivan had been a Roman Catholic Passionist nun. She describes the difficulties of deciding to leave her cloistered order: "A Roman Catholic life in the mid to late '60's was really in turmoil; and their own identity wasn't clear,

[14] Faculty Minutes, p. 2.

much less how to incorporate people in the life of the community. I think that really was part of the issue. For me the loss of—I think it has almost gone—the loss of Roman Catholic life in the American Church is really a great tragedy and worthy of study, really. The oppression, the outside control of women's lives, highly educated women....There are more women religious with Ph.D.s than there are [Roman Catholic] priests in the United States. I mean, a powerful group of intellectual, brilliant, courageous women; and you know, they are kept from really, I think, from reaching their full potential as human beings and as gifts to the life of the whole Church. Now certainly they work it out in all kinds of ways....It has to do with male dominance and all kinds of really pathological group dynamics. Women's communities have suffered greatly; and so to see that continue for me is a great sadness, great sadness." Sullivan left the cloister and, as she says, "wandered around a bit." She was a graduate student in Social Work when she met her future husband at a student Mass at the Shrine of the Immaculate Conception. After marriage, they moved to the country and found the Episcopal Church; and in time she began the ordination process.

At VTS Sullivan developed a close personal relationship with Professor Marianne Micks: "I used to think she was just the smartest thing that ever came down the pike. She used to get frustrated with me because I just couldn't get inclusive language down. I was always messing up on inclusive language, and she would

Rosemarie Sullivan

just get on my case....She gave up chapel once for Lent." Like Horne and Irish, Sullivan found her first job after ordination with the parish in which she had done Field Education as a seminarian. She became the third woman rector in the Diocese of Virginia when she was called to the Church of St. Clement: "That little community had a heart for outreach; and of course being a social worker, my heart is there, too. So we began to work on that particular strength of the community which helped the congregation to regain its sense of self." The parish established an emergency shelter, but the city of Alexandria insisted on an $8,000 shower hook-up: "For us at St. Clement's $8,000 in those days was like 'Holy Cow, you are kidding me!' So I said, 'I tell you what. We are going to invoke the law of sanctuary. Let them sleep in the sanctuary, and don't bother me.' And the city didn't, and they started bussing the people over to us. You have to have a nice congregation with a good heart to do that, to confront the city....'Parish Profiles' are a study in untruth....Every parish, I believe, has a charism. Sometimes they know it, and sometimes they don't. One of the roles of the rector is to determine what the charism is here. How do we live that in a way that really makes sense for us? How can we get behind it?...We need to name that and collect it and understand it and make it who we are and do what we can in that parish to support one another in that kind of work and encourage the Alexandria community. At one point I think we had every

Rosemarie Sullivan

Rosemarie Sullivan

non-profit on the planet holding their meeting over at St. Clement's."[15]

During the time she was rector of St. Clement, Sullivan was a candidate for bishop in several elections. Of those experiences she says, "Women are still not willing to stand for election because we get the starch beaten out of us." After eleven years at St. Clement, Sullivan served for six years as Secretary of General Convention and Executive Officer of the Episcopal Church. Tiring of the constant travel entailed by that position, she accepted the position of Director of Alumni Affairs at VTS until she was called as rector of St. Paul's Rock Creek, Washington, D.C., from which she has just announced her retirement.

Rosemarie Sullivan

Mary Belfry Hansley

Without any record in the Faculty Minutes, the minutes of the May 14, 1986 Board Meeting, note that "[o]n behalf of the Board the Chairman wished Mrs. Hansley Godspeed in her new ministry."[16] After her departure from VTS, Mary Hansley accepted an offer to work part time in a yoked parish in Middleburg, full time while the rector was on sabbatical. Because of her husband's long-distance commuting, she then served as chaplain at the Episcopal Church Home in Georgetown to ease their transition toward closing, during which time she took interim ministry training in Baltimore. In subsequent years she served as an interim in the Dioceses of Washington, Minnesota, and Southern Virginia. But she also spent five years as assistant priest at St. Michael's Church, Barrington, Illinois, the diocese of Chicago, which she valued highly: "I loved the liturgy, and I loved the rich symbolism, and I loved what living in that context does for us. The hard part of being in that environment was I was called 'mother,' and I found that appalling." "Father" and "mother" are not terms that evoke complementarity. "To keep the categories that people limit themselves with as male and female is always a challenge. How do you respect yourself and value yourself as a female when the language around you is not doing that?" She now does supply work on a consistent basis on the Eastern Shore.

The Board Minutes of May 14, 1986, which

---

[15] Interview with Rosemarie Sullivan, April 27, 2010.
[16] Board Minutes, p. 7. The non-renewal of contract of the Rev. Mary Belfry Hansley occurred four months after her full-cover picture and extensive interview appeared in the *Seminary Journal* of January 1986.

noted the departure of Mary Hansley, also record a significant discussion under item #7: "Special Assistant to the Dean. The Dean reviewed the proposed position of Special Assistant to the Dean as described in the May 1986 Board Book. The three-year appointment would include such duties as assisting in admissions work, organizing the Conference on Ministry and orientation week, counseling and advising students, and possibly some teaching....Motion passed unanimously. During the discussion, Bishop [Peter James] Lee expressed his concern about the position as described being interpreted as perpetuating a role model women are trying to overcome, i.e., administrative assistant, arranger of receptions, rather than carrying administrative responsibilities. The Dean was encouraged to continue to search for an ordained woman to fill a professorial position. Dean Reid circulated a curriculum vitae for the Rev. Martha Horne (VTS '83) whom he hoped would be available to fill the position of administrative assistant."[17]

That Fall of 1986 Katherine Ragsdale was a senior at VTS. Ragsdale had been active in the Canterbury Association as an undergraduate at the College of William and Mary when she realized she was called to the priesthood, but the Diocese of Southern Virginia had never deemed a woman qualified for ordination. A male faculty member of VTS advised her to transfer to the Diocese of Virginia; but she recalls, "I needed to do one more check before I thought it was O.K. to move, so I went to the college chap-

Katherine Ragsdale

lain, Sam Portaro (VTS '73). Sam and I have become buddies since that time, but then we didn't get along. So I made an appointment and I said, 'O.K., Sam. You don't

Pat Merchant (Park)

like me. Your opinion is not going to be colored by affection. I need to know if the reason I keep getting turned down by the Diocese of Southern Virginia is because I am a woman, or is it me? Do they have reasons and stuff? I need it from somebody who doesn't like me.' And Sam said, 'If you were a man, you would be ordained by now.' And he fixed me up with Pat Park. He gave me her number and said to call her. I was terrified to call her: She was famous! But I did, and she was so warm.

"She is the thing that changed the ordination of women in the Diocese of Southern Virginia. Somebody called her in to cover for them during a sabbatical; and the bishop couldn't quite bring himself to say, 'No, you can't come in for the sabbatical.' She went in, and I think he probably thought she would support his case because she had a reputation of being so abrasive. You know, just one of those nasty, pushy, abrasive women. She has got that side. She has to. But she is so incredibly pastoral. She went in and loved this parish, and they loved her back; and about the time she left the parish, another parish right near by wanted to call a woman. And it was next to impossible at that point to say, 'No,' given what had just happened with Pat. So I credit her with the Diocese of

17 Ibid., p. 3.

Southern Virginia changing its position."

Ragsdale transferred to the Diocese of Virginia and began the process toward ordination at Westover Parish where Marian K. Windel (VTS '79) was rector. Ragsdale was Executive Director of Common Cause in Virginia immediately before enrolling at VTS in 1984 which, in her own words, "is how I got involved in Church politics. I was a lobbyist, knew how to do all of that, came here [to VTS], had been bumped from a flight sometime during my first year here, and got a free ticket anywhere, which at that stage in life was like a windfall: 'A free airplane ticket! I am rich now!' General Convention [of the Episcopal Church] was coming up in L.A. that summer [of 1985]. My rector [Windel] actually was with me. We both got bumped; we both got the tickets; and she said, 'General Convention, here we come!' So off we went. At the time, Carol Cole Flanagan (VTS '86) was one year ahead of me here and was President of the Women's Caucus. We started talking at Convention. She discovered my history as a lobbyist, and said, 'Excellent. We have several hearings coming up at this convention in different committees where we need somebody to talk and to testify. You clearly know how to do that, so here you go: Here's where to be and what to say.' That was my entrée into Church politics, which I loved; and that has been the thing which has kept me in the Church and active in the Church through all the up and down years….I was officially expelled for missing the day of registration to go to General Convention."

Ragsdale had majored in English and Religion at William and Mary. Her grades were what she characterized as "average/mediocre," but her Graduate Record Examination scores were perfect. Upon looking at those results, the faculty at her admissions interview said, "We think you have a very low boredom threshold….Perhaps you would be happier just doing independent study." Be-cause she began that program immediately upon entering seminary, rather than at the beginning of her middler year as was customary, she registered for her courses and had each instructor sign her registration individually. She continues, "You know, I am awfully independent but, none the less, I thought, 'I am living in a community where people might worry. I am going to make sure. I am going to tell everybody who might wonder where I am and that I am O.K.' So I went to the chaplain's office to say, 'I am going to miss the first two weeks of school because I am going to General Convention. I won't miss any classes be-cause I am doing all independent study.' So I talked to everybody: advisors, the whole bit, registrar, paid registra-tion in advance before I left, all of that stuff, got every-thing signed." Nonetheless, she received an official letter of expulsion. After a great deal of back-and-forth within the faculty, Ragsdale was summoned to meet with Reid and Parrent. "Carol Flanagan said, 'You are not going in there alone, two against one. I will go with you.' So Carol managed to make sure before we went that the seams on our hose were perfectly straight. She was fabulous at in-timidating by looking like Beaver Cleaver's mom, a just completely unexpected piece. So I said to them, 'I am bringing Carol with me.' 'I don't know why you feel you need to do that.' 'Just seems best, you know: two and two.' 'O.K.' So in we came, and I guess it had become clear I was not going to apologize. It being Virginia, somebody had to. So they did: 'I guess you did speak to everybody you should have, and somebody should have pointed out to you [that] you had no business going. If students just start making those decisions for themselves, it will just be chaos around here….We just can't have stu-dents doing whatever they want, but somebody should have told you; so we apologize.' And I said, 'O.K. That will be fine.' 'And you are reinstated.' 'Thanks.' So that was my first expulsion.

"The second one was they made a big deal about how they used inclusive language:[18] that they insisted on it in the classroom, that they graded down papers if you didn't use it. Now, I have no idea what went on in the classroom because I wasn't in them, but my fellow students suggested that was not their experience; and certainly in the chapel it was not the experience. They occasionally fixed the person language. They never touched the God language. So in the old days back before cell phones…before home alarm systems for anybody except the fabulously wealthy, you might remember they used to advertise these things for little old ladies who were panicked. It was a little box with a couple of sirens on it and a remote thing that went by the bed; so if the lady heard prowlers in the night, she could hit it, and the sirens would go off and reportedly scare the prowlers away. That was the closest thing to alarm systems for all of us that existed at the time. So we found an electrician who was able to take the alarms off and substitute buzzers. The battery pack would carry five. We got five buzzers on it. I let him in the chapel one night at three in the morning. It is amazing how many people there are out here at three in the morning walking their dogs! 'Don't come up just yet. O.K. you're clear now.' He went down in the cellar under the chapel, used the floor board as a sounding board, mounted the buzzers, and the main machine in the rafter. I sewed the remote control into the lining of a jacket and various friends, classmates, had used it from time to time. One of the guys said, 'You know, the only problem with this is it is such a feeling of power. And then you go back in the classroom, and you want it there where you really need it.' But nobody had quite really noticed it. And then one day the [chapel] was packed. [In the congregation that day were the Bishops of Province

Three.] And I had it. It might have been the first time I used it, actually. But suddenly people noticed it. And somebody said, 'Well, I know she didn't do it because I was standing right next to her.' Of course everyone suspected me. And another one said, 'I know she didn't do it, and it's funny because everyone knows feminists have no sense of humor.' [Still, she didn't admit to pressing the buzzer each time non-inclusive language was used.] Chapel pranks were a big thing then. There were always the pink flamingoes that would show up in the pulpit and these little icons. Or people would decorate the eagle on the lectern. This was one of the better chapel pranks. Dick [Reid], to his credit, when one of the people who knew turned me in, said, 'You know, chapel pranks are a long tradition here at Virginia, and this one just didn't go over very well.' 'Yes. Sorry about that.'

"But then the faculty were in an uproar that it had happened, and they insisted on a special meeting to vote on expelling me. Mixy was funny. She was on sabbatical right then; but she was still at home, and she was doing an independent study with me on Process Theology, which nobody knew about including Mixy who said, 'I don't know anything about it, but we can read it together.' I was over at her house that day; and she said, 'You know, I have been called for an emergency faculty meeting for your buzzer. I have been here a very long time. There has never been an emergency faculty meeting including the time the police came into class and hauled out one of the students for abusing his daughter. There was no emergency faculty meeting. But for the buzzer there is an emergency faculty meeting. What does that tell you?'….Verna Dozier (VTS '78H) was the Commencement speaker. Her response to the buzzer episode was 'It buzzed every time they used inappropriate language?'

[18] Just a year prior, a proposal concerning inclusive language had been received by the faculty from the VTS Women's Group. This proposal was adapted from comparable policies at Wesley and Union [VA] Theological Seminaries and Duke and Yale Divinity Schools. The proposal was endorsed by the Student Executive Committee and adopted in slightly revised form March 11, 1986, by the faculty.

'Uhuh.' 'Well, my dear, when did it ever stop?'

"[Bishop] Jack [Spong, VTS '55] came in right as all this was breaking. I was over in Sparrow asleep and

Verna Dozier

somebody, my next door neighbor, came in the room to wake me up. She said, 'There is a guy here who wants to see you. I told him you are asleep. He said, 'Wake her up.' I said, 'Who is it?' She says, 'I have no idea, but he said [pause] so I'm doing it.' So I said, 'All right. Fine.' So I threw on some clothes, walked out the door, and recognized him: 'Bishop Spong! How nice to meet you! I'm Katherine Ragsdale.' He came in and said, 'I visit campus a couple of times a year to check on my students. I always ask what has been happening, and all I keep hearing about today is you; so I thought I would check in and see if you are O.K.' Then he said, 'Come to my diocese. We will take care of this.' His diocese was getting mad at him for a variety of things. I wasn't in it, so I don't know what the whole list was. But one of the things they said was, 'We are no longer going to be the place that receives people that can't get ordained elsewhere. We are cutting that off.' So the day after graduation [she did, indeed, graduate in 1987], I had gone up to my room to get something, and the phone is ringing. It is the Canon to the Ordinary

in the Diocese of Newark calling to tell me, 'I don't know what the bishop has told you, but we don't take refugees from other dioceses any more. I'm sorry about that.' I said, 'That is fine. I understand that.' Then something was said that was related to the buzzer; and she said, 'Oh! Wait a minute. You are the buzzer person?' And I said, 'Yes.' And she said, 'Never mind. Come on up. Why didn't you tell me that?' So if it weren't for the buzzer, I would not be ordained….

"It took fourteen years to get ordained, many of them here. I graduated from here seven years after I started the process because, of course, I was all those years in the Diocese of Southern Virginia trying to get postulancy before I came to seminary. Then I got to Newark just as the Standing Committee was trying to prove something to Jack….It became a political pawn, and it ended up taking another seven years. So I remember waking up New Year's Day 1990 and saying, 'That's it. I have spent ten years. I started the process in 1980. I have spent an entire decade trying to get ordained and not doing ministry because [I was] completely absorbed in trying to get ordained. I am absolutely called to ordination. I do not believe I am called to the ordination *process* as a substitute for a life in ministry. I am done. I am out of here.' So I called the diocese and quit and shortly thereafter got a call from either the Chair of the Commission on Ministry or the Standing Committee, I don't remember which: 'Could we have lunch?' I thought, 'If this guy hits the "What can we do for you" sort of thing, I am just going to go ballistic. Too little too late, pal, so forget it.' So we had lunch; and to his credit what he said was, 'It would be such a huge loss to the Church if you get out of this. Is there anything we can do to make this happen which will encourage you to stay?' I was working at 815 at the time; and I said, 'Well, I am concentrating on doing ministry from now on. If you can get me ordained without interfering with my ability to do ministry, terrific. I am there.

At the minute I am spending so much time jumping through hoops that I don't have time or emotional energy to focus on doing ministry. We're done.' And after that, everything fell into place pretty quickly."[19]

Katherine Ragsdale was ordained deacon in 1993; priest, in 1994. It had taken the community fourteen years to acknowledge the gifts of grace this woman brought to the Church. During those years, Ragsdale had served on numerous women's advocacy boards and worked at the Women's Desk at the national headquarters of the Episcopal Church in New York City, "815" as it is called, on public policy affecting women. Women were being ordained in an increasing number of dioceses. By 1989 Alison Cheek had completed a Doctor of Ministry degree at Episcopal Divinity School and joined the faculty there to direct the Feminist Liberation Theologies program. The sculpting of grace continued.

Once ordained, Katherine Ragsdale served at 815 for an additional four and one half years while doing team ministry at a "little starving church on a bad side of the street in Jersey City. We did

Katherine Ragsdale

Katherine Ragsdale

Sunday services and pastoral emergencies in exchange for living in the rectory." She then moved to Cambridge, MA, to pursue a Doctor of Ministry degree at Episcopal Divinity School. Shortly thereafter she answered the request of a small country church to provide supply from Advent to Epiphany and stayed fourteen years, through it all continuing her work of advocacy on countless boards.[20] She had argued against being their vicar saying, "I have all these boards I am serving on. I could get a call Saturday afternoon to do a Sunday morning news show, and I have made a commitment to this work. I would have to take it." "It's O.K.," they replied. "We'll cope. You come back with great stories."

In 2009 Katherine Ragsdale became the Dean and President of Episcopal Divinity School, Cambridge, Massachusetts. She speaks warmly of the support provided her by the current Dean and President of VTS, Ian Markham. But the other reality of women's struggles is ever present: "There is a whole generation of women coming up who don't get it: that there is still discrimination. Eventually if they have any talent, they are going to rise high enough to discover it; but in the meantime, they haven't been part of the movement to fix it. I don't know what the answer is, but we have to find a way to help these younger women know the story, know what is in store for them so they can become activists, become ener-

[19] Interview with Katherine Ragsdale, May 22, 2010.
[20] She served as President and Executive Director of Political Research Associates and on the boards of The White House Project, NARAL Pro-Choice America, and the Religious Coalition for Reproductive Choice, among others.

Katherine Ragsdale

Katherine Ragsdale

gized and passionate and part of the solution before they get a very rude surprise after they are my age and don't have the energy for fighting quite that hard….We have cleared a very wide path up to the point where they are and as far ahead as they can see, and they don't get it that we actually know something about what is farther ahead than they can see. If they are not prepared, they are not going to be able to deal with it when they get there."

Yet again the question of the capacity to recognize grace in the midst of confrontation arises. Having been pushed to the margins, some women clergy have accepted the duty of standing on the edge between humanity's comprehension and God's plan for a new dimension of reality. Desisting from the pursuit of their own needs, their own projections, the self-focused goals for "their" ministry, they listen for the Word that was and is present at creation and in revelation, drawing near by grace. They watch for the future to break into the present. And then they proclaim that Presence.

"I said to my soul, be still," wrote the poet T. S. Eliot,
I said to my soul, be still, and wait without hope
For hope would be hope for the wrong thing;
wait without love
For love would be love of the wrong thing;
there is yet faith
But the faith and the love and the hope are all
in the waiting.[21]
The women who offer spiritual sacrifices listen and watch, waiting for God's house to emerge. Then, like sculptors, they model a new creation.

[21] T. S. Eliot, *Four Quartets* (New York: Harcourt, Brace & World, Inc., 1971), 28.

GRACE
in Motion

CHAPTER EIGHT

"So they remained for a long time, speaking
boldly for the Lord, who testified to the word
of his grace by granting signs and wonders to
be done through them."

Acts 14:3
New Revised Standard Version

Each clergy person comes to the good news of God in Christ from a different perspective, from different ways of looking at the world, from different realities. They also come from different cultures: Some seminary students are from the American South, some from the American West Coast, some from the East Coast, some from the mid-West, some from countries far away from America. These are all different cultures because each area has its own values, its own vocabulary, its own rules and expectations. And even within each area, one encounters cross-cultural events.

Cross-cultural events are liminal: They cross a threshold that is barely perceptible. Some call these liminal moments when life is capable of being changed "thin places." Thin places are found when one stands on the edge of something numinous, when one is filled with a sense of the presence of divinity, when God's absolute presence lifts the veil between the immanent and the transcendent.

In a book entitled *Thin Places: a Pilgrimage Home*, Ann Armbrecht writes, "[T]hin places [are] where one's nerve endings are bare. People make pilgrimages to thin places, places where gods have made their mark on the land. As the legends of the hidden valleys make clear, these journeys are internal as much as external. What the pilgrims encounter—the blessings they perceive—depends as much on their receptivity as on the sanctity of the land they pass through."[1] In writing of gods as plural, Armbrecht is referring to the native wisdom of priests and shamans and such things as maintaining relationship with ancestors or spirits long dead. Doubt, in such cultures, does not consist in questioning the existence of God but, rather, mistrusting the ability of God to overcome the gods of witchcraft.

There are less than positive spirits alive in our internal landscapes, principalities and powers that hold sway in what we think of as more sophisticated cultures. Why else do we pray in the baptismal service to renounce the evil powers of this world which corrupt and destroy the creatures of God? Demonic powers assault us in every conceivable way: consumption as a way of life, busyness as a mark of pride, powerlessness in the face of poverty and hunger. But ritual is "the way that we participate in a reality that has changed around us."[2] In the opening in the landscape created by ritual, "we can see and feel, if only for an instant, a clearing outside linear time where the boundary between worlds is less sharply drawn…."[3] In Baptism, Eucharist, and the Pastoral Offices, the people of God cross a liminal threshold, led by the ordained. If our reality is sophisticated, sophisticated in the sense of deprived of its original simplicity—the simplicity of Eden—the power of the gospel is deprived of strength; for we make it nothing but a solution to problems we can define. Many of the ordained women graduates of VTS have recognized the limits of sophistication, crossed cultural boundaries, stood on the edge of something numinous, and in that thin place been met by God.

– Stepping across the Boundary –

Mariann Edgar Budde [nee Edgar] is a person unafraid to face bare nerve endings and boundaries. In her own words, "I went off to college and there had some experiences of faith and community that brought my conversion to a different level, more in the realm of social justice and doing something that would put my life on

---

[1] Ann Armbrecht, *Thin Places: A Pilgrimage Home* (New York: Columbia University Press, 2009), 87.
[2] Thomas G. Long, *Accompany them with Singing: the Christian Funeral* (Louisville: Westminster John Knox Press, 2009), 165.
[3] Ibid., 176.

the edge somehow. I was very drawn to that kind of dangerous, exciting, challenging world….These were not radical years on college campuses; but…while I was in Spain, the Central American wars were really intensifying….Then when I came back, I found this group of people who were very involved in solidarity movements with the people of El Salvador and Nicaragua. I joined them, and then I became immersed in and inspired by the social justice arm of the Catholic Church and the nuns who were getting killed and the priests who were starting small-group, Christian-based communities in Central America and the people in this country working to stop the funding for the wars….I also became involved in the Catholic worker movement." Because the Diocese of Newark was not particularly open to younger vocations, after college Budde took a job with the Methodist Church in Tucson, AZ, for two years. She spent time with Roman Catholics but was always drawn back to the Episcopal Church. "[The Diocese of] Arizona did not have an environment that was open to women at that time. I went back to my home parish [in the Diocese of Newark] and back to that priest who was never particularly supportive of my going to seminary. But when I told him that I was ready to test [a vocation], he said, 'Okay.'" About choosing VTS Budde says, "I didn't know if I wanted to come here. I was living where I wanted to live, kind of in that edgy place….I really thought I wanted to go to New York….I felt almost suffocated here….When I first arrived, I felt a bit trapped because I had to move into the dorm. Didn't want to do that. People were calling me 'ma'am'….I spent as much time as I could my first year outside of VTS. I took courses in the Consortium. I was

Mariann Edgar Budde

in D.C. all the time, trying to get some remnants of my old world back. I'd almost transferred, I think, after my first semester; but then after the second semester, I thought, you know, I have some work to do and I can do it here….Murray Newman was teaching an intro course at Howard at the time….So I started sitting in on Murray's class. We would drive over together and just sit in his class at Howard, and it was wonderful; and it was wonderful to spend time with him and to listen to him tell the story. Through him I got the story [of the Old Testament], and I got the magic of it and the power of it….He taught me to read the Bible."

Mariann Edgar Budde

Budde did middler field work at Mission San Juan del Obisbo, a Spanish-speaking mission in D.C. Then she married after her second year at VTS and with her new husband spent a year at Tegucigalpa, Honduras, teaching in a home and school for abandoned boys. "I thought for sure that somewhere on the edges of the Church is where I would live my life, but I wanted to come back. I wanted to get my degree."

After graduation from VTS in '88, Budde served five years as an associate at Trinity Parish, downtown Toledo, Ohio. She interviewed for the position one week before her son was born. "Spong was reluctant to release me; but he didn't have any work for me, and he didn't have very good experience with women. He told me straight out that every woman he knew that got pregnant left the ministry....I learned how to be a parish priest in Toledo: how to preach regularly, teach classes, be a good pastor, work with all sorts of people, take initiatives—some that failed and some that succeeded. [The rector] gave me freedom and responsibility. But he was a deeply troubled man, and he self-destructed while I was there.... He was stripped of his priesthood, but actually what was more heart breaking for me was what happens when a priest stops functioning in a healthy way and its effect on the congregation systemically. That's what I saw, and I didn't know what to do about it or who to talk to....Fortunately, I also had a growing sense of call, and assurance, that I could be a rector."

As she began to interview for a rector position, her children were two and five. She recalls, "Gaye Jennings was the Canon to the Ordinary in Ohio when I was there; and when I was interviewing, she really wanted me to stay in Ohio. She set me up to interview with this parish in Kent. I had a phone interview, and it was just dreadful. It went so badly, and I knew, I just knew. Gaye called me and she, in her inimitable way, asked me if I wanted feedback. I said, 'Sure.' She said, 'You led with your weaknesses and your anxieties, and you basically told them every reason in advance why they shouldn't call you.' Then she said, 'Let me ask you a question. Do you honestly feel that your being a mother is an asset or a liability to your vocation as a priest?' I said, 'It's an asset.' And she said, 'Okay. The next time you have an interview, remember that; and don't tell them all the things that keep you up at night unless they ask. But you don't have to start with your weaknesses!'....I think women are more inclined to do that. I've observed that in women. We sort of tend to just give away our authority much more readily. We have to learn how not to do that."

Budde was called to St. John's, Minneapolis; and after ten years, she was a finalist for Dean of the Minneapolis cathedral. Of that experience she says, "I would guess that my being a woman was not in my favor in that one. I don't think that's the only reason I wasn't called, but I don't think it was an asset in that system." Budde and the leadership of St. John's agreed to a commitment of five more years together, a "fruitful decision. We made a lot of headway in those years in terms of the development of the congregation." During that time she also earned a D.Min. from VTS and published a book. Of her D.Min. thesis she writes, "I began by documenting the precipitous, systematic decline of the Episcopal Church in Minnesota; and then I spent time with the leaders of thirteen congregations, like St. John's, that have a worshipping community of 150-300 members. These are large congregations in Minnesota, and we are perceived as being healthy, vibrant congregations. And yet we are quite

Mariann Edgar Budde

small, relative to churches of other denominations. I worked with them to evaluate our strengths and then to imagine what it would take for us to become more responsive to our age and to become numerically stronger in order to reach more people with the message of the Episcopal Church."[4]

Yet Budde continues to work on the margins of the Church, leading mission trips to Central America, supporting the first Spanish-speaking Episcopal mission in the Diocese of Minnesota, establishing companion relationships between her parish and Native American and Liberian congregations, and addressing racial inequality in the city. On June 18, 2011, on the second ballot, Mariann Edgar Budde was elected Bishop of the Diocese of Washington.

Bishop-elect of the Diocese of Washington, Mariann Edgar Budde

The year that Budde spent on the edges of the Church in Honduras was the year Martha Horne became administrative assistant to Dean Richard Reid. It was also Katherine Ragsdale's senior year and the junior year of Ruth Lawson Kirk. As a child, Kirk [nee Lawson] imagined herself a priest serving communion, not unusual for the daughter of an Episcopal priest and a mother who had come from the West Coast to study at Yale Divinity School as a candidate for ordination in the United Church of Christ. At Yale Kirk's mother met the man she married and gave up her ministry to be a wife and mother, and Kirk's sister observes that more of the chil-

Ruth Lawson Kirk

dren's theological conversations were with their mother than with their father. Kirk notes, "My parents were socially progressive and advocates of the Civil Rights movement....My father's ministry ended in '71 within the Church because Eli Lilly was the funder of the congregation [in Indianapolis], and he really objected to my father's ministry. He withdrew his financial resources; and they were in a negative, deficit situation, and the congregation chose the comfort of the money over the radical gospel. My dad just couldn't deal with that kind of hypocrisy, so he left the Church for almost a decade. They divorced....[Mother] didn't want me to suffer in ordained ministry, so there was a piece of her that encouraged and there was a piece of her of 'I don't want you to get hurt like your dad did and so many others do'....My father and mother stopped attending Church, and they said to their five kids, 'You have your own path. You have your own choice. What do you want to do?' Four of the five were involved in the choir ministry; and we all said, 'We are staying. They are not kicking us out, they are not asking us to leave, and this is our church.' So there was some defiance in it but also some 'This is my home; I am not giving this up.'"

But the political ramifications continued once Kirk sought to enter the ordination process: "I came from the wealthiest congregation, the cathedral congregation, and so I kind of had some strikes against me because of that. I couldn't sort out what it was, but something about me was not O.K. Was it that I was a woman? No, never had any resistance for that; but political? Very definitely.

[4] Interview with Mariann Edgar Budde, June 22, 2010.

Somebody actually said, 'I think you are trying to heal your father's broken ministry.' I was like, 'No, you don't get me then. This is not about my dad. This is about me.' So the first time through the bishop's advisory committee they said, 'You need to wait a year.' I was ready. I was charged up. I had done everything the Bishop had asked me. I had been in the real world [as an investigative case worker in child protective services for three years]....The second time they said 'No,' I came back to the Dean and said, 'They said "No."' He said, 'This is ridiculous.' He called the bishop; and there were strange, pulled conversations. Then they said, 'You have to leave the cathedral congregation and may not worship there, teach there, lead there. You have to go and explore other kinds of ways of being in the Episcopal Church because that is all you know'....So the third time the answer was 'yes.'"

Kirk considered several seminaries in addition to VTS: "At [one] the admissions director said, 'You're Peter Lawson's daughter.' And I thought, 'You have just lost me. I can't come here then'....I said to her, 'I can't come here. I can't be his daughter. I have to be my own person and not known through him.' So I went to the bishop and I said, 'I have investigated four seminaries and I think it is Virginia.' He said, 'That's good because that is where I was going to send you.' [I thought] 'You could have saved me some time and money. Oh, well.' So I came with the other postulant [from Indianapolis]. We both were single, lived on campus, and immediately moved into two very different circles of Virginia Seminary.

"This was during some very difficult times at Virginia. I arrived in '86. Martha Horne arrived for her first year in the administration, and people refused to take communion from her, refused to attend. Chapel was mandatory. It was really clear at the very start: If you come here, these are the things we expect from you. But people were not being forced to attend....There were probably six of my classmates who were opposed to the ordination of women. That was the first time I had met anyone who said on a theological basis women should not be ordained. I had never had to make the case as to whether women should be ordained because nobody had ever said to me that I shouldn't [be]. I had never had to come up with justification....So what do I do, what do I say when somebody says to me, 'This is not of God for you to be ordained. It is not in the Bible'....Every Tuesday a member of my group who is opposed to the ordination of women speaks about it on a regular basis: 'It is not wise for you to be here. This is not right for you to be here. You are wasting the resources of the Church. Somebody else could have had your place.' [There was] no systemic address to that in our classes and by the leadership of the Seminary. So that was harsh, and that was the year we did a trial use on inclusive language; and it just inflamed these men. I wrote one of the articles in the student newsletter at the time and had a friend draw a picture of a woman pushing into a men's room saying, 'Oh! I thought that [men] was an inclusive term.' You can't have it both ways, guys. You can't say it is one thing, and then also say it is something else. So there was just a lot of hostility and a lot of repression, too. It was like 'We don't talk about those things here.' I don't know whether that was a Southern thing, but...I was like 'We talk about everything. What do you mean we don't talk about these things.' So I was very puzzled in my first year.

"There was one very painful account: I was also a party organizer and became president of my class. I lived in Sparrow Hall; so we had the downstairs we could use when we needed to, and so we had several parties through the year and invited lots of people over and had a great time. There was a party in the late Spring [of '87] in Aspinwall. It was a beach party theme, and we had kegs on campus. A couple of these young men, including my fellow postulant from Indianapolis, got rip-roaring drunk, and one of them shoved me up against a wall and was on the verge of assaulting me. I was undone by that event and reported it to Martha [Horne] because she felt safe to talk to about it. Then I had to talk with Churchill Gibson. In his lovely Southern way, it was dealt with. I was heard, and there were consequences for those students….These were three of my classmates with whom I was in class everyday for the next two years. So it was not a very safe place…lots of good community but also some unspoken things we don't talk about, things we don't deal with. That was very disconcerting for me. It was like the senior class was the most open/ liberal. The middler class was a pretty good mix of conservatives and liberals, and there were some tensions in that class. Our class did just not gel at all, did not get along. There were very definitely camps and groups in our class….

Ruth Lawson Kirk

"Maybe a third of our class were women. I don't know if we ever engaged in making the case theologically for why we should be there. It was very definitely treated as a justice issue and not because God is calling us and because we are empowered and because we have these gifts for ministry and because this is how God works in the world. We never positively stated that case….We gathered for our twentieth year reunion last year, and it is amazing how many have left the church or are part of the Anglican Church in America from our class….What a telling sign: for the reunion there were five of us. I think there were sixty some students [in that class], so there really was no sense of community or connection in that class. There really wasn't. It was a loss.

"[After graduation] July of '89, I became assistant to the rector in a residential but urban inner-city parish, St. Paul's Chestnut Hill….There still wasn't a [diocesan] policy on maternity leave, and this was 1991/92; so I had to create my own policy and negotiate it with [the rector] for what my maternity leave would be….I was the youngest woman called to be a rector in the Diocese of Pennsylvania. I was thirty-one when I was called to St. Peter's, the woman rector of the largest congregation of all congregations where women were the clergy person, and that was surprising to everyone. I remember the suffragan bishop saying to me before, 'You know you are not going to get this—I don't want you to be disappointed—because you are too young, and they are not ready for a woman.' But the interim had been a woman….I was like, 'Whatever God wants is going to happen, and so we will wait and see.' They called and I went and I was there for fourteen years….The great thing about being in Pennsylvania was getting to know Nancy Wittig and to have her presence in the diocese….She was one of my mentors…. Nancy had her children while she was active in the priesthood, but we never really talked about that. I sort of felt different because most of the other women clergy were either lesbian, single, divorced and older; and I was like this odd young, married, [with] children, sort of doing normal generational kinds of things but having started ordained ministry at an early age….A couple of parishioners were very anti women's ordination, but [thought] I was O.K. They didn't like the concept, but I was O.K. But one couple thought the interim was great because she went to seminary after her children were grown, and that is what I should also have done—I should do the mothering and then do the priesting—and how selfish of me to put my children through all this.…The Search Committee actually stood up for me and said, 'She said she was going to have a child, and we affirmed that we think it is a wonderful thing.' The couple eventually left the congregation. Discrimination…was always present, but it was like 'you can't defeat what I already know inside me is true. You can't tell me that it is not true because you can point to some ancient way that the Church has lived and say tradition trumps the power of God because it doesn't.'"

Before leaving St. Peter's to answer the call to Delaware, Kirk was a finalist in the New Hampshire election in which Gene Robinson was chosen bishop. She reflects, "It was an incredibly excellent experience because throughout my career people said, 'You are going to be a bishop, you are going to be a bishop'; and I don't know why. I have said to people, 'Why do you say that to me? Why do I hear that from you?' [They reply], 'You care about the Church so much. You are passionate. You bring people together. You are a great leader. I just see it.'" She testified at General Convention to the integrity of the New Hampshire process and to her belief that Robinson was called to be the bishop of the Diocese of New Hampshire. Robinson said to her, "You know, you are first runner-up; so if this doesn't happen, you had better watch out." She replied, "Well actually, I am Miss Congeniality."

Kirk arrived at her present parish, Christ Church Christiana Hundred, in September of 2007. This parish had had women assistants, but Kirk is their first woman rector. Among the challenges is the different context for ministry: Her previous parish was middle class; this one, a mixture of socio-economic backgrounds but definitely upper class with parishioners who are the "movers and shakers" of the community. As Kirk says, "If you want to get something done for the homeless, these folks are on the boards and active and making a difference. An incredible church. Both of my predecessors were autocrats and

did empower to some extent, but [gave] very limited responsibilities.…I really felt called to exhibit authority in a different way. I am very collaborative, and maybe part of it is just the male/female way, maybe it is generational. I don't want to be called "Mother" in church. I don't like "Father" in church. I don't think that these parental titles are appropriate for clergy even though I grew up using them for my father's colleagues. So I have people call me "Ruth," and I am working really hard to make the congregation understand that the staff are colleagues in ministry and have various functions of ministry and the congregation are partners in ministry and have the responsibility for x, y, z; and we are there to support them too, help guide them too, encourage, inspire, whatever we can do but neither do it for nor tell them what to do

Ruth Kirk, September 2007

and how to do it. So they are coming through a pretty big transition of leadership style. Often times the altar guild cowered in fear. It was like, 'Is this the way you want it? We don't want to disappoint you, and we don't want to upset you, and please don't yell.' Why would I yell? 'You are doing a great job. You are taking care of things.' But that was their experience, so there have been stutters in transformation. I have been challenged.…I know that it is the powers pushing back, both on my leadership style and on me. I also think it is the powers of dark pushing against the powers of light because we are working on some very good and healthy changes this year, and people are responding, and ministry is being accomplished. My senior associate reported at the staff meeting yesterday that he has heard from many people that they are seeing the youth involved in outreach in a very different way. The kids are doing service projects and are invested instead of going off to this go-kart track or at some person's pool. People are involved in using their gifts in ministry in the church. People tell me, 'This feels like a different

Ruth Kirk baptizing baby

church'.…In the culture in general there is a lot of anxiety and pain in the world, and you know they come to the church to let that go and to grab hold of something else. This is a great ministry, and this is a great place to be."[5]

Like Bonnyman, Kirk has crossed a cultural boundary, a threshold, by being called as leader of a major parish. The women who have cracked the "glass ceiling" which limits

Ruth Kirk at February 2009 pancake supper

Ruth Kirk on Easter 2008

the influence and achievement of many have, by their presence in the realms where power is exercised, changed the nature of leadership from hierarchical autocracy to collaborative authority. But for the majority, such transformation would be a long time in coming.

Meanwhile, the status of Betty Works Fuller changed: "When we moved to the Diocese of West Texas where Frank was a rector in San Marcos,…technically I was the first ordained woman in West Texas.…I continued to do curriculum. I helped Frank as a non-stipendiary assistant; and then in 1988 I agreed to a six-month, which turned into a six-year, stint as the deacon in charge and eventually rector in a little town called Luling which was twenty-five miles away. So I commuted. After I accepted the position, I found out I was pregnant with our [second child, a] son; so I got to be the first pregnant cleric in West Texas and took baby Will in his little car seat back and forth. During that time Bishop Bailey kept saying, 'Betty, why don't you get ordained?' Then he retired, and about that time it was clear to me that it was time to get ordained [to the priesthood]. I can remember Frank and I having supper, the exact location; and he said, 'Quit talking about it. Either do it or shut up,' basically. I said, 'O.K.! How do I do it?' He said, 'You need an interviewing committee.' So I asked a couple of people, brought them together, and one laughed, one smiled, and one cried; and they all said, 'You are already a priest. You just need the laying on of hands.'.…It was a wonderful

[5] Interview with Ruth Lawson Kirk, April 28, 2010.

evening. Frank preached, and we had forty clergy there, and the parish was jubilant and had a big celebration. I stayed another year, and then it was time to move on to campus ministry for two and one-half years….

Then we moved to Corpus Christi [in 1995] and started all over again. Talk about obstacles. [The Bishop said,] 'I want you to be careful where you wear a collar'…. They had had a clergy couple before and that had blown up…so they were very nervous about having a clergy couple. Although the [other couple] went straight from seminary, we were happily married; and at that point we had been married for twenty-five years. So it took a while to deal with that; and I was like, 'Oh, Lord, how long are we going to have to prove ourselves?' It is really clear in some ways. It may have been twenty or thirty years, but it is still a new thing. It is not only the symbolism of a woman with a collar, but it is just the whole trust thing. Then you add in clergy couple. We knew but we didn't know at the beginning that making the decision to marry was not going to be good for our careers, at least where God had called us to live. So we moved to Corpus and two weeks after we got there, the Bishop called and said, 'I need you to go and be the interim….'" Betty Works Fuller served as an interim there for several months, then as interim for thirteen months in a tension-filled, combined parish. From Oct. 1, 1997 to Dec. of 2007, she was the rector at Alice, Texas, commuting from where she lived with her husband. In Alice there was a male parishioner, lay reader for the 8 a.m., who told her that women priests were an abomination. He accepted blessing and absolution from Fuller, but not communion. Because she was concerned about him, she told him, "Go to another parish for sacramental feeding." On the first Sunday of Advent, he took communion. "I just couldn't believe it was wrong anymore," he said. When Fuller left Alice for Beaumont, he

Betty Works Fuller goodbye at Alice, TX

cried. Beaumont is the first time there have been immediate jobs for both of them: She is chaplain at St. Luke's school and half time Christian Education director at St. Mark's where her husband Frank is rector. "Waiting and trying to be sensitive was the only way I could function all these years," she says. "You're a good priest if someone wants you when they're dying." It had taken long years of signs and wonders for a culturally conservative part of the country to acknowledge Fuller as priest; but a continuing question for her is, "Why can't the Church value clergy couples?"[6] That question would arise in increasing numbers in the coming decades.

Christine Whittaker (VTS '90) is a woman who in many roles has crossed traditional boundaries between male and female spheres of influence. She remembers, "I was ini-

Betty Works Fuller

6 Interview with Betty Works Fuller, May 6, 2010.

tially in my early teens thinking that I would study medicine, and I thought about doing some sort of medical mission type of work. I wanted to do something that had a sense of purpose and that in some way responded to God's call in my life….That's what really began a pattern of being aware of some sense of vocation, getting close to it, and stepping back. I think the same thing happened after graduation from [Oxford] University. I came to the United States for a year immediately after graduating from Oxford and then went back and worked in the British Civil Service for two years. That was a position which was well-regarded and extremely competitive and, incidentally, accepted only about 10% women in those days."

During her years at University, Oxford had a ratio of four men for every one woman undergraduate. After two years with the British Civil Service, Whittaker earned a Masters degree in the history of medicine from Yale University and began to look for a job on Capitol Hill, Washington, D.C. "I thought that I would work on some of the health policy issues, such as national health insurance and a single payer plan that were a hot topic then; and that was, of course, thirty-five or so years ago. I was astounded to find that I was being asked not only if I could type but whether I took shorthand, and here I was with a degree from Oxford and a degree from Yale. I would not have had that experience in Britain because of the particular job that I'd had there, and I was astounded because I knew that that wouldn't have happened to a man with my experience."

Whittaker then went to law school. "I was working at [the Washington office of a large New York law firm]. I sort of knew this really wasn't my call in life; but I also knew that it was a good job and it paid well and I wasn't sure what I was supposed to do. I stayed there for

Christine Whittaker

six years, and then I moved to the Justice Department which I liked a lot. I was an appellate lawyer in the Civil Division arguing before most of the federal courts of appeal around the country and working with the Solicitor General's Office on Petitions for Certiorari before the Supreme Court. It was really stimulating, interesting, and worthwhile work; but I still had this nagging feeling that I needed to pay more attention to God."

After having served as Senior Warden at her parish on Capitol Hill, Whittaker was invited to preach at an informal Eucharist on St. Andrew's Day. "It had been an unnerving experience, when I felt that the gospel for the day…was speaking directly to me. The impact was strong enough that I went to talk to my priest, telling him that I thought I needed to learn how to pray.

"I began spending ten minutes or so in silence every morning, before the rest of my family got out of bed. At first, that time seemed long and empty, and I wished that I was still in bed. But gradually, that silence was less empty and seemed to encompass a presence. Then one morning, totally unexpectedly, in the midst of this prayer time, I heard in my mind the words, 'Here am I, send me'….The feeling was compelling enough that I started praying about this and talking to my priest about this feeling that God was calling me to do something.

"Over the next few months, I started exploring what this sense of vocation might be. I reflected on which areas of my life were satisfying and which seemed to be going nowhere. I started to do things that challenged me to venture outside my comfort zone—like training to be a volunteer in a new hospice program at D.C. General Hospital. That made me confront the fact that I lived most of the time in a head-centered, analytical world and I needed to learn to act from my heart as well as my head."[7]

As Whittaker tested the invitation to cross a liminal boundary, it was "as if God were saying, 'Don't worry about your unworthiness. I have a job for you, and only you, to do. Get up and do what needs to be done, and I will support you with my grace." She entered VTS and was a seminarian, and later associate, at a lower middle class white parish which was becoming a multi-racial, multi-cultural parish. "Not only were there middle class white parishioners, there were African American parishioners, including people with graduate degrees and professional jobs. There were recent immigrants from West Africa—from Liberia who were refugees from the terrible civil war there and Ibos from Nigeria....There were people from East Africa, and there were quite a large number of people from the Caribbean who brought their Anglo-Catholic tradition. Having all these relatively new arrivals in the parish did not make for an easy [community] life. There was a fair amount of conflict in one way or another."

Following her two years as seminarian, then eighteen months as full-time curate at Church of the Ascension, Sligo Parish, Silver Spring, MD, Whittaker was called to a parish in Georgetown, the Diocese of Washing-

LEFT TO RIGHT: *Jane Morse & Christine Whittaker*

ton: "In my parish in Georgetown there was a parishioner whom I loved dearly who thought that I could not be a priest because I was a woman. He was an active, faithful parishioner; and when I was the assistant and the rector was a man, it didn't cause any particular problems. He would receive communion when the rector was the celebrant. He didn't receive communion when I was the celebrant. He was always supportive. When I became the Priest-in-Charge, he was even more supportive: He chaired the Worship Committee, he made brilliant suggestions on liturgy, and he gave me really good feedback about sermons. He supported me in conversations with people in the parish, and he would from time to time go to another church in order to receive communion. He and I talked about this and agreed that we both loved God and loved the Episcopal Church and that the Church was bigger than our differing perspectives on the ordination of women. We did not want it to affect our being members and serving God in that particular parish. He was a retired foreign service officer, and so I suppose a background in diplomacy...made it easier to think of negotiating solutions rather than declaring all-out war."

After Georgetown, Whittaker moved to Massachusetts, served as an associate at Trinity Church, Copley Square, Boston, and has now been a rector for thirteen years. Comparing the two dioceses, she notes, "Both the Diocese of Washington and the Diocese of Massachusetts very early elected women to be suffragan bishops....So I

[7] Sermon preached at St. Michael's Episcopal Church, Holliston, February 7, 2010.

Christine Whittaker

think the diocese and the diocesan clergy have been open to women. I think it's taken much longer for women to be chosen or called as rectors of large or 'Cardinal' parishes….I was aware when I was in the Diocese of Washington that the clergy still felt very much a male-dominated group. I remember walking into the clergy association and feeling that it was a fairly competitive atmosphere. I recognized it, I think, because I'd practiced as a lawyer. I knew that sort of environment, and it felt similar. It did not at that point feel particularly collegial. I'm sure it's changed now. When I got to Massachusetts, I found that clergy women in Massachusetts had had a history of gathering separately during clergy conferences to support one another because there were few women in the diocese. That was something that I'd not been used to and was not really comfortable with because I have generally preferred situations where there are no separate groups, rather than to divide or segregate people on the basis of gender or anything else. Once at Trinity, Copley Square in Boston, a state senator was wanting to have some sort of memorial service and wanted only women clergy to officiate at it. My colleague who was the associate priest for Outreach at Trinity asked me if I would be there; and I said, 'No,' that I would not do it if I was being invited to do it only because I was a woman."[8]

Grace in motion can be stopped when human will erects artificial boundaries, preventing an appreciation of the all-encompassing fullness of God. One must ask whether it is ever appropriate for communities to segregate and isolate rather than cross cultural thresholds to take into account the values of minorities. How can the Church better be multiculturally catholic while at the same time allowing each particular community to construct its own truth? What would intercultural theology look like? How many traditions can be sustained by one interpretive network? Such questions do not generate ready answers. Rather they instantiate a hermeneutical process, a revisioning of the world.

Katharine Babson's (VTS '92) experience of liminal moments began early in her life: "I used to ride my bike down to the church as a little girl…and go in and just sit and listen to the pigeons on the roof and the timbers creaking and wonder how I fit into this great mystery that I perceived. I wouldn't have used those words at the time, but I was very much drawn to the church. More than once I walked through the entire church, opening doors, and sat in the rector's chair when everything was still open as if I were looking for something. So later the story of Eli and Samuel's call made sense to me because that was very much part of my childhood.

"I consciously understood my call to the priesthood when I was in a transfer interview at Williams College. After having spent several months there on exchange from Vassar, I decided this was really where I needed to be. So I went in for my transfer interview; and at the end of it all, the gentleman said, 'Well, Kitty, after you graduate, how do you think you might give your gifts back to the world?' And I said to him, 'The Church doesn't ordain women now; but when it does, I believe I'm called to be a priest.' And it was one of those moments where these words came out of my mouth, and I was totally unconscious of having thought anything of this kind before….I

[8] Interview of Christine Whittaker by Jennifer Andrews-Weckerly, Oct. 5, 2010.

stood up, and it's as if the whole world had tilted. I walked out. I remember being afraid I was going to trip over the rug because I felt so off balance by this pronouncement out of nowhere.

"And then I went to India for my senior year… with that sense of vocation very active in my mind….I found myself fathoming my understanding of myself and my culture and my religious tradition in new ways as I sought my identity in such a very different place."

During that trip while she was alone and ill with dengue fever, a man tried to break into her room. She managed to fend him off by throwing India ink down the front of his garment. "The next day, this man from the Rajasthani Folklore Institute came, betel nut dribbling down his chin, scraggly looking. He said, 'Come with me.' I packed my bag and I went. He helped me down the stairs, put me in a pony cart, took me to his family's house. His wife and his daughter took me into this beautifully darkened room with a bed laid with fresh linen, a mosquito net over it. They laid me into the bed, tucked me in, and said, 'Sleep.' I don't know how long I slept; but when I awakened, they poured a hot bath for me; and I realized, 'This is a good Samaritan.' And I began to make the linkages between what I was seeing in this other culture with what was so seminal to me in my own, and suddenly the whole of this story came alive for me in ways that had never been alive before. Though it had always been meaningful and attractive to me, I was living the story and in a culture that was as close to first century Palestine as I had ever experienced in my life: people still driving around or going places in ox carts and fueling their stoves with cow patties."

After college as a young wife and mother of two, Babson set about volunteering: managing the Sunday school program in her parish, volunteering at Hospice, becoming one of the first AIDS volunteers, managing the education policy at a local preschool, and substitute teach-

ing. To fill in some gaps in her background in order to accept a teaching position in Art History, she began to attend Northern Virginia Community College. One night in class the thought came to her, "'You don't belong here. It's time for you to go to seminary.' Again, that sense of being so off balance. I practically stumbled out of that classroom and down to the parking lot in the rain." She talked with her husband and her rector and started the process toward ordination, immediately taking Hebrew and Mission courses while balancing her husband's travel schedule and their children's needs. One of her fellow students was John Wilme, a priest from Myanmar who was to have a significant role in her future.

Kitty Babson

Her husband had just been offered a position with the World Bank in Jakarta, Indonesia. Had he accepted, seminary study would have been postponed for eight years. Thinking he had "killed" his career, he gave up that opportunity; and Babson said to him, "If you ever have another opportunity to work overseas, I will go with you anywhere because there are ministries to be served everywhere, and we will figure this out." Thus, in the Fall of 1989 as Babson accompanied her husband on a business trip to East Asia, visiting the Philippines, Hong Kong, Bangkok, Kuala Lumpur, and back through Tokyo, she made a point of meeting with each of the Anglican bishops in those places.

"The bishop in the Philippines was very excited. They were about to ordain their first woman. So that was very positive. The next stop was Hong Kong. I didn't meet with anyone there because Tiananmen was happening, and there were huge demonstrations….Our next stop was Kuala Lumpur where I had an extraordinary experience." Told by his secretary to call the bishop at home on his day off, Babson did so. The bishop made arrangements for his canon to show her churches in the diocese that afternoon: "This Chinese priest pulls up. He's very cordial, opens the door of the car for me. I get in. We take off. The first thing he says is, 'We don't ordain women here.' And I said, 'Oh.' He said, 'Because they talk too much.'"

The next day at the end of a lengthy interview, the bishop asked Babson to read the gospel for the celebration of the Feast of the Annunciation. After the Eucharist, she was invited to join him and his priests for a luncheon celebration of his birthday. At lunch the bishop asked Babson, "'Do you listen to your dreams?' And I said, 'I do.' And he looked delighted. But there was another long silence. And then he said, 'I must tell you, Katharine, yesterday when you called, I had just awakened and I was journaling what was a most extraordinary dream. I dreamed that a woman was standing in front of me surrounded by colored lights….Yesterday when I opened the door and saw you standing there, I was so surprised because you are the woman in the dream.' And I thought, 'I'm not saying anything about this. I'm just going to be totally quiet. I'm not going to presume whatever is going on here.' But I thought, 'He dreamed of Mary. He knew. He knew it was the Day of the Annunciation. I didn't, but I was wearing a pale blue linen dress.' He said, 'Yes, you are the woman in the dream. I was so surprised, I didn't know what to say.' And then there was another long silence. And then I said, 'Well, I do listen to my dreams and last night I also had an extraordinary dream. It had three distinct parts, very brief.

'In the first part, I was being attacked by lions, and I had been badly mauled and knew I was bleeding to death. I was dying, and then that part of the dream was over. In the second part I had been given something sweet and metallic to eat, and I realized after I had eaten it that it was poison and I was dying. In the third part I was trying to hide under a chair. I had been shot, and again I knew I was dying.' I said, 'What do you think of this dream?' And without hesitation he said, 'I think it means that you are supposed to die to your own culture and come minister here.'"

Katharine Babson was ordained to the diaconate on June 13, 1992 and to the priesthood on December 16, 1992. Though Babson's ministry would take her to other parts of East Asia, she and the bishop of Kuala Lumpur corresponded for many years. There were obstacles to his ministry because, as the only non-Chinese bishop in the Southeast Asian constellation of dioceses, his spirituality was quite different from the Chinese: His was rooted in South Indian culture; and theirs, in Confucian understanding. Babson, too, was to encounter barriers both spiritual and political in the jockeying for power that is characteristic of the countries and cultures of Asia. The following conversation is illustrative of the boundaries over which she crossed: A bishop, wagging his purple ring, said to Babson three times, "'Katharine, you have been confused and misled.' I said, 'By whom?' He wouldn't entertain the question. He said, 'I cannot license you to be a priest in my diocese because your priesthood is not ordained by God, indicated by scripture, or sustained by the tradition of the apostolic succession.' Silence. I said, 'Well, I've been called to serve in this Church. How, then, do you think I might use my gifts and abilities?' 'Katharine,' wagging his finger again at me, pointing at me, he said, 'You have to understand that I cannot allow you to do any of the ministries that are for the laity to do because that's their calling, not yours.' And I said, 'So you are recognizing my priesthood?' 'I have to because a fellow bishop ordained you.' I said, 'Well, you put me in a total Catch 22 on this, then. How, then, do

Kitty Babson

you imagine I might use my gifts and abilities here?' 'Katharine, you have to understand that Christ calls us to give up our gifts for the good of the community, and it's not good for this little Christian community, in this troubled land, to see the due authority of the Church compromised by someone who cannot be a priest.' And he stood up…and walked away," leaving her to fend for herself in Southeast Asia.

"One of the things that happened soon after all of this was, I received an old-fashioned telegram…from John Wilme, whom I met here at Virginia. He said to me, 'My wife has a rare opportunity to go to Jakarta for Christian education for a month, but she cannot take the equivalent of any more than $17 out of Myanmar. Will you please meet her at the airport and give her $500 so she can live in Jakarta? Faithfully, John Wilme.' Well, $500 in 1993 was a lot of money. Brad and I looked at one another and thought, 'Wow! On the other hand, how could we refuse? How else would she ever have this opportunity unless we helped? Here we are. We've been asked. We'll do it.' So I met her at the airport, and I gave her the $500 and a silver class cross from Virginia Seminary….And off she went with a cross and the money. I didn't hear anything for months until late December, I got a crackly call: 'Hello?' He sounded a million miles away. 'This is John Wilme calling from Myanmar. I've been elected Bishop of Toungoo, and I would be glad if you and your husband could come to my consecration

and enthronement. They'll cut the phone line in three minutes. That's all I have; but if you can come, I'll send you details.' I said, 'I'll come.' Chop. I was cut off."

So Babson made the first of what was to be over thirty-five trips into Myanmar: "Increasingly, as the friendship developed, they would ask me to do more and more things when I came. But it still was hard to have advanced communications that would allow all the details, so it usually happened that I would arrive in Yangon. Someone would meet me, put me on the train, which was then a Chinese diesel. I would arrive in Toungoo, where John Wilme was bishop. And he'd say, 'We're so glad you're here. The clergy, the priests, they're all coming down out of the mountains tonight. They're coming by bicycle; they're coming on foot. Some are able to find trucks to bring them part way. They're arriving tonight. Tomorrow morning, we will have Morning Prayer at 5:00 and then a Bible study. Breakfast at 7:00. And then there will be three lectures tomorrow, four the next day; and I would like you to give the lectures. The theme is grace. The biblical quotation is this. Each of the lectures is two-and-a-half-hours long. Please feed them. They are so isolated. They're so glad to see you. Give them something to eat. Let's have the lectures. Three a day….And the preschool teachers need some encouragement. Please tell them anything you can about early childhood education, especially discipline and how Christians discipline. I want to take you over the river to meet all the students from St. Peter's Bible School. They are all training to be catechists. Please give them something to eat, feed them in some way….Just whatever you feel you want to say. Please be available for prayer with anyone who wants to pray with you. Oh, and Phil's ordination to the diaconate is Sunday. Will you please preach his ordination.'

"And this was classic. At first I thought, 'How am I going to do this? How on earth am I going to do this when the electricity goes out at 11:00 or midnight and all

Kitty Babson in Sittwe, Western Myanmar

I have is candles? All I have is my prayer book and my Bible and myself.' And I did because they were hungry and I was new....I loved it. I absolutely loved it. And I loved hearing their stories and being a part of their world and seeing how they feed on manna. I think that's been one of the greatest gifts to me of all. It probably took me a couple of years before I realized that I'd really been given this extraordinary gift. That if I hadn't been kicked out of [an unfriendly SE Asian diocese], I would not have had the time to give myself into this ministry in Myanmar....I was a connection to the world that they didn't know, but

that they longed to meet."

Babson continues to raise funds to travel to Myanmar at least twice each year. On this side of the world, she ministers part-time to a small mission in Maine, reading the Bible through a missionary lens. In accepting their call to be priest-in-charge, she said, "I would be willing to be considered only if they could comprehend the Myanmar ministry as something they also wanted to be a part of. That I couldn't give that up. But if they could embrace that, then I would be delighted to have my name put in. They selected me unanimously; and they said, 'Ab-

Kitty Babson at the parish of the widows, Mogaung, Kachin State

transcendence and immanence. Clergy balance on the very real boundary between the way things are and the way things ought to be, equipped to "mediate [God's] absolute presence within a relative world."[10] The formation of Christian leaders is for the purpose of mediating transcendence, according to Urban Holmes, mediating those moments of grace when the barrier between heaven and earth is broken. Thus does the clergyperson model grace, exhibiting to all the face of love.

Kitty Babson, 1996

solutely! What you're doing there is outreach to us, and it enriches our understanding of how God is at work in the world.'"[9]

Like the mission that called Katherine Ragsdale and rejoiced in the perspective she brought to their isolation, Katharine Babson's worshipping community now finds God present in the world in amazing new ways. God testifies to the word of His grace by granting signs and wonders. For it is of the essence of God to be in relationship, the nature of God to take the initiative in search of relationship; to reveal Himself as the source of life itself; to pursue us. As both the divine source and the end of life's meaning, God passes the barrier erected between human will and God's will, crosses the boundary from transcendence to immanence. Thus, lament uttered from the edge of understanding is always voiced with the expectation of satisfaction. Lament cries out with the confidence that God will penetrate the boundary between height and depth, between absence and presence, between

---

[9] Interview with Katharine Babson, May 19, 2010.
[10] Urban T. Holmes, III, *Ministry and Imagination* (New York: Seabury Press, 1976), 8.

GRACE
in Motion

CHAPTER NINE

"Above all, maintain constant love for one another, for love covers a multitude of sins. Be hospitable to one another without complaining. Like good stewards of the manifold grace of God, serve one another with whatever gift each of you has received."

1 Peter 4:8-10
New Revised Standard Version

When Janet Tarbox (VTS '92) went on pilgrimage to Iona, she was among a group of ordained Episcopal women: "We were given charge of leading worship one evening...in a tiny little chapel on Iona. All of us took part in the Eucharist. At the end of the service, the woman who was our logistics person sat in the pew weeping. We didn't move. We just sat there; and for fifteen minutes at a time, she would weep. Then she would get all right, and then she would cry some more.

"Finally, somebody reached out and asked her if she were going to be all right. She said, 'Yes. Iona—there's a lot of graves of very important people; but back at the little convent, there are all these stones with no names on them. None of the nuns was named.' And what this woman said, after all of that was done, was that all of those nameless women were cheering because we had done that service and we were allowed to do that service and how far we had come and how happy they were for us."[1]

Janet Tarbox

Even as a child, Janet Tarbox was a contemplative: "My dad was a Type A. He had a lot of work to do; and if I were sitting on a bench, he'd say, 'Don't you have anything to do?' So I lost that piece for a long time.... There was this sort of fun movement asking people what their theme song was; if their life were a movie, what would the opening music be? Early on, before seminary, that wonderful line 'Intercessor, friend of sinners, earth's Redeemer, [plead for me]'[2] was extremely important to me because I have lived a very fearful life of being out of step, being wrong, being conspicuous, of not wanting to be any of those things. And so as I've struck out to examine what I thought was call, that piece of that stanza of that hymn was very, very important to me. Not so much anymore. That wouldn't be it anymore, though what is it now....'When we feel confused and fruitless, dawn upon our restless night; give us faith's imagination, hope's renewing, love's delight'[3] is sort of my next step from 'plead for me.' I'm 56 years old, almost 57 years old, and I am only now realizing that the whole creative part of me has been locked away all of my life. I'm just beginning to explore that, and I got there through Ignatius and all of his imaginings....That's the piece that is so important to me is that faithful imagination, not doctrinal by any wild stretch, but faithful imagination. What does it mean? Where might I go? What's it going to look like?

"The trouble with that is where I live in the American South....Where I am there's not really a place for me to be authentically vocal....When people ask me a question about 'the' Bible or 'the' faith, they're not looking for information. They're checking it out to see 'if I fit or not,' and so I tend to stay rather quiet....I'm far more taken by phrases out of music than I am phrases out of Scripture. Now, the music comes from Scripture; but in my experience, Scripture has been so misused. It's been used as a club so much: 'The Bible says *this*; so this is what that *means*; and this is what you have to *do*; and this is who you have to *be* because of what the Bible

[1] Interview with Janet Tarbox, May 25, 2010.
[2] William Chatterton Dix, *The Hymnal 1982* (New York: Church Hymnal Corporation, 1985), 460.
[3] Carl P. Daw, Jr., *Wonder, Love, and Praise* (New York: Church Publishing, 1997), 782.

says…."[4] What I long for is conversation and being able to disagree, but still able to have conversation. What I find is that the faith is so strong and so fragile at the same time that any suggestion of a different way to look at it, and [they] shut down immediately….The freedom to explore and not be afraid is what I yearn for, and I can't do it there….

"I think for me the jury is kind of 'out' on parish work actually. I don't think I was wrong in saying, 'The seminary is where I need to be' and 'The church is where I need to be.' I think I was right for the time, and I've been in some wonderful parishes and in some wonderful locations. But what I am beginning to discover is, I think, the call now is to accompany people who are intensely serious about the spiritual life. They can't say a whole lot that will frighten me, and I don't want to do to anyone what I have perceived happening to me, and that is—because of belief or lack of belief or wrong belief or whatever it is—being discounted or no longer accepted. I mean, I can take the not being accepted. That's really okay. But I certainly don't want to do that to somebody else who is seeking, searching for answers, for their own answers and trying to perceive their own path."

LEFT TO RIGHT: *Dena Bearl & Janet Tarbox, 1992*

"Like good stewards of the manifold grace of God, serve one another with whatever gift each of you has received" one reads in 1 Peter. Janet Tarbox learned to do that very thing as a student at VTS: "I didn't want to let shyness get in my way. I didn't want not knowing how to do things [to] get in my way. I was raised never to ask a question; stay quiet, and you'll figure it out. Life is so much more interesting if you ask questions. It really is. So I came here determined to enter in the community and not stay on the edge, and I did that. So I was in student government and took classes at the Consortium and branched out. I would do more of that now, but for me at that time it was a brave new world; and I really, really thrived here. And I was treated as though I was a—I wasn't the smartest person—but I was treated as though I were gifted. Not that I wasn't, but it was the first time in my life when it soaked into me that I wasn't second best. The gifts that I had were enough; and if the Church could do that, it would be really amazing; but this place did that for me.

Janet Tarbox

"Now, there were some hard things….There was tension between [some of the professors]….Having to learn to deal more directly with conflict was hard. My class followed a very unhappy class…but my class was amazingly close except for the tension over women. That was still very strong, and the whole gay thing was getting really tuned up here. Those tensions were hard, but it was the air of conflict. I wasn't deeply involved. On occasion I

---

[4] See Robert D. Putnam and David E. Campbell, *American Grace: How Religion Divides and Unites Us* (New York: Simon & Schuster, 2010) for documentation of this phenomenon.

weighed in, but I tended not to.

"[A female student] approached [a male student] one day because he was using the word 'men' for humanity. Until you get used to saying something, it's awkward saying something different. It's very awkward. She could be politic when she needed to be; and she said, 'Could you try?' And she didn't say 'humanity' or 'humankind.' She didn't give him an example. And he came back at her. This was in small group. He came back at her, 'Well, what do you want me to do? There's the word "wo-man" and "fe-male." So I just refer to "fe's" and "wo's"?' It wasn't funny at the time: He was very angry, and she was very angry.

"I was on Dean's Table when Dean Reid decided after lots of prayer to accept the invitation to preach the installation sermon at Nashota [House Seminary]. He had a meeting of women on campus to try and explain why.[5] It was well received by some and not by others….The Seminary itself, I think, was fine with women, but the women were pushing for more [and] there was some pushback from some of the men….Somebody's got to be the one that's out there pushing."

In sixteen years of parish ministry Tarbox served a variety of parishes. In some she was the first woman priest they had ever had. In one she "was on a theological collision course with the rector from day one." The Personnel Committee hired a corporate life coach for the rector and begged Tarbox not to leave. But when she was told by the rector, "I

Janet Tarbox

don't want people to see you as the spiritual one," she resigned. Now having retired as vicar of three yoked missions to spend more time with her eighty-four year-old husband, Tarbox is, in her own words, "at a crossroads, [in] uncharted territory."

Janet & Tal Tarbox

Tarbox is providing spiritual direction for a number of people and recently served on the Search Committee for a new bishop for the Diocese of Upper South Carolina. She says of parish life, "The minuses outweigh the pluses, to be honest. They really do: What color the carpet is going to be. I mean…worrying over things that to me are just rearranging the furniture. It's having a *Club*, and I see more devotion to mission at the National Wild Turkey Federation where they're dedicated to wild turkey habitat. I see much more passion in places like that than I do in the Church….Katharine Jefferts Schori had a session with diocesan clergy the day before the consecration of our new bishop (May 21, 2010), and Susan Heath (VTS '83) asked her about the Church operating outside the Church [as an] institution. So the two of them had a very interesting exchange about that; and the Presiding Bishop sort of came right out and said, 'It's essential that the institution get outside the institution.' So I don't know. I may be headed in that direction. I am not sure. But the institution provides us the place to talk about it, if there can be conversation; and I think that's the stum-

[5] Though they permitted women students to enroll, Nashotah House Seminary did not support the ordination of women. The majority of their faculty and students refused to receive communion from female celebrants at inter-seminary gatherings.

bling block right now: Conversation is being shut down through society. Throughout society, it's being shut down. There's a lot of shouting going on, but not a whole lot of exchange. And the Church mirrors that. The Church is society. It's the society inside the institution, and so we see it there….I have a very clear sense of still being led along a path. I'm not frightened at all about where it's leading. My interest is piqued. So I'm not terribly sad over not being in the parish right now. I'm not terribly sad over not being in the institution [of the Church] right now."

Janet Tarbox

The vision of possibilities for ordained woman began to expand in the 1990's, and women began to stand in solidarity with one another. The *Virginia Seminary Journal* of August 1991 reported that "The National Network of Episcopal Clergy Associations held the 'Clergywomen in Leadership Conference' at Virginia Seminary in March 1991. The conference was co-sponsored by the VTS Center for Continuing Education."[6] Among the VTS graduates in attendance were Shelley Baer (VTS '90), Gwyneth Bohr (VTS '79), Jane Dixon (VTS '81), Carlyle Gill (VTS '76), Martha Horne (VTS '83), Pat Merchant (formerly Park, VTS '74), Thelma Smullen (VTS '84), Noreen Suriner (VTS '76), Elizabeth (Ibba) Peden Tappe (VTS '77), Darlene Tittle (VTS '81), and

Marian Windel (VTS '79). Barbara C. Harris had been consecrated the first female (suffragan) bishop in the Episcopal Church U.S.A. two years earlier. This gathering of women began conversations about the need for other female bishops, and the possibility of making and keeping networks to work for the election of female bishops was explored. That was the Spring of Tarbox's middler year.

Clergywomen in Leadership Conference

On Saturday, May 30, 1992, after six years as rector of St. Phillips, Laurel, MD, Jane Dixon was elected suffragan bishop of the Diocese of Washington. Marian Cover, co-chair of the Nominating Committee, was a member of St. Luke's, Washington, D.C. The rector of St. Luke's, Sheldon Pollen, was not supportive of women and, on the day after the election, announced to the congregation that the election of the new suffragan was not valid because she is a woman. Whereupon Marian Cover walked up the aisle to the chancel steps, turned and said, "Are you women going to put up with this?" Forty women and men followed her out of the church, including the former rector's wife.

The following Monday, June 1, the Diocesan

[6] p. 45.

Bishop of Washington, Ron Haines, received a letter from five rectors:

1) Sheldon Pollen of St. Luke's, D.C.
2) Richard Cornish Martin – St. Paul's, K Street
3) Arthur Wooley – St. Luke's, Bladensburg
4) The interim at Ascension & St. Agnes
5) Claude Bonbrest – St. Bartholomew's, Latonsville, MD

The letter stated Dixon would not be welcome to come for visitations to their parishes. The strategy of Bishops Haines and Dixon was simple: Give them time. Haines wrote a letter to each of the dissenting rectors suggesting they have Dixon preside at Evening Prayer or do education at a forum hour, but nothing episcopal.

The consecration of Dixon occurred in November. There were two protests: One was because of her support of gays and lesbians. The other had to do with "Anglican unity."[7] Martha Horne was one of her presenters; Carolyn Irish, one of the litanists; and Verna Dozier, the preacher.

Three months after Dixon's consecration, the Church of England, in a close vote, affirmed the ordination of women to the priesthood after nearly twenty years of debate; but the arguments, even in the United States, over whether a woman priest could participate in the transformation of the elements at the altar because of her femaleness persisted. In February of 1993, the following poem by Frances C. Frank appeared in *The Episcopal Voice*, the diocesan newspaper of the Diocese of Olympia:

> Did the woman say,
> When she held him for the
> first time in the dark dank of
> a stable, After the pain and
> the bleeding and the crying,
> "This is my body; this is my blood?"
> Did the woman say,
> When she held him for the
> last time in the dark rain on
> a hilltop, After the pain and
> the blooding and the dying,
> "This is my body; this is my blood?"
> Well that she said it to him then,
> For dry old men,
> Brocaded robes belying barrenness
> Ordain that she not say it for him now.[8]

Sheldon Pollen retired, and Dixon's first visitation to St. Luke's, D.C., was a glorious occasion. The parish went out of its way to welcome her: hired professional singers to supplement the choir and gave an elaborate reception.

Then Claude Bonbrest changed his mind. Dixon did not know all the parishioners by name so made it a practice to have representatives of parishes (rectors and wardens) come to her office two weeks before a visitation to prepare. Bonbrest would not come; however, he did in-

Bishop Jane Dixon celebrating

[7] *Newspaper of the Washington Diocese*, December 1992, p. 5.

[8] Originally published in a Roman Catholic journal, *New Woman, New Church*, which advocated for the ordination of women, publication dates are no longer available. Published in *The Episcopal Voice*, February, 1993, p. 12.

vite her to lunch at the rectory the day of the visitation. She followed the parish's customs, including celebrating at the altar facing east. In 1995 when Bonbrest was dying of cancer, Dixon visited him at the hospital, in part to assure him that although Ron Haines was on sabbatical, she would make sure that Haines did Bonbrest's requiem. As she was leaving, Bonbrest said, "Bishop, will you give me your blessing?" God's grace had been in motion and was in that moment tangible.

But there were three parishes still resistant to her ministry. St. Paul's, K Street, refused to have Haines and Dixon visit. Representatives came to Church House to register an adamant "No." Evening prayer is not an episcopal function, was Haines's view. In the course of the conversation, Haines became so irritated that he pushed back from his desk and said, "She *will* do a visitation in the Spring of '96." It was to be the Second Sunday of Easter.

Meanwhile, in February Dixon was to visit St. Luke's, Bladensburg. There was heavy snow. The *Washington Post* on the Saturday before ran pictures of the rector and senior warden who said the rector would be on retreat and that the church wouldn't be open. Dixon's oldest son called that night and said, "Mom, you can't just have groupies go with you. Are there people in that parish who want you?"

Bishops Ron Haines & Jane Dixon

Dixon called the rector of St. Matthew's, Hyattsville, a good friend, and asked if any of his altar guild knew

members of the altar guild at St. Luke's. They did. Those women were contacted and said, "Bishops come and go. The office [of bishop] is the office. The church will be open." When she arrived the next morning although the sacristy was locked, the lights were on and the church was open. The elderly members of the 8 a.m. service had tramped down the snow. About sixty-five people were present, about half members of the church. There were some protesters but also supporters of Dixon. Dixon had brought chalice and paten and elements; but a woman with a Giant grocery store paper bag walked down the aisle bringing Wonder Bread to make sure they had bread for the celebration. The manifestation of grace takes many forms.

Then came the visitation at Ascension and St. Agnes. David Booth Beers recalls, "I was asked to try to work out a compromise—indeed, there was a group in the parish that had asked Ron Haines if I could mediate the issue because I have some friends there—and declined. Jane was going to go that way, full bore. But they would have accepted her preaching.… Either they were going to agree to the absolution or the final blessing, not both; and she would preach but sort of gracefully yield the altar. And she and Ron said, 'No.'"[9]

At 9 p.m. the night before the visitation, Paul Cooney, chancellor of the diocese, called to say a lawyer representing the parish had phoned with the message, "They can't promise to protect you." Dixon called Jim Anderson and asked him to remind her of what Bishop Walker had said when told by Southerners "Nigger, you go to your people." His response was, "You *are* my people." Dixon was accompanied by her family, the Rev. Richard Downing, rector of St. James and president of the Standing Committee of the diocese, and the Rev. Enrique Brown, missioner. African Americans Marsha Harper and

[9] Interview with David Booth Beers, June 10, 2010.

her husband, who had marched at Selma, also escorted her. Mr. Harper said the confrontation reminded him of Selma: There were protesters with such signs as "Nazi, go home" held by an eight-year-old girl. The people of the parish did not show up but the church was full of supporters. The interim sat at the back of the church reading the *Washington Post*. All prayer books and hymnals had been removed from the church, the top of the lectern had been removed, and the bathrooms were locked. Once again, Dixon had brought elements; so they had Eucharist and sang lustily. After the service, Dixon asked the interim for the record books. He slammed them down. She signed them and left.

Next came the visitation to St. Paul's, K Street. Dixon prepared carefully to follow their customs: The organist practiced with her. She used the Anglican Missal. She was taught to cense the altar. The VTS seminarian acted as her chaplain. The Master of Ceremonies was hospitable. She vested in the sacristy and said to Richard Martin, the rector, "I don't expect you to stand at the altar with me." The church was packed, with more people than on Easter. As the service started, someone in the back screamed out, "Jane Dixon supports abortion." The Easter celebration begins with the singing of Alleluia on D and, by the grace of God, she was right on key. There was a reception following; and a woman came up to Dixon and said, "I need you to know that I'm having surgery tomorrow, and I told my doctor that the surgery needed to wait until I could experience a female bishop celebrating in my parish."[10]

By 2002 all of these congregations had changed. Dixon visited each of them two more times; and by the third visit, Bladensburg gave her a lovely reception; the new rector of Ascension and St. Agnes, Davenport, couldn't have been nicer; and the new rector of St. Paul's, K

Street, Andrew Sloan, had her for dinner with the wardens prior to the Sunday visitation, although he didn't stand with her at the altar. She invited Sloan to be chaplain at her last convention when Chane was elected. There have been no visitations by female bishops at these parishes since 2002, a sadness for Dixon; although Geralyn Wolfe has done a Quiet Day.

The confrontation at Accokeek was of a different nature. Dixon had visited there when Peagram Johnson was the rector. Then the parish called Sam Edwards as rector. The Sunday in May of 2001 when she went there, they barred the doors. She was prepared to celebrate and did so on a card table in the covered basketball pavilion. Ron Haines, Tom Andrews (president of the Standing Committee), and JoAnn Macbeth (chancellor of the diocese) accompanied her. They had received a warning that they were going to be arrested for trespassing. When Macbeth saw the two Latino policemen the parish had called to keep them off the property, she said to them, "Obispa"; and they became Dixon's protectors! The junior warden began yelling at her menacingly, and her husband stepped between the two with his hands up. This resulted in an accusation of assault that went to trial. The day of the trial, the junior warden called it off. However, other court actions were necessary to rid the parish of Edwards who refused to sign the Declaration of Conformity required of a new rector. The decision of the federal court in Oct. of 2001 that he vacate the property was upheld on appeal to the Fourth Circuit Court of Appeals in a May 2002 unanimous decision. Dixon's responsibility as Bishop was to protect and defend the Church, and she did so.

During her tenure as suffragan, Dixon served on the Board of Trustees of VTS and on the Search Committee which nominated Martha Horne as Dean. She reflects, "[Martha Horne] and Bishop Lee asked a group of us

[10] Interview with Jane Holmes Dixon, June 16, 2010.

shortly after she became Dean to talk about our vision for the seminary, and I was able to talk about the inclusion of gay and lesbian people in the life of the seminary. Go ye into all the world and preach the gospel was the theme of my talk to the Board of Trustees, and it seems to me that 'all the world' is all the world. They're not folks restricted from that 'all.' So I made the plea for that. Then, shortly after that, Bishop Frank Vest brought up in the Board meeting what I had said and that we needed to consider the mission of openly gay and lesbian people, and I will always be grateful for that, that I was at this place at this time to be a part of that, to raise that issue."[11]

From 2001 to mid-2002, Dixon was the Bishop pro-tem of Washington. Since that time she has taught at George Washington University, worked at the Interfaith Alliance, and is now director of Foundations for Spiritual Leadership, a Lilly-funded program for newly ordained clergy.

Of the new year that began Dixon's episcopate, Martha Horne recalls, "There was a new Chairman of the Board [in 1993], Peter Lee; and the first thing he did as Chair was to appoint himself Chair of the Search Committee [for a new Dean]….I knew that Dick Reid was planning to retire when he was sixty-five: He had been very clear about that. I assumed that would be the time for me to move, as well. Don [Horne] had been looking at some other positions during those years; in fact, during the time of the Dean search, he actually turned down a position so that I could take this position. (I did not know that until later.) When the Search Committee was first formed, I was asked to be a candidate; and I said, 'No, definitely not,' and meant it. There were other people interested in the position, some of whom I thought would be excellent. I felt their credentials were much better than mine, and I had never expected to stay at VTS.

Martha Horne at the altar, Seminary Chapel

For reasons I still don't understand, one person whom I especially thought would have been a very fine choice was not chosen as a finalist by the Search Committee. Three members of the Search Committee came back to me and said, 'We really want you to reconsider. Would you please be a candidate?' They then outlined some of the reasons that they wanted me to take into consideration as I thought about the position. I went to Fredericksburg to talk with Bishop Lee….I remember saying, 'I understand that you want to have a woman on your slate, but I have absolutely no interest in being the token woman….This is what I have been told that some of the issues are and these are the ones that I think I might be able to address and these, the ones I am interested in; but I really need to know whether this is a serious inquiry or not because I really don't want to go through this process just so there can be a woman finalist.' Bishop Lee assured me that the committee was very serious. Two additional finalists were selected and interviewed….

"I talked with Jane and Cally. In seminary we began the process of sharing all of our vocational decisions; first, mine about staying at St. Andrew's; Jane, about going to Good Shepherd, Burke; Cally, about going to Epiphany. We did that again for the next round of placements: when Jane left Good Shepherd and went to St. Alban's, D.C.; when Cally moved to Michigan; and when I went to Christ Church. Still later, we discussed my

[11] Interview with Jane Dixon, June 8, 2010.

decision to come to VTS, and the Episcopal searches for Jane and Cally. We talked together about all of those decisions. By the time of the Dean search here in 1993, Jane was Suffragan Bishop in Washington and a member of the VTS Board. She was a member of the Search Committee too, so she had to be very careful about what she said. But we talked about the issues facing women in the Church. We talked specifically about what it was like to be—or what we thought it might be like to be—a woman in leadership in the Episcopal Church. I did talk once to Pam Chinnis (President of the House of Deputies). I had not contacted her, but we were together on an occasion that provided an opportunity to talk about these issues for women. I believe I talked with Betty Wanamaker. I am trying to think if there were any other women, but I can't remember any other women with whom I talked about the search process or the issues that might face me as a woman and…the only woman Dean of the eleven Episcopal seminaries….Even though I had been working here for eight years, and I

LEFT TO RIGHT FOREGROUND: Frank Wade, Martha Horne, Loren Mead

had been working close with the Dean, there were sensitive and difficult dimensions of the job that I just didn't know about. Jim Fenhagan (former Dean of General) became a wonderful mentor. I remember saying to someone—Jim or maybe someone else—that I had no idea I would spend more time talking to lawyers than to theologians during my first year as Dean….

"One of the things that persuaded me to be a candidate was the knowledge that there were going to be some very significant retirements and that was a source of huge concern for people. Losing Dick Reid and Charlie Price, with Murray Newman not far behind and Reg Fuller, there were concerns about the future. Within a fairly short time, VTS would lose a group of people who had defined the faculty and, I guess, largely the theological ethos of the place for many years. From about 1992 until the late 1990's, in that block of time, there were many faculty retirements and a lot of concern about what that would mean for the Seminary. I believe I ended up appointing eighteen faculty members during my thirteen years as Dean and President [from 1994-2007]."

After two years of teaching at Bangor Seminary, Katherine Grieb returned to VTS as Assistant Professor of New Testament in June of 1994, the same month Martha Horne assumed her duties as the first female Dean and President of an Episcopal seminary. In January of 1995, Marge McNaughton was called to VTS as Assistant Dean for Admissions and Community Life. There are at this writing eleven women and twelve men on the faculty but no ordained women in the Dean's Cabinet, the principal decision-making body of the faculty.

When asked about the joys and difficulties of leadership, Martha Horne reflected on her years on the Council of Deans: "There were many years when it was a very good experience. When I went to the first Council of Deans, however, I came home saying that I would never go again….The next year, I did go back, and

Katherine Grieb

LEFT TO RIGHT: *Amy Dyer, Marge McNaughton, Stephen Cook*

it was very different. Some of the other Deans were very supportive, and we became friends….

"There were frustrations, however. We met each year at least once, and sometimes twice, and shared responsibility for leading worship. For most of my thirteen years I was not able to celebrate the Eucharist because the Dean of Nashotah House would not participate if I celebrated. (I should note that I had a friendly relationship with Gary Kriss when he was Dean, and he invited me to preach at Evensong when the Deans met a Nashotah; but he did not feel that he could participate in a Eucharist for which I was the celebrant.)

"The Deans met for several days each year: first in December, then in January. For several years we also had a shorter meeting each year and tried to move around, meeting at a different seminary each year. When we met at VTS, I invited them all to dinner at the Deanery. I cooked the dinner, and we were all seated around the dining room table. (There were two or three deans absent, and Don [Horne] had joined us for dinner; so we were a group of nine or ten men with me as the only woman at the table.) Don later told me that he had known for years that I was the only woman among the deans, and he had heard me speak about the occasional problems or frustrations that presented for me; but when he saw all those men in their suits and my being the only woman, he had a completely new vision and understanding of how diffi-

cult that must have been….

"It was lonely. And there were similar dynamics at work when I attended the ATS [Association of Theological Schools] biennial meetings during the early years. Of approximately 230 schools accredited by the ATS, there were only about ten women presidents in the early years of my tenure, and some of them were Roman Catholic women who headed programs in religious educa-

Seminary Deans meeting at VTS

tion. Walking into plenary sessions of the biennial meetings always left a knot in my stomach: literally rows and rows of men in black suits, with only occasional women in attendance, most as academic deans. There was—and still is—a dinner during the biennial for women presidents and senior administrators, however, and that was both a blessing and an occasion for much interesting conversation!

"I was asked to chair an ATS advisory committee of women who were presidents or academic deans of ATS schools, as part of an initiative to support women in positions of senior leadership in theological schools. We planned and implemented conferences and workshops for women in positions of leadership in ATS schools. Several members of the advisory committee became good friends over the years: some were academic deans rather than presidents, but we were all able to share with each other—and with women attending some of our workshops and conferences—the issues that we faced as women leaders of religious institutions. (I am happy to report that the number of women presidents has been growing in recent years: slowly, but steadily, with women now heading schools in all the mainline Protestant seminaries, and in some others, as well. Roman Catholic women presidents and Baptist women are now also serving as presidents)....

"One of the real challenges for all of us as women—and I certainly have struggled with this myself—is to try to be as objective and clear as possible about the nature of our conflicts. It is very hard to do that in the heat of conflict, to ask 'is this problem because I am a woman or is this something else?' I think some of the people who were not happy about my being Dean were not happy for theological reasons or because they thought I didn't have the proper academic credentials or perceived me as being too liberal or too whatever—and yet, in some situations I could not discount the fact that my being a woman was a major obstacle for some people."[12]

LEFT TO RIGHT: *Unknown woman, Martha Horne, Alison Cheek, Barbara Harris, & Jane Dixon at General Convention 2000*

Horne retired as Dean of VTS in August, 2007. Since that time she has served the Church as Dean of Presidential Leadership Programs for the Association of Theological Schools, on the Vocational faculty of CREDO, on the boards of In Trust and the Episcopal Evangelical Education Society, as consultant to theological schools with the Auburn Center for the Study of Theological Education, and led retreats.

For seventeen years as an active lay woman in the Diocese of Texas, Ann Normand (VTS '95) had led a program designed to train laity for their part in the work of ministry: "Equipping the Saints." By that means, and many others, she was well known in her diocese. She recalls, "I was one of the ones that the bishop would call to ask for prayer for particular clergy. A lot of clergy sought my counsel....As I look back now, I know that I had a gift for pastoring and to offer counsel that was based on Scripture as well as just the heart of a pastor. I had been what my rector and I called 'soul friends' with him, but it really spread far and wide around the diocese; and I had been really close to all these clergy, to most of them, and many did call me for prayer or my thinking on this, that, or the other in relation to what was happening in the diocese or Church....

"The first thought I had about ordination was my attending a very large conference in England. The sum-

12 Interview with Martha Horne, March 31, 2010.

mer that I began to study Greek, I went to England to a conference of approximately 7,000 people. During one of the sessions, we prayed one for another, and a young English lad of sixteen years of age prayed for me: It was that I would serve the Lord if He called me to do so.

"When I returned, I began my first full semester at Austin Presbyterian Seminary in Austin, Texas. The Academic Dean called me in between semesters and told me to go to my bishop and tell him to ordain me. And I informed him that no one went to my bishop and told him to do anything, and it was indeed the very thing that he would not want to hear. But ultimately, at the end of the second semester, I had had enough nudging that if there were indeed a call that I did go to my bishop who asked me why I was there. I said, 'I think I'm called to be a priest.' He said, 'Thank God you have come. My wife has asked me everyday for ten years, "Did she come today?" because I told her that I couldn't tell you that you were called. You had to tell me. So now I can go home and tell her that, "Yes, Ann came to me"'….

"I had finished my first year of seminary, not as a postulant, but as a student. The bishop determined to leave me at Presbyterian for another year. I was active with tutoring Greek and Hebrew; and so he said, 'I know you well enough that you're not going to step out of the Presbyterian seminary and walk six blocks over to the Episcopal seminary and be fully engaged in that community. I want you to go to Virginia for your last year of seminary and have (what he called) the "Anglican dip."' Which is what I did….

Ann Normand

"Because the bishop had been waiting for me and I knew many on the Commission on Ministry, from June [1993] when I talked to the bishop to September when I went to the Commission, I was made a postulant. So there were very few obstacles. The biggest discussion was between the bishop and the Dean of the Episcopal seminary in Austin. They wanted me to go there but wanted me to repeat all I had done at Presbyterian, and the bishop said, 'No. She'll go to Virginia.' So that was about my only obstacle.

"The hospitality from Dean Horne, the faculty, and the senior class was wonderful. Frank Allen was there and, of course, Andy [Doyle] was there; and that was very helpful. I particularly enjoyed getting to know the international students. I'm still in touch with one of the students, Andrew Norman. He became a Canon for the Archbishop of Canterbury, and he's now the head of Ridley Hall at Cambridge. I actually visited Lambeth Palace and stayed in the Palace because of that. There was a man named Oliver Duku from the Sudan, and I was able to learn so much about the Anglican Communion and life in other parts of the Communion and the trying times that many of the countries were having and still are. So that was very beneficial for me. I was able to read Greek with Reginald Fuller, which I count among one of my big, big blessings. So it was a tremendous experience. I had done my field work in Austin, so I visited many, many churches and got to see many different styles of worship….

"I was not ready to leave Virginia when I left. I was not ready to be through [with] seminary. The Academic Dean at Presbyterian called me in and said, 'You must wait three years to start a Doctor of Ministry program.' I said, 'Yes, sir, but I'm going to ask after two.' I was in maybe the third wave of women clergy. They had just begun to be able to be rectors of churches in Texas. In fact, I think I was maybe the fifth or sixth woman rector in the diocese after I was ordained and served as curate for two years. The price had been paid by women who had gone through the process earlier….

"I was ordained a deacon and did CPE at St. Luke's in Houston. Then I was assigned to St. Paul's in Waco, a large downtown church. I interacted with [the seminary at] Baylor. Did quite a bit of speaking as a woman, talking about new beginnings and led any number of retreats about that. So I stayed there two years and then took a call to Marble Falls, Texas. I was there for ten and a half years. It was a family-sized church: I think fifty worshipping on a Sunday. We rapidly grew and actually bulldozed the existing building and built a new church and quadrupled financially and in membership….I was at the church three months, and I started the D.Min. program [in Benedictine Spirituality]. One of my mentors and readers was Esther de Waal. I spent two summer sessions with her in England. So that was a rich, rich experience for me and helped guide my thinking." After Andy Doyle (VTS'95) was elected Bishop of Texas, he asked Normand to serve as Canon to the Ordinary. In that capacity, she works now with 160 parishes.

Bishop Doyle and Ann Normand

The Center for Lifetime Theological Education at VTS sponsored a conference for women in ministry February 24-26, 2003. It had been 29 years since the Philadelphia ordinations, and there were still questions: "What has it meant to honor the masculine and feminine

Alison Cheek at 2003 Conference on Women and Power

in this visible and primary way within our faith communities? How have women experienced taking this prophetic step for 25 years out of 2,000 in a church dominated by men? What are the special issues and concerns of women as they make their way into major places of leadership within the church? What are the challenges they still face? What does it mean for women to enter positions of power?"[13] The talk Sandra Day O'Connor, Associate Justice of the Supreme Court, gave was entitled "Women in Power"; and Associate Professor of New Testament Katherine Grieb gave a lecture entitled "Leading Women in the Gospel of John." Among those leading workshops was Alison Cheek who, in retirement, had established Green Fire, a women's ministries retreat center in Tenants Harbor, ME. Carlyle Gill joined Cheek in "A Conversation about Women in the Priesthood Over the Past 25 Years." Margaret Ann (Sam) Faeth (VTS '96) led a workshop on "Women in Leadership." Stephanie Nagley (VTS '93) led a workshop entitled "Women Working with Men in Ministry." Lucy Anne Lind Hogan (VTS '81) preached at Morning Prayer and Evensong. Jane Dixon celebrated and Martha Horne preached at the concluding Eucharist of the conference.

Katherine Grieb was to expand the range of her theological contributions to the Church by serving on several Anglican Communion Commissions while continuing her work as Professor of New Testament at VTS. In

[13] *Virginia Seminary Journal*, July, 2003, p. 27.

Luke Timothy Johnson & Katherine Grieb teaching New Testament

her years on the faculty from 1995 to 2009, Marge McNaughton would move to becoming Associate Dean for Community Life, Ethnic Ministries and Admissions, reflecting a major change that took place in the Seminary in response to a mandate from the ATS to pay more attention to racial and ethnic diversity at every level of the institution.

The history of Virginia Seminary and its intersection with the issue of women's ordination took major steps with the consecration of Jane Dixon as Suffragan Bishop of Washington, the installation of Martha Horne as Dean and President, and the addition of women to the faculty. Moreover, the relationship of VTS to other seminaries and the broader Anglican Communion was affected in ways that are still being discovered. But whether women serve in high profile positions or small missions in out-of-the-way places, with faithful imagination each individual offers her gifts; and the impact of those gifts is multiplied beyond individual ministries. Rejoicing in the fellowship of unnamed women who had gone before, the women graduates of VTS would move forward knowing in their hearts and minds that the manifold grace of God is more than sufficient.

Marge McNaughton with international students

GRACE
in Motion

CHAPTER TEN

"Stir into flame the gift of God which is within you....For the spirit that God gave us is no craven spirit, but one to inspire strength, love, and self-discipline. So never be ashamed of your testimony to our Lord…but take your share of suffering for the sake of the Gospel, in the strength that comes from God."

2 Timothy 1:6b-8
New English Bible

As the Church lived into a new habit of priesthood, she did so with one foot anchored in past tradition and the other foot reaching out for firm ground. It was a time of transition, a time of negotiation between diverse societal and generational expectations. Different parts of the country and different age groups reacted in distinctive ways: Older women who had ministered as laity when ordination was not possible for them began to heed the urgings of God within, yet still dealing with the mind-set of family and friends brought up with them whose views of reality had not shifted. As Dr. William A. Spurrier had observed in the 1975 Zabriskie Lectures at VTS, prevailing values work to prevent change: "We have a Church structure which has built-in mechanisms to prevent change….Thus, in our recent turmoil over the ordination of women, one never heard the majority pleading for taking new risks for the Gospel. Instead, all we heard were fearful complaints about upsetting traditional procedure, or possibly violating one of the Canons, or establishing an unwise precedent, or acting with precipitous haste, etc…. The prior issue is not the validity or invalidity of the ordination of women; it is the Church's order and peace that seems to matter most. But where were criteria which raised the question of 'Is this the Loving thing to do? Is it fair and just? Can we limit the means of Grace?'….I think we must come again to the conclusion that today our Church is very good in its pietistic and priestly tradition, but very weak and virtually atheistic in its prophetic and Gospel tradition, and that our chief ethical battle is *not* against evil people, but against Principalities and Powers."[1]

Against the Principalities and Powers the only armor is God-given insight. Sight is the grace which bursts into flame in times of transition. Thus, "stir into flame the gift of God that is within you" is not a spirit of cowardice, but rather a spirit of power and of love and of self-discipline. This admonition, prompted by Timothy's struggles with transition at a time when doubts about his profession and doubts about himself threatened to render the ground beneath him a swamp, became a clarion call. Not only were older women more openly questioning the adage: "stay in your place, within the realm determined by custom"; but also young women were apprehending new possibilities. For several decades the Church had been telling its young people that they needed to go from college to a non-Church vocation in order to obtain "life experience" before ordination. Now even that practice was in transition as more young women saw female priests at work and began to imagine themselves capable of leadership in that vocation. Like the ministry of Timothy's grandmother and mother, the ministry of ordained women would not be measured by success, but by fidelity to the One who calls with a holy call. Leadership is not to be evaluated by skills or accolades, but by being tested, as unashamed servants. "Remember, remember," the passage from 2 Timothy says to all who would proclaim the Gospel: "You have been created and formed by no craven spirit but by the same power that gave Egypt as your ransom, Ethiopia and Seba in exchange for you because you are precious in God's sight. Remember, remember. The power at work in ministry is not merely the power of human beings. The power at work in ministry is God's power. Yours is not a profession whose goal is the passing on of a package of teaching. Yours is a vocation, a calling to proclamation enabled by the same power that was at work in the death and resurrection of Jesus Christ. Remember, remember; and never be ashamed of your testimony to our Lord—but take your share of suffering for the sake of the Gospel, in the strength that comes from God."

[1] *Virginia Seminary Journal*, June 1975, pp. 20-21.

Nancy DeForest (VTS '96) was forty-five years old when she entered VTS and had worked for the Texas public school system for twenty-two years as principal of a high school in Friendswood when she began serving as part-time youth minister of her parish. She was volunteering for many things at Good Shepherd and asked her high school daughter for permission to work with the youth group of which she was a part. She relates, "The more I worked for God, the more I felt affirmed and drawn to that work as opposed to what I was doing in my secular job. It energized me. It inspired me. It excited me to watch young people make faith commitments, struggle with issues, and have a source to go to which was way beyond them and way beyond anything that they could experience in their peer groups, at school or anything else. In some ways, as they were awaking to their faith, so was I. So I went to my rector and told him that I felt possibly called to ordained ministry. His first response was, 'No. That is not a good idea'….He was concerned that [my husband] Bill would feel that God was taking me away from him….

"Bill knew that my spiritual fires were being lit; and I can remember sitting there at the kitchen table and saying, 'Bill, I think I am supposed to go to seminary.' And he reached over and patted my hand or something and said, 'Now I know that you have had a spiritual awakening, but let's not go overboard about this.'

"But that burning desire never left me. Knowing that our daughter was a senior in high school and that Bill wasn't totally supportive of my choice, I decided that I would pray for him for the next year, that he would have that same passion and fire that I did for our Lord and Savior. And prayers work.

"So the following Easter Sunday unbeknownst to me, the rector had asked him to preach the sermon. So he preaches a sermon; and he goes through the process at the church with the discernment committee of the vestry; and I am thinking, 'What about me? This was my idea first,' and I didn't feel like God had let me go. So we wrestled with that for quite a while. And for that year, for one year, we did have a moratorium. We just did not talk about it at all because it was causing too much strife in our family and our marriage; so we just put it aside. But that burning desire was still there.

"So then eventually he went through the process, and a month later I went through the process. In between those two times, Bill was called to the diocesan office to meet with the Bishop and then later the Commission on Ministry. I was going along as the little lady, the little spouse. Because his dad was an Episcopal priest, he got to the diocesan office and everyone was patting him on the back and saying, 'Oh, we knew this was going to happen. We knew. Your dad is just wonderful. You are following in his footsteps.' At that time we hadn't said anything to the diocesan officials about my calling. So we get in the room with the bishop. Bill and I had decided that when we were finally in the room with the bishop, face-to-face with him, that we had to say something because if I denied my calling as he was going through seminary or if I went and he couldn't go, it wouldn't work because we both felt called.

"So when we finally got in front of the bishop, Ben Benitez, he centered everything on Bill first. Then we went, 'Excuse me Bishop Benitez. This is a dual call.' We had already been told by our rector…that Bishop Benitez was not in favor of clergy couples, and he had told us four or five different reasons why Ben had that stance. Sure enough Ben ticked them all off. Then about forty-five minutes into the conversation he went, 'Oh, sure. We will send both of you. Nancy, get your paperwork in.' So the one person who had to say 'yes' said 'yes.' All these other people before had said, 'Are you crazy?' or 'No' or 'It won't work.' But the one person who had to say 'yes' said 'yes'….

"When I am teaching confirmation classes and I talk about the movement of the Spirit and how the Spirit can be such a strong and powerful force, I talk about it like that whole scenario was like watching an atomic meltdown: from 'Absolutely not' to 'Sure, why not?' So I know that the Spirit was alive in that room. Of course we also had sixty people praying for it. We had just been part of a Cursillo team, and they knew that we were meeting with the bishop; so they were praying for us….That was the end of April, [beginning of] May; and by August of that year, we were heading up to Virginia."

The DeForest's daughter graduated from a private college within a week of their graduation from seminary. "It's the children," DeForest recalls, "When you have to say to your children, 'No, we don't have money to fly [you] to come see us.' Rachel felt that she had lost her home, because we had moved from Texas and didn't have a house there anymore. She didn't have a house or parents to go back to because she was still in college in Texas. It was very different to have John in public [grammar] school in Alexandria [and] not to be able to buy him blue jeans when you needed to or tennis shoes when he needed. That part was hard. The studying itself was demanding. The course work was stimulating and challenging but wonderful too, wonderful. But life in general was hard for those three years….

"I was the first female seminarian to be placed at the Falls Church….That wasn't the easiest place in the world either, being the first woman, being not accepted by the entire congregation, having to break that ice. At first I thought, 'I am supposed to convince them that it is okay to ordain women.' And then God said, the Spirit led me to believe, 'No, that is not your role, Nancy. It will be the Spirit that will convince them. Your role and responsibility is to be faithful in what I have called you to do.' So once I received that insight, it was much easier being there, and it wasn't such a struggle….

"The end of the second year, we went to Jerusalem. That was a total gift from two members of my family who allowed us to do that, and it was life changing….Mary Wilson was the one who took care of John when we were over there….There was an anonymous donor who bought both of us the senior cross that was commissioned for our class. We didn't have the money to do that, but somebody anonymously paid for our crosses, so we were able to have them."

The Diocese of Texas places its seminary graduates: "Bill was placed at the most liberal church in the diocese, and I was placed at one of the most conservative churches of the diocese. So everybody at the time said, 'We wish we were flies on the wall in your bedroom so we could hear what you were talking about' because the church life and orientation was so different."

Nancy & Bill DeForest wearing class crosses at graduation

After ten years in that position, DeForest realized, "It was time to leave. When you have been there that long you get to know the underbelly of the fish. When you are not totally in agreement with the hierarchy of the church and how money, power, and influence are used and how employees are treated, it is time to leave. For several years it was just a soul killer. I am an upbeat and joyous person, and it was robbing me of my joy. It was a great position financially, and sometimes I think of it as having golden handcuffs on. But even the golden handcuffs came off because my soul was more important....I ended up going to St. Luke's Episcopal Hospital for over a year; and during that time, I did supply work because I still missed a pulpit and altar....

"As part of an earlier conversation [the diocese] said, 'We want you to go to Beaumont. They had asked me this two years before, and I went home and told Bill, 'They want me to go to Beaumont.' He went, 'What would I do?' So we ended up not going to Beaumont at that time. But this was two or two and a half years later, and I realized that I was not going to get a job in Houston, that we were going to have to move if I were ever going to have a chance at advancement. So I came to St. Stephen's, Beaumont, full time, in March of 2008 as acting rector. So they had a chance to look at me, and I had a chance to look at them. I was the seventh rector in seven years, so they had gone through lots and lots of turmoil. Not all of those were their fault....There was one person on the vestry who was adamantly opposed to a female clergy, so I had a three-hour sit down, face-to-face, with him to let him know who I was. He said, 'Well we have only had one other little female around here. You couldn't even see her because

Nancy DeForest baptizing

she was so little. You couldn't even see her behind the cross.' I had intentionally worn my highest boots because he is a big, big tall guy. Big and tall. And I stood up to him, and I said, 'In case you haven't noticed, John, I am a large woman. That won't be a problem with me'....So I had to show him, or he had to experience me as someone you can't muck around; and he became one of my supporters. Now he shudders when he sees me coming because he thinks I am going to ask him to do something, and he will have to say 'yes'....

"I can remember living in Houston and even this past Council waving to Betty Masquelette and saying, 'I still thank you for all the hardship you endured so that we can be here.' Those early people—Helen Havens and Betty Masquelette [the first woman ordained priest by a bishop of Texas]—we have no idea. Has it been hard for us? Yes, yes, it has been; but not anything like it was for them....The discrimination and the sexual harassment and a lot of those things are still there."

DeForest and her parish have moved from an average Sunday attendance of 161 to 175 and a deficit budget of $140,000 to being in the black for the last two years. She notes, "It is just amazing that that passion and fire for outreach is being seen more globally now. It is not that the local [outreach ministries] have suffered anything, but they are really seeing if they can go and do a variety of things,"[2] including starting a ministry to Uganda called "Runners for Hope." Clergy couples continue to juggle vocations to priesthood and marriage: Accepting the call to Beaumont meant that Bill and Nancy DeForest lived in two separate cities for a year and a half. At this writing both of the rectors of the two Episcopal churches in Beaumont are married to clergy: Frank and Betty Works Fuller are at St. Mark's. Nancy DeForest is at St. Stephen's. Bill DeForest has retired.

[2] Interview with Nancy DeForest, May 6, 2010.

Nancy DeForest preaching

"Stir into flame the gift God that is within you" is not only tangible for DeForest but also for Mary Wilson (VTS '97), the fellow seminarian who cared for the DeForest's son while they traveled to Jerusalem. When Wilson was a teenager, she was sitting in the pew one Sunday morning in a Methodist church when, as she describes it, she "felt God's call. I really didn't know what to do with that. It wasn't like an audible voice, but I just felt His call; and I looked up front, and there were three men standing there. I felt a little bit confused about that. I really didn't have anybody I felt comfortable enough to discuss that with, so I just decided it probably meant I was to be the wife of a minister because that made sense in my generation….

"About two years after I had started attending St. Matthew's [Austin, Texas], we called a new priest [John Pitts, VTS '87]; and so I made an appointment to go and talk with him about the curriculum we were using for the healing ministry. When I walked into his office, he said, 'Well, Mary Wilson, what have you come to talk to me about?' And the hair on the back of my neck stood up; and that little call that I had tucked away so long ago—I could feel the fire starting to burn. So I immediately started talking quickly. I said, 'Well, I have come to talk to you about the curriculum, blah, blah.' When he had finished talking to me about the curriculum, he said, 'Well, what else do you want to talk to me about?' I said,

'I don't know what you are talking about,' even though I had a clue. I wasn't really ready or prepared to discuss that. But he said, 'O.K.! You can come back later and talk to me about that.' And I said, 'No! I would like to know what you are talking to me about right now.' And he said, 'I understand you want to go to seminary.' And I burst into tears uncontrollably, and he started laughing and said, 'Well, it looks like you have thought about it'….

"I was a single mom with two children, so I was very concerned about that as well; but I began the process. At St. Matthew's at that time, you worked with a lay committee for nine months….I had two people who were against women's ordination on that committee [one female, one male] and one person [male] who was a little unsure about it….John asked me if I would like to have those two people who were against women's ordination taken off my committee; and I said, 'Absolutely not. If I can't make it through with the committee and if we can't discern whether or not women are called as clergy, then I will never make it in a parish; so I want to go.' Even though I knew it would be difficult, I wanted to step into it; and actually, probably it was one of the best things, although difficult things, I had done in my life. So we met monthly, and my life was kind of an open book. They were free to ask me whatever they wanted, so it was difficult….The gift the committee gave me was the support and freedom for them to really discern women's ordination and for me to discern my call to the priesthood. So together we did that; and at the end of nine months, John met with the committee, and they unanimously approved me. Even the two….

"When I was in Virginia Seminary, coming from a conservative diocese by the way, I was very aware of you women professors, clergy, and watched how I saw you interact with people and deal because I had not been around a lot of women clergy. There were some in our diocese but not that many….I was raised in a very small town with very clear-cut roles for women, and you didn't usually go outside those roles; so I was always curious how you got to where you were….

"When I graduated, I came back to work as an assistant at Christ Church in Tyler; and I was there for three years. From there I became the rector of St. John's in Silsbee which is a little, small town in East Texas. I was there for five years. Then I was called to St. Richard's in Roundrock as rector. I was there for four years. Today, here I am at St. Martin's as the senior associate rector for Christian education and spiritual formation."

Mary Wilson has been the first woman in each of the positions she has held. In each she reached out to those with doubts about leadership by a woman: "One of the old faithful members of Christ Church, who was also very involved in the diocese…was very concerned about women's ordination and was not really happy with the rector's calling me. I asked to meet with him right away, the first day I got there, and shook his hand and said, 'I would really like to meet with you and [for] us [to] get to know each other.' He was one of my best supporters; so I have to say it's not really about what we are wearing. It's about relationship, which is what Jesus always taught us anyway." East Texas is even more conservative: "It was a difficult five years in many respects….I watched [I want to meet with you and talk about this] form part of my beginning with a group of lay people who were against women's ordination from the very beginning; so I think that is what started my realizing that we may agree to disagree; but unless we have built a relationship, we will never even know. We can all make judgments about people when we don't really know them, or sometimes when we do; but when we are really in relationship with people, it changes how we relate….[Silsbee] was a difficult place to be received as a woman in authority….A woman had her place, and that was where she was supposed to stay. More of the older generational, you know, 'You can be a

secretary, a mother, and a teacher but not a lawyer. Certainly not a rector.' I think that it was difficult for me because people still carry hand guns there on their personal being, and so they were still coming into church with their hand gun in their pocket. Segregation there is still very deep. I think the first year I was there, three black homes were burned in the Christmas season accidentally. The [Klu Klux] Clan is still on the corner in Beaumont recruiting people. Those kinds of things were very concerning for me, very difficult and prevalent. We think that most of our country has moved through those things, but it is very deep-seated there."

From a family-sized parish in Silsbee, Wilson moved to a program-sized parish with $120,000 in debt: "Average Sunday attendance [was] between 300 and 350. I was there for three years doing it all by myself. We were in the black by the end of the first year….We were one of only seven parishes in our whole diocese able to hold up their asking and their assessment, so we felt like we accomplished a lot there. The parish got on board and were very giving and really loved that church. We are good committed Christians….Six months before I left, because I had no idea I was leaving, I called my first assistant; and he has just been fabulous. I believe that the average parishioner sitting in the pews needs to see the fullness of the altar with male and female, all the way around, lay people, lectors, chalices….There really had not been an interim. I had done the interim work at St. Richard's, and I realized that I had really been called there as an interim and not as a rector. I was the rector, but not the next long-term rector."

Wilson was called to the staff of St. Martin's in Houston by rector Russell Levenson (VTS '92). Of her decision to go there she reflects, "You know President [George H.W.] and Mrs. Bush go here. They wanted to have a little reception for the clergy in their home about three weeks before I started. So Russell e-mailed me and said would I be able to come. Actually, I already had a commitment that evening that it was scheduled; so I said, 'I am so sorry, but I can't.' They e-mailed me back and changed the date so that I could come, so I ended up going to their home. It was a lovely evening; and when I got home and wrote Russell a little e-mail 'thank you' I said, 'You know, I had to look around the room and say "How did I get here?"' He e-mailed me back and said, 'You got here because God called you here.' So I think that is what we are all praying for: to be obedient to our call to God. I have never taken a position without really truly wrestling with it as a call from God and not just because I wanted to go or because my ego felt good about it, but that I was called there for a purpose whether or not it will be my serving the way I think it is to be. Like St. Richard's: I thought I was going to be there for ten years and have a long and happy service as the rector of a program-sized church, which I was very honored to do. But it didn't turn out that way. It turned out I was to have a short term there. I was to move on and let someone else come in and do that. I think that is just my prayer always, to be as faithful as I can be."[3]

Mary Wilson with small group at St. Martin's, Houston

St. John of the Cross wrote, "[Christ is] a living flame of love that tenderly wounds our soul in its deepest center....So greatly God has descended in order to excite us from the inertia of sleep, so to ignite us with the fire of his affection...that a divine fire always burns within."[4] And so it was for a much younger woman than DeForest or Wilson: Kate Moorehead (VTS '97). "I can't imagine God would have given me this huge desire and passion if it wasn't something God wanted me to do," reflects Moorehead. "I think the love of God comes very early, and how you express it in your vocation slowly develops over time....I saw a woman priest before I was really thinking about what I was going to do with my life, so I consider myself second generation in terms that I didn't have to do that heavy lifting of the first ordained women who really had to display a fortitude to their vocation because they had no role models; and they ended up being battle-scarred because they had to fight for their vocation. I didn't have to fight. I had someone ahead of me, showing the way. So I felt very blessed in that way, not having to have had that. But on the other hand, I have been the first woman rector in every church I have been in; and I am the first woman Dean here. So I have been the first woman everywhere I have gone, apart from curacy.... There is always a small group of people who are upset that I am a woman, although most of that is appeased by visiting them and getting to know them personally. Some of the older women and men, once you love them and get to know them, I find that they don't have a hard time getting used to it. There have always been one or two who have left the parish....I don't think it furthers the cause if I ram myself down people's throats!

"I was part of that movement, the gathering the next generation movement, to try to call the national Church to ordain young people because they were still at

[3] Interview with Mary Wilson, May 6, 2010.
[4] *Ex Instructionibus sancti Columbani abbatis, de compuntione*, 12, 2-3.

the point where they were ordaining mostly older and second-career women. Even in seminary at Virginia in my third year, I think I was the youngest person there, or maybe the second youngest. [Moorehead had taken one year off between college and seminary.] I felt as if there were more young men than women…."

But even for Moorehead's generation, the stereotypes of a woman's role vis-à-vis husband and children were still prevalent: "With regard to after seminary, I had a very interesting journey because I assumed that I was going to be a mom and a part-time priest and my husband was going to be this high-powered lawyer and I was going to sort of follow him around. My husband actually hated the law. I love being a priest. So he came one night when I was pregnant with our first child and said, 'You know, you have to find your own church because this doesn't make sense. You love what you do, and I hate what I am doing. So why, just because I am the man, why should I work and you not when you love what you do and I don't.' I didn't think I could do it. There weren't any young women rectors that I knew of; but he sort of pushed and said, 'I really think you can do this, and you will be happy.' So my first church that I took as a rector was in rural South Carolina….It was there I encountered the most push-back to my being a woman that I ever had. It was in the buckle of the Bible belt, and there were no women ministers anywhere. The ecumenical Christian group sort of broke apart because some of them wanted

Katherine Bingham Moorehead & John Lewis at graduation

me there and some of them didn't. I ended up preaching a lot at the big Baptist church because the assistant minister wanted me to preach. But the head pastor didn't want me in the building; so I preached on the lawn, which was really interesting….[My] church sort of exploded because I was a woman, too, because anybody who was curious about it or thought it was a good idea came. So in about a year's time the vestry told me that I had to slow down. They didn't recognize people on Sunday, and it had 'grown too fast.' I realized I couldn't stay there for a long time because they didn't want to get that big." Moorehead went from South Carolina to a parish of 175-200 in Wichita, Kansas: "By the time I left we were doing five services on Sunday, and I realized they just didn't want to expand the sanctuary; and again, I really did feel called to bring people into the Church and teach them about Christ….By then I had a staff of about twelve….There was a little four-year-old girl in my parish in Kansas who asked her mother, she said, 'Mommy, can boys be priests too?'…."

Kate Moorehead is now the Dean of St. John's Cathedral, Jacksonville, Florida. Of her journey to this position she says, "I think there was a lot of assumption that because I was having babies I would be an assistant for a really long time, and I would have if my husband hadn't pushed me. If my husband had been happy with the law, I would probably still be an assistant somewhere, which tells you a lot about women, because in a way I was still deferring to him. It just so happened that he wanted me to be a rector! I think that it is interesting because there are still a lot of women my age who are in small parishes or are assistants because they have either stayed where their husbands were working, or they have wanted to make their family their first priority in a way that men are not inclined to do so. It is very interesting how God has worked in my life because if I hadn't married this particular free spirit guy who really didn't want to work really hard and loves being a dad, I wouldn't be where I am. So it is not like I am a really independent-thinking pioneer…. He is getting a lot of pressure to work full-time, and the implication is that he is sort of a slouch if he stays at home with the kids….

"I think that the Church is going to be greatly blessed by the presence of women priests, and that is only just beginning. I think that some of the 'black and white' divisions that we have been having, women would have done it differently: I think that we are going to be consensus-builders in a way that men have struggled with, and I think we are going to bring a richness to the priesthood that we are just beginning to touch upon. Women are still discovering who we are as leaders. I feel like the baby. People keep asking me to make decisions, and I keep working around them for somebody to ask and then realize I have just got to figure it out! I do think we are going to bring a peacefulness and an insight that is very pastoral. I think we are natural pastors. I think we are going to have to live into our authority more. We tend to defer a great deal to authority; and I think the more we see more women around us, the more we will claim who we are. The Church is changing a great deal. I look back to the Reformation and the printing press and how the Church changed. We are

Presiding Bishop Frank Griswold & Kate Moorehead

definitely in a similar period with the advent of the Internet and technology, and things are going to have to be done very differently in the next decades. I think women will be an integral part of whatever kind of Church emerges in the next decades. It will be an exciting time."[5]

The mental and spiritual transitions Sheila McJilton (VTS '99) made were several. Her father was a Southern Baptist minister. When she was about twelve or thirteen, McJilton told him that she wanted to be a preacher like he. His response was, "Little girls can't do that." McJilton married an Episcopalian and was confirmed two years later. After their son was baptized in 1978, she became "fairly active" in the Church and sought spiritual direction from a priest in a nearby town. When she told him what she thought she was supposed to do with her life, he said, "Run like hell as long as you can because if it's something you are meant to do, then you won't be able to get away from it. It will be like a freight train bearing down on you. You won't be able to get away from it." McJilton recounts, "So I threw myself into my work, which was radio broadcast sales, until I just became so unhappy that I really had to do something; and I began to think about it….Then two friends of mine…both of them at different times, and within six months of each other, said, 'I don't know why you just don't go to seminary and get this out of your system,' which was interesting, that confirmation of calling came outside the Church completely. But I felt very strongly about my calling as a mother. I was at that point a single parent to an ADD child and just felt it wasn't the time to…work with that idea of ordination, the process….My first look was the year that Addison opened, '94….Then I walked away thinking, 'No, this is not my place. It's way too "good old boy" for me….By the time I came back, it felt like a very different place….

[5] Interview of Kate Moorehead by Jennifer Andrews-Weckerley, July 8, 2010.

"The night that I went to the Commission on Ministry interview, I knew something was up. I didn't know what, but another priest in the diocese had called. First of all, he had left the Episcopal Church and gone with one of the offshoots, the Charismatic Episcopal Church; and he and I had met each other a couple of times, but we didn't know each other. He apparently called half the Commission on Ministry and 'outed' me. I didn't know that at the time.

"Harry Bainbridge was the Chair of the Commission on Ministry, and he kept grilling me about authority and Scripture and accountability; and I am feeling like a bug pinned to the wall here. I am not sure what's going on. Finally he said, 'Well, you know, only you know the right questions to ask or the right answers; and so I would just ask if there is anything that we haven't asked you that you think should come before us.' And I said, 'Yeah,' and I just told him. I said, 'You know, Harry, you and the Commission on Ministry, you should be aware of this, but I have the bishop's full support, and he has asked me to go through the process celibate, and I don't agree with the bishop about that, but he's the bishop.' And I said, 'I need to say also that I'm tired of this Church talking about sex.' I said, 'We are too busy worrying about what people are doing in their personal lives, and we should be putting shoes on people's feet and feeding them and taking care of our brothers and sisters and quit worrying about that stuff.' And he said, 'I agree with you.' And I thought, 'Well, you either just sank the ship or you are going to seminary. I don't know which it is. And I just looked around the room and said, 'Does anybody have any questions?' And they said, 'No.'

"But up until the last 'hurrah,' at the ordination, I never was sure someone would not stand up and object; and so that was very nerve wracking. It was difficult to be on this campus and not feel like I could be myself in lots of situations. I made it through because of good friends."

Upon graduation McJilton served as associate rector at Christ Church, Kent Island, MD, and was a deputy from the Diocese of Easton to the General Convention of 2003 which endorsed Gene Robinson as Bishop of New Hampshire. She recalls, "We had a huge amount of fallout in [Christ Church] where Bud had been the rector for thirteen years before he was elected bishop [of Easton]. I have always felt that people's anger about Gene Robinson was misplaced, that they were just angry because Bud had left. There was still the grief over Bud's leaving, and there were a number of folks who were very angry and very vicious. The interim at that time, Thelma Smullen, was very supportive of me. She had a couple of adult forums on a Wednesday night where she talked about Scripture, reason, tradition and went through that, then had questions and answers. I went the first week, and a couple of people stood up and said unbelievable things. Thelma said to me after that, 'I don't think I want you to come back next week. You don't need to endure hearing this if it's going to

Sheila McJilton upon winning the John Hines Preaching Award

be like this.' So there was a fair amount of ugliness. Then the obstacle, of course, for everybody at that point who is gay and lesbian was finding a job after that. My challenge was I had been there for four years. I needed to move on, and finding a rector's position was going to be a challenge.

"So I ended up as a priest in charge in a small parish for two years and then became an interim for a year and a half in Delaware….And I said, 'It takes too much energy to be this closeted. When I go as a rector, I want to be able to say, 'This is who I am.' If they don't want me,

Sheila McJilton

then I don't want to be there….As most people who are minorities know, you don't get the real reason often why they don't call you: 'Oh, you just don't fit our profile.' Right."

McJilton has now been the rector of St. Phillips, Laurel, MD, for three years and is working on a Doctor of Ministry degree. In the years between Dixon's and McJilton's rectorships, this parish was in a difficult place: Before Dixon was elected suffragan, there were as many as 350 in attendance on a Sunday. By the time McJilton arrived, attendance was down to 130 and the parish was saddled with debt. She reflects, "I am a good administrator, and I see lots of big pieces and can put them [together]. My senior warden said, 'I have finally got you figured out.' I said, 'What?' He said, 'You get people to do things, and they think it's their idea. I'm not going to tell them.' He said, 'But the best part is you don't let your ego get in the way, so you let them think it was their idea; and then they own it, and then it gets done.' I said, 'Well, it isn't about me. It's about enabling them to get the work done.' So it's fun. It's just a kick….I think coming out of a Southern Baptist background, I am particularly aware of the grace in doing what I do. Some days it feels like you are being nibbled to death by ducks. And some days you think, 'God. They pay me to do this. How wonderful. I get paid.' Other days you think, 'Oh, can I retire yet?'….

"I don't know if there is another frontier, but I think it's a shame that the House of Bishops doesn't have more women in it. I truly believe that at its heart, the

Sheila McJilton

issue with sexuality is really against women. It's masked, but that's what it is. If anybody needs a good example, look what just happened to Bishop Katharine in England. The Archbishop of Canterbury allowed her to preach at Southwark Cathedral and asked her not to wear her mitre….I had a conversation with David Jones last week; and he said, 'Oh, this went back into the '80's, Sheila'….I

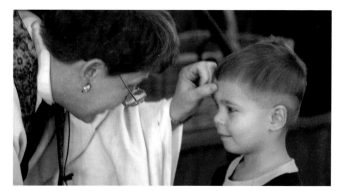

Sheila McJilton

think [it's] a misogynist kind of culture, and I don't think the young women are that aware of it."[6]

Another woman who *is* well aware of this dynamic is Kit Carlson (VTS '00). She says of herself, "I feel like I am in a transitional generation between the first women priests and the younger [recent college graduates]....I also have been in just a terror about Bishop Katharine, realizing that if I went to England—because Jane Dixon ordained me a priest—I would actually not be able to function as a priest in England because I was ordained by a female bishop. They don't recognize female bishops. I was like, 'Well, how crazy is that!'"

Growing up in Florida in the early '70's, Carlson belonged to a "really, really rigid Anglo-Catholic church where they told me I couldn't be an acolyte because if I got too close to the altar, I might get the mistaken notion that I was called to ordination and wouldn't that be sad.... Jack Iker came as the assistant and then became the rector at Redeemer. So when Wendell and I got married, he did the wedding. I have pictures of him in my wedding album, and it is just tremendously fun to me that Jack Iker did my wedding."

By the time Carlson and her husband had one child with a second on the way, she felt a strong and incessant call "to be a priest"; but it took ten years, "from 27 [years of age] to 37 to do therapy, get my kids a little older, do all the discerning I could do on my own so that when I went before the Commission on Ministry and the bishop, I was clear that I could no longer answer the questions. The Church had to answer the question for me....It was up to the Church to say, 'Yes. We see those gifts in you, and we perceive this calling. Go forward'....It did work out at that point. And some of it is related to being a woman and a mother. In that sense I finally decided, 'You can have it all, but you can't do it all.' Or 'You can't

Kit Carlson

have it all at once,' or I couldn't do it all at once....So I'm not the first generation of women priests; but in many ways, I am that first generation of women who really had the opportunity to go do something. You know, the women in the 70's, the early feminists, the early priests made it possible....My seminarian supervisor was Luis Leon (VTS '77) who came through here at that time. He said he saw these women as having to put so much energy into being icebreakers for everyone coming after that they almost couldn't have typical, normal ministry experiences....But women in my era, I think, have the same expectations [coming at them from others]. I commuted to Gaithersburg [her parish] from Silver Spring [her home] for seven years. I commuted here [to VTS]. My kids never moved. They never left their schools. They never left their friends. And still they were resentful that I was a priest. 'Look at these people. Look at these families. They all moved across the country with their kids. Stuck them in the Alexandria schools. You're lucky,' [Carlson would say to her children]. 'No. You ruined our lives. You became a priest.' And my son could be very eloquent about that always. He has kind of outgrown that now, but he would rant to strangers. They would be like, 'Well, how do you like your mom being ordained?' and he would go off. That was tough....

"The Church itself did not throw obstacles at me

[6] Interview with Sheila McJilton, June 20, 2010.

because I was a woman. [Now] I think, VTS is a lot different from the way it was in the late '90's. When I came here, it was really clear that the normative model, no matter what they said, was preparing single, young, white men out of college for ordination. I got here the year after they decided to admit openly gay students. And it was a weird class. I mean, a lot of the class were young married people. There were women in the class, but I still felt this sense that you couldn't use feminine language for God…. There was just this aura of old school, old boy. [A female classmate] used to call it 'The Plantation.' She said, 'We are on a plantation.' At VTS I had the feeling my whole class had a hermeneutic suspicion about the administration and everything. We had a hermeneutic of suspicion about each other, too. It kept us, I think, really from bonding as a class because we were in that transitional period where the rules were changing. Martha was the Dean. It was Martha, Marge, and Mary.[7] You know, the holy trinity, which was great to be in a place that actually was run by women. But they were women who knew how to do it by the rules. I wish Martha would write a book about how you change an institution without ever going out and planting the flag and going, 'We are going to change the institution.' It was all stealth, subterranean; but you know, she did it. But to be there in the transition, I think, was difficult because you never really knew what the rules were. You never really knew if people said what they were really thinking. The class after us, I think, developed better ways of talking to each other about their disagreements: about gay ordination and things like that. Our class didn't have a model for healthy conversation. We frequently felt like things were happening, and the administration would give us an official line about what it was and then say, 'Oh, it's personal and confidential. We

Martha Horne & Mary Hix

can't really tell you what happened.' So there was always this, 'Well, one day so-and-so was here and the next day they're gone.' What really happened?….

"There are many people in my class I'm really fond of….I think our working together was incredibly challenging. I was the vice president of the class senior year, and we were trying to do senior year projects and just could not get people to agree on a cross, a gift, anything. Then they're like, 'Okay. We need a big healing and reconciliation service, and nobody went. It was just [pause] it was wacked. And then also dealing with the whole plantation mentality and the old guys who were left who came from another time. They just did. But I didn't want them really doing my formation. I didn't want to be a person from the other time. I wanted to be a person from the 21st century."

After seminary Carlson served Ascension in Gaithersburg, MD: "I stayed for seven years. [Joe Clark] retired, and I was the interim….I think I sought out men to be my mentors because the system hadn't messed them up; and I wanted to see how to do it if you were just doing it, and you weren't doing it in fighting. Because they could do it—not to say our male rectors are healthy, but they had a healthier vision of their ministry and Church structure and stuff. I just wanted to see how to do that if you weren't always thinking all the time, 'Is this be-

[7] Martha Horne, Dean and President; Marge McNaughton, Assistant Dean for Admissions and Community Life; Mary Hix, Vice President for Administration and Finance.

cause I'm a girl?'"

Carlson is now the rector of All Saints, East Lansing, MI. Of accepting that position she says, "It was so God's call it wasn't even funny. I'm back in the church where I was an acolyte for the first time, in the town where I went to school for two years. And it's lovely. I am fifty-one. I want to be here until I retire, and I want to somehow successfully hand down this community of faith to a new generation; and I'm not sure, given the culture and what is happening with Christianity in the wider culture, if that's doable. But that's my personal goal for the next fifteen years is to somehow get people committed enough disciples that they attract other people in to be committed enough disciples to somehow manifest the body of Christ in that place in some way that is so meaningful that it can't help but continue to thrive."

A local colleague, the chaplain to Michigan State University, is Sarah Midzalkowski (VTS '04) with whom Carlson teamed up to counter the effects of a threat to burn the Qur'an on the lawn of a Florida church on September 11, 2010. "We were talking about the guy down in Florida, and we both went to the University of Florida in Gainesville. We thought, 'This guy is going to be burning this book.' And [Sarah] said, 'We should be reading it.' And I said, 'Yes. Let's just—during the time that he is supposedly burning these—on that Saturday night, let's just read it. So we let the congregation know that we would be reading it and looking for readers to read it in English. I have the news director of the NBC affiliate in my church, and the woman who writes for the local weekly. I sent them both an e-mail; and I said, 'If you're interested, this is what we're doing.' Well, it went everywhere. I mean, I did media interviews—that was a Wednesday—I did media interviews all day Thursday. My poor secretary handled all the crank phone calls all day. I handled them when they called me at home at night. But we didn't have any threats or anything. Most people were

LEFT TO RIGHT: Mrs. Charles Price, Sarah Midzalkowski, Mrs. Phil Smith, Bishop Phil Smith

just really confused: Why we would read from a heathen book in the house of Jesus. And I kept saying, 'All of you people wouldn't come into an Episcopal church on a Sunday anyway. You think we are all going to hell. So why now do you get to tell me what to do with my sanctuary?'

"But it really was showing the community what Christians can be like. We had probably a third Muslims in attendance. There were people from the community. We had 350 people. The church was packed. They sat there for two hours and listened to—if you read Deuteronomy straight through you would be pretty bored. The Qur'an is not that interesting to listen to read straight through. But people from the Islamic center came, and they chanted in Arabic which makes it an official reading, you know, if it's chanted in Arabic. If you read it in English, it's just a translation. So the Ara-

Kit Carlson being interviewed by the media

bic is the real word incarnate for them. And people from the community read, students from Michigan State read, the local rabbi read, local clergy read….So we had a good time.

"So the Qur'an thing was wonderful. Someone burned a Qur'an and left it on the Islamic Center's doorstep Friday night; so the leadership of the mosque knew that this had happened, and they came anyway for the reading and didn't publicize [the burning of the Qur'an]. They let the police know. They didn't want anything to overshadow the observances of 9/11. They didn't want to have anything overshadow this community expression of good will. So nobody knew about the burned Qur'an until Sunday. It was an amazing time. East Lansing always has an interfaith Thanksgiving service. So it's a kind of community that is supportive anyway. And this was a chance for the community to step up and say, 'This is who we are and we love our neighbors and we tolerate each other and we are willing to listen to each other's sacred texts and not be afraid.' It was amazing. There was Holy Spirit to go everywhere."[8]

"There was Holy Spirit to go everywhere"… echoes across the years: "They were all together in one place. And suddenly from heaven there came a sound like the rush of a violent wind, and it filled the entire house where they were sitting. Divided tongues, as of fire, appeared among them, and a tongue rested on each of them. All of them were filled with the Holy Spirit and began to speak in other languages, as the Spirit gave them ability….And at this sound the crowd gathered and was bewildered, because each one heard them speaking in the native language of each….In our own languages we hear them speaking about God's deeds of power….I will pour out my Spirit upon all flesh, and your sons and your daughters shall prophesy….both men and women, in those days I will pour out my Spirit; and they shall prophesy."[9] The threat of evil flames was countered by the stirrings of flame within. For one evening the Principalities and Powers were conquered by insight given to women by God.

[8] Interview with Kit Carlson, October 5, 2010.
[9] Acts 2:1-4, 6, 8, 11, 17-18

GRACE
in Motion

CHAPTER ELEVEN

"I give you the end of a golden string. Only wind it into a ball. It will lead you in at Heaven's gate, Built in Jerusalem's wall."

Jerusalem
William Blake

In the eighteenth century, the poet William Blake gave the name "Jerusalem" to all that is tender in the human soul. Blake's poetry suggests that the route to the tenderness of the human soul is something like a labyrinth an individual follows through life. The end of the golden string is the grace given to each in his or her developing search for identity.

Many women—in a cross-section of ages from 20's to 80's, gay/straight, black/white/Hispanic/Oriental, pastors/missionaries/academics, single/married, from different geographical/societal contexts here in America and abroad—feel within their souls a love for God but seek a diversity of ways to learn about God more deeply. As they follow their respective paths, there are times when others see in them a grace they cannot see themselves. Mentoring on the part of both women and men is a grace bestowed from without that can enable discernment of grace within as faith seeks heaven's gate.

Kim Coleman (VTS '01) left Tulsa, OK, where she had gone after graduation from college to care for her seriously ill grandmother, because "the mentality or ethos there in the Bible belt was 'you are here to get married.' These dynamics did not fit well with my aspirations. Now would be a different thing, because now the idea of being well-established with family and community is precious and valued in my heart. Then it had not entered it." At her Baptist church in Alexandria, VA, she met resistance to the idea that a woman could assume a pastoral role. Her love of serious Scripture study made leaving the Baptist tradition difficult, but she found herself "throwing up my hands and saying, 'O.K., Lord. Where do you want me to go?' And all these Episcopalians came out of the woodwork! Every time I went to a job placement, there were these Episcopalians there saying, 'Well, aren't you an Episcopalian?'….

"Susan Goff, rector of St. Christopher's Church in Springfield, hired me as her Administrative Assistant. I went there first as an employee, then stayed as a member, and eventually was formed and shaped by that congregation for ordination….It is hard to find mentors/people who will commit to the God in you and say, 'I am going to support this person.' Mother Susan was able to exemplify for me that kind of welcome and hospitality and generosity and affirmation that are so crucial to individuals as we struggle to find our way in being open to and obeying God's will for our lives….I have encountered women who supported my ministry to a point, the point it did not challenge tradition or it could be accommodated within an existing vision or it called for people to think differently….Some of the support I received was circumscribed by the political and social realities of the time. There was a time when women were permitted voice and place, but they had to stay in their place and within that voice….There are great costs, great costs to supporting and to breaking down the barriers that I believe God calls us to break down; and not everybody is willing to pay that cost, whether that means supporting and mentoring someone or putting the Church through yet another level of angst. We could all use a little peace once in a while. So I think any deficit in women mentors has a lot to do with change and ethos, the struggle that goes along with that, and finding the courage, first of all, to believe that God really is up to something and that our support of people is not about ensuring that they have their next job. We have got to learn to trust God for a large portion of this. Thanks be to God for every woman who has touched my life and particularly the ones who have mentored it….

"I absolutely loved my time at Virginia Seminary….The colleagues that I met here have been extraordinarily supportive and continue to be throughout my tenure as an ordained person. The faculty, the staff, everyone was very supportive. I just thoroughly enjoyed it….The spiritual direction discipline and practice of meeting with someone on a regular basis gives me a new lens to see God at work. I could not be as healthy as I am right now in ministry without having embraced spiritual direction, and VTS introduced me to it.

Kim Coleman

"My first stop [after seminary] was St. George's in Arlington, VA. It is a congregation which probably averages 300-350 in Sunday attendance. Urban ministry is something that I delight in. First as a deacon and then associate rector, my ministry focus was Christian education, evangelism, and pastoral care. From there I received a call to Trinity Episcopal Church in Arlington. I will have been there eight years in November 2010. This congregation is a diverse, multi-cultural, and—as I have just learned—multi-faith congregation that has about 100 people in attendance at worship services on Sunday and a full, thriving ministry of outreach to the community….I was and am the first woman to serve as a rector at that parish and the first African American woman to do that, so it has been a learning experience for us all….

"[One of the obstacles I have encountered] has to do with our tendency as human beings to want to fit people into our image of God instead of having people conform to God's image. For me that has meant 'I expect women to be motherly. I expect women to be soft.' What then do we do with a woman who is strong, who can be authoritative, who can be decisive, and who can lead? Well, we can either try to have that person fit into our expectations and become the person that that person is not, or we can allow that person to be who they want to be.

"That glass ceiling of opportunity is still present. As a woman and as an African American, I believe it finds different expressions: 'We don't see any positions in the Church right now that we believe you would be called to.' Shall we let God make that decision? I cringe hearing people say, 'There is some music we don't have to learn because it belongs to another culture or another color.' Rubbish! Rubbish! That's the glass ceiling assigning color to particular types of music. That glass ceiling also says things like, 'You know, if a woman or African American is at the table, my conversation, our conversations, may have to change. Our level of accountability may be different from what we have experienced in the past. Since I don't know if we are ready for that, I don't believe that opportunity or that appointment will work.' These are the kind of things that we as people, and especially as people of faith, have as part of our DNA that God is working out because it stands in the way of Kingdom of God living. In God's kingdom there is no Greek, no Jew, no male, no female but all nations, people, and languages gathered around the throne.

"It's a privilege and an honor to be serving the Church and to have the opportunity to serve the Church. I am so thankful. It's a joy. It's really funny: Part of my time since being in seminary, I have worked with the Office

Kim Coleman

for Black Ministries for the Episcopal Church and also have had the pleasure of coming back to VTS to work on our Oral Interpretation of Scripture class as well as to work with some of the students who have been placed at Trinity for Field Education. These are all times that keep my involvement in the broader picture alive. I have en-

Kim Coleman

joyed it a lot….I see the younger generation, and they live in an electronic world that for much of the Church is an option, not a necessity. I have delightful people of a more mature age that aren't thinking about checking their e-mail, even if they have it. Watching all of this leads me to ask questions like, 'What happens when the incarnational part of our lives as Christians—that is, being physically present— is no longer vital to our relationship-building? People can establish relationships on line. What happens to how we understand God and value Jesus Christ coming to life? It is a fascinating process as we watch the Church grow. Being a woman in the middle of such change has allowed me perhaps to be more open and less confined by tradition and expectation than others might be. Because I know that

Kim Coleman

Kim Coleman & Bishop Shannon Johnston

tradition and expectation have not always worked in my favor, I relish the favor of being able to do God's will. It's nice being a woman. I like it!...The lessons that Susan Goff taught me about investing in the God in people and not being reluctant at all to do that continue to be a prime expression in my life. It really is a gift to be able to support other people in ministry—both laity and clergy, male and female."[1]

Mentoring that supports a person in becoming the Kingdom worker God wants them to be can take unexpected forms. Coleman's classmate, Connie Jones (VTS '01), found such mentoring coming from a man many years her junior. Jones grew up in the Church and never fell away. As a pre-teen she "had this feeling that this was where I am supposed to be, but there was no place for me because there were no acolytes that were girls….Women were not able to be priests until I was about thirty-five years old." Jones was a very active lay person—senior warden, lay reader, choir member—at St.Mary's, Anchorage, AK, when she began to consider what she would do when she retired from her job as a top level executive in local government. "So I completed all the things I needed to do to go to law school: the LSAT's, the applying and getting accepted. Then a young man who had been in a class with me took me out to lunch; and he said, 'I really need to talk to you.' He went into law as a second career, and he said, 'You are not going to be happy. I know you. You are not going to be happy. Even the studies will not interest you. It's very detailed and dry and dull. Besides which, what you want to do is save the world, and you are not going to save the world in the small back office of someone's law firm. At your age you want to do what will be meaningful.'

"His own mother had become a priest in her fifties. So he said, 'You need to do what my mother did.' And I sat there just sort of stunned. I thought, 'Why did I not think of this on my own? This young man has to come up with this. Well, he's right. That is the whole motivation. I want to do pro bono work. I want to work with people who have no money. I want to do all these things with the law that probably would never pay back any loans I had, and going through that education would

probably not be that much fun.' So I immediately left that lunch and called all the law schools I was going to visit and said, 'I have changed my mind. I am actually going to seminary!'

"I didn't even know how one did this; so I quickly checked with my rector. Once I had made that [mental] shift, every door opened. There were no obstacles. There was nothing holding me back. My discernment committee was quickly formed. I wanted to go to seminary in the Fall, and it was coming up on a deadline on that. By chance I was able to meet quickly with the Commission on Ministry, and they okayed it. I mean everything, everything fell into place. It was amazing. I interviewed at VTS, and they offered me a spot right then. I thought, well, I didn't expect that. So I was ready to go. The obstacles just weren't there, so I really did see that as providence….

"Because of my age and my growing up in the time that I did, all of my mentors, true mentors, were men….Chuck Eddy, my priest, had been a graduate of VTS ['66] in the days of guys right out of school go to seminary….I had visited CDSP because it's closer to Alaska; and what I found there were, and it may be changed today, but women were mostly my own age or a little bit younger and mostly my same political, theological persuasion. And I thought to myself, 'This is not going to challenge me at all. It is going to be the same people that I talk to all the time.'

"So when Chuck suggested VTS, which in many ways still had the gloss of being too conservative with us up in Alaska, I agreed to go visit and ran into marvelous students that I talked to about coming there. They were in the minority, but they were of my persuasion about the progressive side of the Church. Professors gave that wonderful talk where they all spoke to us. They were just now

[1] Interview with Kim Coleman, April 6, 2010.

coming there or had been there for a year, coming from other seminaries. I knew they were going to be sort of the new face of VTS into the future. I met Martha Horne, who just bowled me over; and I thought, 'Oh, a female Dean. This is fabulous. This is the way it is supposed to look!' So I was sold. Even to go that far geographically, I was sold. My experience there was really never anything but wonderful. It was absolute joy….The most impressive thing was that there was a belief in community.

"I went back to our Rotary meeting [in Anchorage], just visiting; and the Roman Catholic priest from a nearby town was speaking. I went up to him afterwards, and I told him that I was in seminary and was really enjoying it. I must have looked like I was enjoying it far too much because he said, 'Keep in mind, it's not the goal to love seminary. It's the goal to go out into the world afterwards and bring what you learned and what you have been so enthusiastic about to the people that you will serve.' I thought, 'Oh, man. I really must have been just bubbling over with "and I love VTS!"'"

Jones served St. Mark's in D.C. as a seminarian and found their style of dialogue sermons a "terrific experience." There again, she was mentored by a man. With only approximately five salaried priests in the whole diocese, Alaska is a difficult place to find a position. "I did a

lot of interviewing out East because my bishop had told me, 'I am not going to have a place for you.' I interviewed a couple of places that offered me jobs, and I thought, 'Well, this is odd. I am almost 60. What do they see in me?' I was not going for top jobs. I had done that all my working life….But Pittsburgh did me in….I really liked the church. I really liked the rector. I wanted to be there. I didn't know how long she would be there; but I thought, 'Oh, we could work together. This would be great.' But I got homesick for Alaska driving home. It is beautiful country. It's that lovely road going from Pennsylvania back to Virginia; and I am thinking, 'I have got to go home. You know, my family is up there. I have to go home.'

Connie Jones

"So I graduated and came back to Alaska not knowing at all what was ahead of me. Didn't have a job. I was interviewed down in Juneau….They loved me, offered me a job. I liked them a whole lot; and I thought, 'This is it'….I got back to Anchorage, and the rector of the church who had just replaced Chuck Eddy asked to meet with me." After a five-hour conversation, he offered Jones a job. "So my ministry for seven years was as associate rector [of St. Mary's, Anchorage], and I loved every single bit of it." About two years before she retired, Jones went to part time ministry because she was on dialysis three times a week, four hours at a time. On March 22, 2011, she received a kidney from a woman in her church. She still serves on the Standing Committee; flies down to Kenai to a very, very small church once a month because they have no priest; mentors three individuals in their pursuit of a

LEFT TO RIGHT: Connie Jenson, Connie Jones, Connie Jackson

Master in Divinity degree from Vancouver School of Theology; and serves a very small church in Anchorage once a month.

As a member of the Standing Committee she recently took responsibility for filling in at a service: "It was not until I walked into that church that I remembered that this church does not think kindly of female priests. I just think there had never been a female priest in that church. I am walking down the aisle, and I hadn't time to even process that thought before I am into it. I gave the sermon, did the Eucharist; and then I went back." The return visit occurred because as the Standing Committee prepared for the visit of the Presiding Bishop, they suggested Schori visit that church. Jones responded, "'I don't know that that is a good one. You know, they are not fond of female priests, much less a Presiding Bishop.' They said, 'Well, it's the best one for her to go to because it has an almost entirely Filipino congregation, some of the customs in Alaska that she would not expect to see.' I said, 'Okay, okay.' I went there before [Schori] did, and some of the same people that I had thought would not be comfortable with me as a priest ran up to me and embraced me, called me by name, and welcomed me. I thought, 'You know, it is the same old story. You need to have an experience of a person who is the other to know what that might be like'….And they welcomed the Presiding Bishop with open arms, too. It was a fantastic celebration. So you know, I am thinking now, 'Don't make assumptions about a church' the same way we don't make assumptions about how individuals are or might behave….

"I learned at VTS, because there is such formation there, that you are not in the process of just taking courses toward a degree….You are not preparing for a career. You are preparing for a life. Even though the biggest barriers can appear that others might consider formidable, my reaction is, 'This is my life, and I am now in the process of finding ways that I continue to live that life which is all about bringing the Word to the people'…. This is what I learned at VTS: This is a life that I prepared for. I have been formed all of my life for the life I live now."[2]

Preparing for a life, grasping the end of a golden string, began early for Shirley Smith Graham (VTS '02), who entered college at the age of sixteen. Halfway through her Bachelor of Arts degree, Smith (her surname at the time) found herself in her rector's office saying, "I'm feeling like I should go work among the poor or the homeless and not just pray but have my acts mirror my prayers and help me with this….Inside my heart of hearts did I wonder if maybe this was a call to the priesthood? Yes. But I had never seen that before, and I just couldn't imagine what it would look like….There weren't any female priests when I grew up in Northern California. I mean, some had been ordained, but that was back East; and, you know, people back East do funny things, and that does not happen out here….It took about eight years from that point to entering the diocese in the process for ordination, in part, because my parish priest knew that the guidance of the bishops at that point was, well, we want you to go and have a life first. We want you to have life experience….So that was sort of my eight to ten-year discernment process….

Shirley Smith Graham

[2] Interview of Connie Jones by Jennifer Andrews-Weckerly, September 8, 2010.

"I had a mentor in business….I got to a point where the company was asking me to make a long-term commitment…and I finally had to say, 'I'm hesitating about this because I feel like I'm called to the ordained ministry.' And his response was, 'Well, what are you waiting for, then. If God is calling you to do this, you have to do this.' It was totally not to his benefit to take that position because he had certain things in mind that he wanted to do. But that's the way ministry has always been for me: That there is no big division between inside the Church and outside the Church, that God seems to go before and is working in both realms. So there's been mentors inside and outside.

"I had a great time [at VTS]. I loved it, you know? What do you mean, I get to quit my job and spend three years learning stuff? Woo-hoo! You know, this is heaven, right?….Being able to go to Kenya and Uganda and, thereby, having confidence to later go to Sudan as part of that teacher's program, and just realizing that that wasn't just about going out into the world, but that that was forming me to be a missionary every day of the week where I am….It's really about being a missionary at the 7-Eleven and in the parish and when someone wants to really let me know how disappointed they are in something I have done to think, 'Where is God cracking open reality for this person and sharing the abundance of the Kingdom?'

"I cannot think of a single instance while I was at seminary where my gender and call presented a challenge to someone. After seminary, yes, but not during seminary….It's so much easier being second generation or third generation female ordained. Those who went before us didn't have the privilege of playing out their ministry the way I have, which is, 'You don't want to take communion from me? That's fine. Here's my male colleague.' You know, it's not that I'm going to convince anybody to think differently. I don't have to. I just have to meet their

needs pastorally. But first generation didn't have that luxury….So I have it easy and know it….

"It wasn't a seamless road from graduation to employed ministry in part because of the marriage. Ernest and I got married after he graduated and had already been accepted as part of the Foundations for Leadership Program at Christ Church, which is a two-year program. He, in part, chose that program because he knew I had another year to finish [at VTS]. Our experience has been all the way along because we have chosen to be together and family together, we have not done the things that otherwise we would have done….So we said, 'Okay. We're going to make it a primary value to be together. I was so helped by my sending bishop, Bishop Lamb, who had said in his wonderfully pastoral but clear way, 'You must understand if you choose to be married, your priorities of relationships will be God, your family, and then the Church. If you cannot live within that framework, I would advise you not to be married.' I mean, he said it that clearly. It was wisdom, and thus it has ever been since. There have been times when a couple of those really struggled mightily against each other; but, you know, almost ten years down the line, I think we're getting the hang of it now. And it's a lot more whole a life as a result….

Shirley Smith Graham

"What I passionately wanted to do when I finished seminary was find a way to do chaplain programs with seriously mentally ill people out in their neighborhoods or at the homeless shelters or wherever they were; but after a lot of research and talking to a lot of community advocates—I mean, you know what I'm going to say: There is no funding for that. That is not a job. That is not a paid job. But I heard on the street that Randolph Charles at the Church of the Epiphany was really into this and had a whole homeless community gathered for worship on Sunday mornings at breakfast and 'maybe you should go talk to him.' So I just cold called him….He and I agreed that there was a job for me there, but they had no money….Grace: Christ Church Alexandria was looking for an outreach director….Christ Church paid me full time, and Church of the Epiphany had me on Fridays and Sundays, so I got to do both.

Shirley Smith Graham

"At the end of that year was when Christ Church called me to be an associate rector there, and that's how I spent the next four years. By that time, I had developed enough experience with people's lives to realize that the brokenness and the intensity and the need for affirmation of God's presence that I was witnessing in the lives of the seriously mentally ill was there, present in the quasi-affluent, middle-class folk also. It was good to have the experience of working as part of a multi-clergy staff of a resource-size parish. From there I was called as rector at St. Martin's in Williamsburg, a large program-size [parish].

"There were always choices. I think our ideal setting out—I'm kind of embarrassed to say this—was, well, if we get a call from a diocese that has two positions open, that will clearly be God's will for us. That would have clearly been God's will, but that wasn't ever the way it worked. The only way it ever worked was we'd get a call from somewhere saying, 'We really want one of you and oh, by the way, I'm sure the other one of you can find something.' Clearly the diocese then said, 'Yes, we really need your skills, but the congregation isn't open to having a female rector.' So what Ernest and I discovered—and as we talked to other clergy couples for the most part this is what we're saying—is that one of us gets called, very clearly, definitively called to full employment. The other one comes along and is usually underemployed or finds great life fulfillment….I would like to say, 'Okay, this is my turn with the big job, and next it will be your turn with the big job; but I think we've lived long enough together now to know that that's idolatrous. You know, trying to exercise more control than we really have….

"I can't say strongly enough how important it was for me to be a priest of the homeless first before I became a priest of the home-full. I mean, I really learned from that community what people at that Maslow kind of level of survival need, and it is true of us all….You need to exercise power gracefully and lightly and collaboratively. This takes me back to the early sense of call and living in community, too. My role is the abbess: How can we structure this community so that people can treat each other well, so that the Kingdom of God can be revealed here today? So it's not some far off thing; but that when people then turn to this property, they feel a sense of sanctuary but also boldness to draw aside that veil and see the one who is here already and know themselves to be different because God is immanently here already….Vision is important, but I think vision has to be collaboratively developed with the lay leadership, not the other way around….

"It's not my gender that I've had a lot of people question. It's my relative youth combined with my gender where I've gotten the resistance….I used skills from my secular work to overcome that obstacle in the Church. I think we're in the middle—hopefully, we're in the middle—of a big transition generationally going on where we do regard younger persons offering of themselves with

Shirley Smith Graham

more high esteem than we used to….I think the practice of ministering and how it gets funded is in the middle of being changed radically. And the model of a parish that can raise the funds to support a clergy person is a model that already in large parts of our country isn't viable. We're sort of insulated from that reality in the East; although in Southern Virginia, we're not insulated from it because we have got a lot of churches that can't afford their own priest and are doing cluster ministry or total ministries. So I wonder if we all as clergy are entering an area where we need to be more entrepreneurial. I wonder how women are going to intersect with that. We are used to being a little more entrepreneurial because we often have to find ways into existing architecture. But that's a question I have."[3]

Sandra McCann (VTS '03) was not interested in grasping the end of a golden string to find her way into existing architecture. All her life she had wanted to be a missionary: "I always had mission in my heart from a child. It just was there. It was not anything I fostered: It was there." McCann and her husband Martin were both medical doctors. Martin McCann had worked in surgery, orthopedics, and pathology; Sandra McCann was chairman of a radiology department and loved being a doctor. By the time she had reached the height of her career, the two of them had done mission trips to Haiti and South America with an eye to being medical missionaries when they retired from their respective practices in Atlanta. When Martin reached the age of fifty-five, he was ready to retire. Sandra was not; however, she told him that if he were able to do his tropical medicine training at Johns Hopkins or the Armed Forces Institute of Pathology in D.C., she would retire because she had always wanted to go to the Servant Leadership School at Church of the Saviour. Driving a car up to Yale to give to their daughter for her last year of college, he found out that he had been accepted at Johns Hopkins and called her from the road. "I literally put the phone down, picked it up, and called my business manager and said that I was putting in my three-month notice. I had never breathed a word. And [the business manager] went, 'What?' And I said, 'I would really like to leave in two' because I knew Martin was starting July 6, and that was only two months away. It was just that sudden. I didn't think about it or anything. I just did it. About two days later, one of my partners called me up and said, 'Sandy, are you going to sell your house?...I would like to have first dibs'….Within five weeks we had sold the house….Catherine was finishing her freshman year at Columbia, and Elizabeth was finishing her junior year at Yale. They came home, and we put up these two big plastic tubs and said, 'Whatever you want in the apartment goes in here. Everything else we are selling or giving away or storing.' I walked out of the office, closed my door on July 3 at 1:30, and I never looked back….

[3] Interview of Shirley Smith Graham by Jennifer Andrews-Weckerly, August 30, 2010..

"On July 6 with a box of books, Martin's microscope, and two suitcases, we were on our way to Johns Hopkins. We felt like we were free. We felt like we were on our honeymoon, just taking off into the wild blue yonder. I mean, it was wonderful. We stayed at Johns Hopkins in the student married housing and had a ball."

By August of the following year, Martin McCann had finished his course but had to wait until January to do his field work in Peru. Sandra McCann recounts their next steps: "I always wanted to go to the Church of the Saviour Servant Leadership School; so we got in the car and went down to Washington, D.C….We found a furnished apartment because all we had were these two suitcases. We rented it, and I went to Servant Leadership School….I didn't even know Virginia Seminary was across the river. I had never thought about seminaries….

"We went to Peru in January….While I was there, we went to the local Episcopal Church, and I met the Bishop of Peru….I would go out and visit with him, and I realized that I could be very happy working with the poor, which really wasn't a surprise. But I confirmed in a foreign country that I really loved doing it and that that was what I wanted to do." It was also in Peru that McCann had her first experience of someone seeing in her a grace she had not realized: At the Church of the Good Shepherd in Lima on Good Friday, the priest was delayed when it was time to do the Stations of the Cross. "The priest's wife asked me if I would lead it, and I said I would. A couple Sundays later the priest said, 'Barbara said you should go to seminary. You should be a priest.' But at that time I never took it as a serious thing. I took it as a compliment meaning that she thought I did a good job and that I was serious and that I imparted good information. I mean, I didn't take it to mean 'This is a call from God.'

"So we came home….It's mid July or the end of July; and we looked at each other and go, 'What will we do?' We had no idea. We had no idea that the Episcopal Church even had missionaries, number one….I guess we just had this romantic idea that we would go to a foreign country and build a medical clinic and practice medicine. We had no idea that you had to have visas to get into countries, and you had to be invited….So we called up our former priest, Charlie Roper (VTS '56), and said, 'We really don't know what to do here.' And he said, 'Well, go back to the Church of the Saviour and join a discernment group….And you might go across the river and take a few courses at the Seminary.' 'What seminary?...Okay.'"

The McCann family then drove both daughters to New York to Columbia, one to medical school. "Then we toddled down to Virginia, found [the Seminary], drove up to it. It was the last day of registration….Marge [McNaughton] said, 'Well, the classes are full. It's a very big year. We have fifty-five students….Do you think you need the Gospels or Paul more?' I had never read the whole Bible; and I said, 'I think I had better start with the basics.' So she put me in New Testament…. There were no other first year classes." On the advice of another student, McCann took a course from Mark Dyer which was full of senior students. "Those were the two courses I took. I studied day and night. I was petrified. First of all, I didn't know how to use a computer….I was a chemist and a mathematician and a doctor who loved God, but I had no background for this at all….I knew I was going to mission. I was just there to increase my knowledge, and so it was very frightening to me. Then I met Dr. Jones and told him we wanted to be missionaries. I joined the Missionary Society

Richard Jones lecturing

right away, and I did really enjoy that. Shirley Smith Graham was in that and Eileen Weglarz (VTS '02). Those were people I could really identify with. They had been to Africa.

"Then [Dr. Jones] told us about the Yale Conference in January, so we went to that….Then I got in the Master's of Theology [track]. So then I was enrolled and started in the second half of Old Testament and the second half of Church History….What were the obstacles? It was fear. I just had no knowledge of what I was [pause] I was just there for a totally different purpose. I didn't identify. I didn't know the language they spoke. I mean, it would be like your going to medical school and starting in your third year of med school without having had the first two. But I really enjoyed the studies….

"The summer after my first year [in seminary], we were at home in Atlanta for just a couple of weeks and I went by and saw [Neil Alexander]. He had just been consecrated: He was a 'baby bishop.' He was not the Bishop when I had come to seminary. I said, 'I just wanted to tell you that Martin and I are in your diocese; and if anything comes across your desk for missionaries, medical missionaries, we're ready. We are just marking time in Virginia.' So he said, 'Sit down.' And we talked for a while. He said, 'Why aren't you going to be a priest?' And I said, 'Because I don't want to be.' And he said, 'Well, why not?' And I said, 'Well, everything I have ever heard about being a priest doesn't fit me'….At the end of October, he walked into the refectory; and he said, 'Hey, how are you doing?' And I said, 'I don't know. I think I am kinda foundering.' We sat down and talked; and he goes, 'Well, why don't you go into discernment?'"

After graduation from seminary and before departing for Africa, McCann had met with the Commission on Ministry in the Diocese of Atlanta. "Then I went to Africa, thinking at that time that I had done the little hurdle that [Neil Alexander] asked me to do. Of course

Sandra McCann & man with leprosy

they didn't like it that I hadn't discerned everything. One of them said to me, 'Well, when you come back from Africa, do you plan to take a church?' I mean, I was only sixty years old. Like I am going to come back and take a church after I come back from Africa? Of course, I would never have had the call in America because there is nothing that interests me about being a priest in the U.S.: vestries, fundraising, Christian Ed. I have always had a wonderful priest, but I have never wanted their job. I loved being a doctor. I never had a priest who made me feel as a lay person that I was less than they. I have really been blessed. So, it was never there. Why would I want to go back and, you know, meet with the flower committee…?

"I went to Africa thinking I probably wouldn't be odained….Actually, it was in Africa that I got my call…. When I got to St. Phillips after we went to language school in Tanzania there, we stayed in St. Phillips in Kenya for kind of an internship with the woman who was the woman principal Ph.D. and a male physician who

Martin was going to work with. And there was no priest at the college. Everyday we would go to chapel, and there would be the altar but there was never communion. I guess I just never knew what it was like not to have communion. And I had this overwhelming urge to give communion, and that was really my sense that I wanted to….So then I wrote home to Neil; and we picked St. Luke's Day for me because it was a good time for me to leave the school to come back and because I was a physician. Neil set up everything…."

McCann was ordained a deacon at St. Thomas, her home parish. But when the time came for her ordination to the priesthood, Bishop Alexander came to Africa to ordain her in the Church of the Holy Spirit: "I didn't realize. You know, I am new to this. I didn't know it was a big deal. I didn't know it was historic. People use the word 'historic' here because an American bishop had never been here. So everybody knows about my ordination. Not because I am a woman or the first or anything. I am not. It was because he came. It had nothing to do with me except I just happened to be the one he came for."

In Africa McCann's ministry has evolved to suit the needs presented: She has taught sacramental theology, liturgics, Mark, Corinthians, other courses in Old and New Testament, and practica. As she says, "Whatever was open, you taught it. I remember a lady [in her first African location]. She was not a theologian. She had a couple Master's degrees and a doctorate, but in business.

Sandra McCann

She was teaching Church History. I said, 'How do you do it?' And she said, 'I get a book.' I loved it. I really loved it. I only had sixteen students. I loved them. I hated leaving [the first location]. We had a tiny house, no running water. They'd all crawl in and gather on the floor, look at pictures on my computer; or we'd have them for dinner. It was such a sweet place. I learned a lot from that lady.

"Then I came here [to Msalato] and again just taught. I realized something here: that I couldn't go as low as I needed to go….I didn't know the subjects well enough to be able to answer all the nuanced questions…. They've never seen a map.

Administering communion

Sandra McCann

They don't know anything about World War Two, the Holocaust, the Civil Rights Movement. Most of them wouldn't know who Tutu is. So you have nothing to grab. There's no foundation. And [English] is their third language. That's how bright they are that they could pick up enough English in a total Kiswahili school….Kiswahili is not a rich language. [Consider] how many words we have for red, for instance. They have one word. And they have three colors: Black, red, and white were the only colors of the original….Poverty is so absolute here and so severe. It's going to take a generation or two before they'll ever be on their own….We need their voice. They have a lot to teach us….Transformation is a slow process. I hoped it were a little faster, but we definitely see things much differently than we did when we came. A short-term mission isn't enough to do it. It might open your eyes to something, but to really start seeing through another person's eyes and to change your world view takes generations.

"People used to do witchcraft, all the Christians.

It's been five generations. No one changes their religion like that….Moses, our principal has written about spiritism and why people here have double mindedness….Esther Mombo (VTS '07H) writes about perseverance theology in Kenya: The wife of the bishop is always head of the Mother's Union; and some, but certainly not all, will preach to the women, 'You've got to forgive your husband' and use biblical words, phrases, and verses to justify that they should persevere. They don't want the house to fall. Their husband is the Archbishop. He doesn't want his priests to look bad…."

McCann remembers learning, "At a meeting in Kenya the women were bringing up before the priest the problem of wife beating; and they said, 'Oh, you're exaggerating everything.' The women said, 'Do you want us to take off our blouses?' because they had the marks on their backs.

"Rape is a huge problem here in the schools. Huge. The teachers rape the girl students….The Head

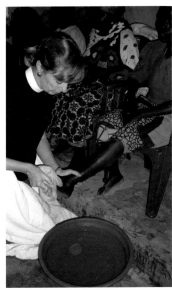

Sandra McCann performing Maundy Thursday foot washing

Master at St. Paul's School in the Diocese of Ruvuma said to me, 'Our biggest problem is pregnancy. The girls have to do their own cooking. The fishermen along the lake give them food for sex.' The highest concentration of AIDS will be around the mining town or around the fish-

Sandra McCann

ing industry because the girls get food….You go to a village and practically every girl of child-bearing age either has a child or there's one on her back….I know one girl who told me she changed majors at the University of Dar three times because you had sex for grades. I remember Jimmy Carter talking about the rumor that you won't get AIDS or to prevent it you have sex with a virgin when that was an African myth. But it's true they hunt the younger and younger girls. So it's a huge issue here: girls and sex and having babies young…. AIDS goes up where there's prostitution and money. In the city it's higher among the educated and the wealthy because they can afford prostitutes. In the remote villages it's still low. Families watch the children; and if you get pregnant, you're going to marry the boy. It's a closed unit. They haven't

been exposed to the outside. The husband may still fool around with other village girls.

"Polygamy was very common, even among the Christians. I had one student in Kenya who had seven mothers. There was a girl who graduated from here who was the eighth wife. Her sister was the seventh or sixth wife, and she couldn't bear children; so the parents had to give another woman….She was given by her father. She did not have a choice….We had another woman last year who is a second wife…but she can't get ordained, and she's good. She can't get ordained because she's a polygamist…. Adultery is treated lightly, which upsets me. [On the other hand] they are upset about homosexuality, and I'm not. It's a world view. But I will say this: You ask the children of a polygamist marriage if it's good; and they'll all say, 'No.' They'll all say, 'No' even if they are the first [child]….A lot of witchcraft comes out of the family unit. It's over jealousy. They'll report that the first wife is a witch….Witchcraft with violent overtones almost always comes out of the family unit. In some places they may even kill the women that are accused of witchcraft; or they will send them away to a witch city, a witch town, or something like that. Once you're declared a witch, your life is over really. Some of the priests here are afraid to stand up for them because if you stand up for a witch, it means you're in collusion. It's a very scary thing. The priests here don't want anything to do with it because they have great fear of it. There is negative evil power, and they know it. We don't acknowledge it, but it's certainly biblical: demons and principalities…. The liminal screen is very thin here between the spirit world and this world. The Enlightenment has not hit here. There's a very closed world between the ancestors and the spirits. The ancestors

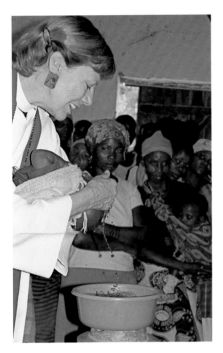

Sandra McCann baptizing a baby

Sandra McCann

Sandra McCann

here are the mediators. They are the ones that are closer to God....When there's drought or sickness, they go to the diviner. He decides who in the community has caused it. He talks with the ancestors. They may say the whole community is doing this and so they have to sacrifice; but usually they will pick out a person, and then that person is ostracized....Some tribes believe that evil was created. Now, that's a hard thing to explain: how God could create evil. But it's the same problem we have, isn't it: Why is there evil in the world...?

"Our theology is way too small for here. Especially in spiritism I don't even believe it, so how can I help them? There is a man who is getting his Ph.D. who talks about a leopard or lion that comes around their house at night and protects them. In our Western mind-set we just say, 'This is bizarre'; so I can't help them. They have to work out their own theology and the sacrifice in all of this. We can't help them. What they're learning at Virginia is not translating to the village Christians....I am passionate about African theology by Africans in Africa. That's why I'm working on this endowment so that we can start a Master's program here and get a library....George O'Koth said to me once, 'Sandy, I came back from Virginia where I printed a page again if I had a period wrong, and here I can't find a pencil.' That is no exaggeration....We need them at the table because we're living in 'la-la land.' We need African theologians at the table, but not African theologians who have been trained in the West and don't know. We need them telling us where God is in this and

Sandra McCann

book to be proud of their own traditions and to let the Holy Spirit work like Roland Allen wrote in his book about Paul's missionary methods.

"The issue here is how you become a responsible giver and not become Santa Claus and make the people dependent....In Kenya the old priest who worked at the school said, 'Sandy, your missionaries taught us to be dependent. They came to my village and said to my father, "Give us your best boy students. Give us your smartest children, and we'll educate them and take care of them completely." I came to boarding school at six years old; and the teachers told us, "Whatever you need, we'll give you." I saw my family once a year. They took my language, they took my family, and they gave me everything I needed, including an education. That's why I can speak English. That's why I'm teaching here. So you taught us to beg. You taught us. You made us beggars....'

"They colonized the mind: Everything white is better. The girls here lighten their skin. These beautiful

Sandra McCann

how to tell their own people. They need to work out a way to go back to their own people and say, 'We don't need the witch doctor.' But as long as they're afraid of the witch doctor....I think my role is encouraging them to be proud of African theologians, to read African theologians, to take what is good from the Gogo religion. I challenge them and say, 'Why should a Gogo become a Christian? What do you have to offer? Why? What should we baptize in the Gogo tradition?' I have them reading Kerwin's book and Donovan's

Sandra McCann

black people lighten their skin. Many want to marry a white person. Many think everything white is better…. When you help someone, you mess with them. It's true. No matter if it's good, you mess with them. You really do….I want to write about how to be a good giver and how to come and do mission. Come and see. Come and be with the people. Come and go to worship with them. If you're going to paint a village, come and paint with them. Don't come in and run to the village and build their church without them….We have left a legacy of honesty, personal honesty. That is the one good legacy. We didn't bring them God in any sense of the word, but

Sandra McCann & Maundy Thursday foot washing

[4] Interview with Sandra McCann in Tanzania, June 27-30, 2010.

we brought them the knowledge of Jesus, of something fuller; and they will always thank you for that….There are twenty-seven, maybe close to thirty, women now who have been ordained….It's just inch by inch….But both men and women consider coming to Msalato like going to Yale or Harvard. They call it the doorway to heaven, the gateway to heaven."[4]

Inch by inch along a golden string in Africa and America, women wind a ball to heaven's gate. The friends of Stephanie Parker (VTS '03) joked "that I was the most religious person they knew that hated church. But when I finally found the Anglican tradition as it was discussed in this very social-justice church in New Brunswick, Georgia, it opened a great feeding frenzy for me, to fill in all the gaps that my intuition had already attained but my intellect had not. I didn't have a vocabulary for it. This idea of a transcendent God being flesh and in the people that I was with in the congregation took shape for me in a way that it had not done before. It was sort of an explosion of passion. In EFM [Education for Ministry] within two or three months, I met with the priest and said, 'I want to learn. I want to learn everything I have missed up until this point.' It ignited a fire that had always been there. In about three years there was a huge emergence in tradition, scripture, and faith. I became one who was leading some of the education programs. It was the collision of my incredible thirty-odd years of hunger colliding with a tradition and a community where I could articulate it, just sort of exploding toward this community that identified me as priest and pushed me. I resisted mightily…but my community recognized in that explosion something that needed to be nurtured and given to the wider Church. It was really an unleashing. 'Explosion' is still the word that pops out when I have time to reflect on that particular time and on things that excite me about the faith: relaying that excitement, conveying that excitement and inviting other people into this really explosive, transformative reality that I think we sometimes miss.

"When the idea of priesthood first surfaced, I perceived it through dreams. Here we go into the mystery: You don't want to articulate your dreams too much to Commissions on Ministry! But I was vulnerable enough in sleep to hear, to receive what I refused to hear in waking. That lasted about six months, and it was six months of tenseness and terror. I had pressure from my faith community: 'Have you? Why don't you? Have you talked about?' And I was, 'No, no, no.' Until one morning there was such intensity that I threw off the covers and shouted at the ceiling, 'O.K. I'll go to Liam.' So finally when I articulated it to Liam, my priest, my rector at the time, he was, 'Well, it's about time.' But more importantly for me is that I felt like I drew clean air for the first time in six months. From the moment I was sitting there in Liam's office, where I still had the idea that two or three years from now maybe I would go to seminary or maybe we would explore this thing a little bit, it was like I was plopped into a locked flume and shot off. It was eleven months later, August 2000, and I was at orientation at VTS.

"After seminary I went back to Georgia to serve a little mission in Swainsburgh which was literally ninety miles from a town of any size. It was a ninety-mile round trip to the movie theater. It was the rural South to an extent, but the socio-economic context of Swainsburgh was the educational system it had. It was the county seat; so all of the schools were there, and it had a two-year system of the University of Georgia. So it was a very interesting congregation of about seventy members, and it was a very rich experience. It was part Tennessee Williams, part Prairie Home Companion with a little bit of Minnesotan good life mixed in; so it really had a lot of the whole drama of southern small town life with a lot of its graces

and surprises. I had never lived in a small town before, so I discovered how complex relationships can be when there is nothing else to do but know the people around you; and since you are going to be in relationship with them forever, you have to just sort of forge ahead.

"I was ordained to the priesthood in September 2003, and you may recall there was a little event with a fellow named Gene Robinson just prior to that day that sort of blew up a few churches in the land. I thought, 'Oh my gosh! Here I am in the middle of central Georgia in a small, tiny mission church. What is going to happen here?' But it was amazing. Nobody let it be a ripple on the water there. Not because they were all liberal, and not because they all agreed about this by far. There were staunch conservatives there. There were some of the few 'out' gay and lesbian members of the community. All of them had had an experience in their Protestant mainline faith of being excluded because of divorce, because of orientation, or because of some reason that they could not control. They had been punished by the institutional Church in one way, shape, or form; and they were not willing to be that body or be that person. It was the greatest gift that any church has ever offered a graduate from seminary: just a really deep glimpse of the redemptive side. People can come back; and even though their basic ideology may not change, their understanding of forgiveness and for making room is changed forever when they themselves have been the target of exclusion. I don't know if many places in the world outside of that environment provide that anymore…small towns.

"While I had my own fears and objections early on, particularly during that time when my congregation was trying to get me to be a priest and I really didn't want to be, one of the self-objections was, 'I am not going to put myself out there for that. I don't want to carry the flag for women. I am "realized."' Until I had my own sort of epiphany with that which was that I ultimately decided it wasn't up to me as to how other people felt about women's ordination. It only mattered what I thought about it and to leave that to everybody else. So the question I was asked constantly, both during discernment and by the wider Church after I was ordained, was, 'What do you say to people who don't agree with the ordination of women?' And my answer was, 'Go in peace.' I mean, what am I going to say to them? That is their journey, not mine. I still to this day, in many respects, don't feel like I experienced any real challenge with that. I haven't. I have colleagues who have. Either I have and have just been too obtuse to notice or too stubborn or just…well! But the funny thing: The place where I have been challenged most and where I felt it most was when I moved to Southern California, the bastion of liberal thinking. The Diocese of San Diego was incredibly conservative-thinking and still incredibly embattled over the question of women's ordination."

After two years in Georgia, Parker had been called to St. Paul's, Palm Springs, by its rector, Andrew Green. "He intentionally brought a woman to St. Paul's as an associate. So here is someone I trusted always in that regard. It turns out when we were going to the first clergy conference, I asked about worship, how that was going to go. I asked that question because in the Diocese of Georgia if you were new, your head was on the block: You were going to preach. This is how they introduce you to the rest of the forum. They make you preach or lead worship. So I just wanted to know, 'How does it work here in the Diocese of San Diego?' And he said, 'Only the Bishop does any of that.' And I said, 'Well, that's interesting. I haven't seen that before.' 'Well, we agreed to this a few years ago because our conservative brothers and sisters weren't coming to clergy conference or diocesan events if women were allowed to celebrate the Eucharist. So we just decided the bishop would do that.' And indignation welled in me so deep because my being a woman on the ordination path or being ordained had never, not in Georgia, made any impact. But suddenly what I heard and what I told him was that I was just astounded that someone I knew who supported women's ordination the way he did would go along with what I thought was just a horrible thing. I said, 'Here is what I hear. Let's pretend it is 1975 in the South and I am a black person and you are a white person and I walk into a restaurant and they say, 'We've got some of our friends here who aren't comfortable with the fact that black people can eat with white people. We know it is the law of the land, so you can come in. You just need to either not join at all or you need to go over there and sit in the black persons' section.' It just felt like betrayal. It really did. It felt like 'it's okay if they think that.' But how could you, if you're in the front line for this, how could you agree that it is better that these people…for women to just be pushed out this way to make them comfortable rather than pushing the prophetic edge saying, 'Come to worship at God's table or don't.' So that was the first time that being a woman who was ordained felt challenged in a way that wasn't a philosophical thing for me anymore. It felt like an emotional, physical thing. It was an assault. That was the first time I really felt violated by the Church in terms of being a woman, or by a segment, by a diocese, I don't know, or by a dead philosophy. I don't know what it was, but it just felt horrible. I didn't realize I had been carrying a notion of second-class priesthood because of my womanhood because it hadn't really been enacted from without. It was still a reality of my existence, not only in my diocese, but in the wider Church and much of the Communion. My priesthood was not valid for a large enough number of the Communion.

"I didn't worry about it. It didn't affect my day-to-day. But this is a story that has been foretold: It was a Sunday. I am sitting there in my chair sort of watching TV and both my cell phone and my home phone start ringing. I pick up my cell phone, and it was Andrew [call-ing from General Convention]. He said, 'They elected Katharine Jefferts Schori!' I had sort of been disconnected from it: I had been at church all day, seeing people; and I never thought it was a possibility. And I burst into tears. I did. I was like, 'Oh my God!' because I thought, 'Wow!' It surprised me. I thought, 'Why am I so emotional about this?' It was sort of like the Holy Spirit: 'What on earth is going on?' It was like this wonderful thing could happen, and the big epiphany in that for me was that I hadn't real-ized how much I cared about it until I had this release of emotion around that kind of validation. The phone kept ringing: It was people from [Good Shepherd] Swains-burgh, it was people from [St. Mark's] Brunswick, it was all the sort of people that had journeyed with me. I had never articulated that. I just had never experienced that as a troubling part of my journey, my womanhood, my ordi-nation and all that stuff. But they were all so excited. Somehow they just had to tell me, 'It's a woman!' I got a dozen of those buttons sent to me: 'It's a girl!' that they immediately came up with. That was another profound time I hadn't really expected. It was somehow like some-thing lighter and greater in the world….It was something in the world about mercy and justice and compassion had happened that even our lesser angels could not stop. Those are the only two times that consciously or emotion-ally my gender and my ordination have collided in ways that were very turbulent, both good and bad."

Parker is now rector of St. Stephen's, a major parish in the Laurelhurst section of Seattle. Of search processes in general she says, "I have to find a clever and humorous way to let them know I am not a lesbian, or at least declare my sexual orientation, because there is a lot of suspicion around the fact that I am in my forties and single." Asked her favorite thing about parish ministry,

she replied, "Getting to teach and share that excitement, getting people excited about their faith in a way they didn't even know they needed to be or wanted to be, being part of people's curiosity and their own unfolding and telling them that they are actually beloved of God. The biggest shock and the hardest challenge I have had as

Stephanie Parker preaching

a priest is convincing people of their belovedness….One parishioner described it: 'It's like a Bible study run by Oprah.' My favorite thing is getting them excited about their faith and about the narrative of the sacred story and about the fact that we are actually meant to be formed into community. So many of our churches are communal isolation: You just come in, and we are 200 individuals just sitting in a pew; so how do we become church. I don't think they know there is an invitation there. I try to open their creative pathways to say, 'This is your tradition. Know it, learn it, love it, go and live it for all you are worth.'"[5]

The path to all that is tender in the human soul begins with the recognition that each step is preparation for a life. Mentoring which makes it possible for women and men around the globe to live their faith "for all they are worth" is being facilitated by a partnership agreement between Msalato Theological College, Dodoma, Tanzania and VTS. Through this partnership, faculty, staff, and students have been and will be exchanged for purposes of study and teaching. The summer of 2010, Leslie Steffensen (VTS '06), Robin Gulick Razzino (VTS '08), James Livingston (VTS '11), Susan Lukens (VTS '11), and two faculty members traveled to Tanzania to strengthen ties between the two schools and global partners in neighboring countries.

Lukens joined McCann at Msalato in mentoring Tanzanian women who are studying for ordination. In their turn, the women of Msalato College taught

Live your faith for all you are worth.

Lukens how Africans share: A cache of fifty colored pencils brought by Lukens to Africa to teach Godly Play, broken in two, became grace for the imaginations of 125 children on the dirt floor of a parish church. Then toward evening, Lukens took the end of a golden string and formed a labyrinth which she and the women of Msalato walked together in prayer, bound for heaven's gate.

[5] Interview with Stephanie Parker, April 22, 2010.

GRACE
in Motion
CHAPTER TWELVE

"Therefore, since we are justified by faith, we have peace with God through our Lord Jesus Christ, through whom we have obtained access to this grace in which we stand...."

Romans 5:1-2a
New Revised Standard Version

Standing in grace on the horizon of wholeness, women and men perceive a vista on the verge of transformation. Transformation takes different forms at different times, challenging all to consider statements of truth and how cultures might alter them. As societies change, women and men begin to negotiate between the remnants of old expectations and the openings of new possibilities. The freedom to make choices, to elect new options transforms their frame of reference and enlarges the contexts of those whom they encounter.

– The Horizon of Wholeness –

The class that entered Virginia Theological Seminary the Fall of 2001 bonded in ways never before experienced on the campus. That bonding began with the news that the husband of an entering woman student had suffered a near fatal heart attack as they were loading the van to move out of their house in Texas and travel to Virginia. To understand the significance of their persisting in coming and the reaching out to them and to one another on the part of the VTS community in that instance and in what followed, one must know first something of that couple's background.

Susan Kennard (VTS '04) was the daughter of an Episcopal priest. The earliest church she remembers his serving as rector was an inner city, primarily African American congregation: "For as long as I can remember, I loved Jesus and I loved the Church; and when I sang 'I sing a song of the saints of God' and Christmas carols and all of those things, I believed them with my whole heart…." At St. James the Apostle in Conroe, Texas, the Kennards married, brought up their daughter, and were active for twenty years. "It was there that [the calling came]. My calling, as best as I could articulate it, was just a desire in my heart to serve as an ordained priest. I wanted to go to seminary. I wanted to learn theology and to learn to preach. If I thought about myself as a priest, I thought about myself preaching. But I was very content to say simply, 'I want it with my whole heart. I want it more than anything else' and then just to allow the Church to decide whether that was a call or not and to allow the diocese and the whole process to say, 'Yes' or 'No'….I was working as a hospice nurse. The chaplain who was on our team said to me, 'Well, what will you do if they say, "No"? Will you go to another denomination?' I said, 'Well, no. I really feel called to be a priest in the Episcopal Church.' He said, 'If you will accept the answer of "No," then that is not a true call. If you are truly called to ministry, then you would continue to pursue that in another denomination or in another way.' That was really food for thought; but at the end of the day, I said, 'That is not who I am. This is my tradition, and this is my Church home; so it will be here, or it will not be anywhere….' But there was always something else happening…." Kennard's parents were ill and needed personal attention. The costs of a college education for their daughter loomed. Finally, their daughter's sophomore year of college, Kennard's husband Bill stated firmly, "One day you are going to wake up and be too old, and you are going to wish you tried. You just have to say it and see what happens."

Dena Harrison came to Conroe to be rector in 1997. "I had never heard a woman celebrate communion in all of my life until she came to our congregation. I had had the opportunity to see a woman preach once or twice at some kind of other event, but I had never heard the prayer of consecration said in a woman's voice. Her whole demeanor just made it real. It just made it a viable possibility in a way that had never been for me before….

"I look back on that congregation as being a body that raised me up, that raised both of us up and just loved us. I was serving on the vestry when Dena presented to the vestry the idea that there was an aspirant for holy orders in our congregation….With me sitting there she kind of described how that process worked and said, 'Susan is here in that capacity, and this is an opportunity for you all to ask her any questions you may have....A life-long friend of ours said, 'Well, I have a question.' Everybody was quiet, and I will never forget it as long as I live. 'I would like to know if you have given any thought to what it will be like for us here after you are gone?'....

"We were loading the van to make the move [to VTS when Bill Kennard had a near fatal heart attack]. We had both quit our jobs already....That congregation in Conroe just virtually moved us, just cared for us during that whole period of time: the hospitalization and the few weeks after that. [They] packed our stuff, cleared out our garage. I called our friend Phyllis when we were finally leaving and said, 'Well, you need to send out a giant message that people can go back to their day jobs because the Kennards are finally gone' because it took that many people to physically move us. But what I remember most poignantly is he had a heart cath on the day he went into the hospital and then a repeat heart cath 48 hours later. He was able to receive an enzyme in the ambulance that dissolved the blood clot that was in his heart and so had a really miraculous recovery from that. But the day of the second heart cath with all of us there, waiting in the back to hear the results of that cath, Bill was winding down a different hallway. They were taking him to a different recovery area, so he didn't really know where we were. We wouldn't have known it was he except that he didn't have his hearing aids with him because he was in ICU and so talking quite loudly as the nurse wheeled him down the hallway, getting the whole story from him of what happened. I can just hear him in the loudest possible voice explaining to her, 'My wife is called to be a priest in the Episcopal Church, and we are moving to Virginia Theological Seminary as soon as I am discharged!' That is what I will remember because in that hour 'Is it too much, is it too far, is it too soon, should we wait a year, will he even

tell me if he thinks he needs to wait a year, do we need to go to Austin instead?'....Just to hear that very large voice telling that story as if there were no question that that was what we were going to do....When I think back on how on earth we did it, I am not really sure how. But we handed out all of our car keys: Our daughter drove a car; our nephew drove a car; and my brother drove a car; and we both flew so that I got to attend chapel on the first day of the August term with my class. This, too, was a sign of the ultimate healing: I got up and got dressed for chapel. Bill did not approve of the blouse I had put on or something, so he got out the ironing board at the hotel and said, 'You cannot wear that to chapel on your first day at Virginia Seminary.' So it was just an amazing beginning of a new life for us."

A message went out to the VTS community for all able-bodied souls to come help the Kennards move in, and they did. A few weeks later, on Saturday September 8, faculty member Mark Dyer's son Matthew died. The community rallied around again. Then on Tuesday, September 11, terrorists attacked the United States. Buildings on campus shook as if coming off their foundations because of the Seminary's proximity to the Pentagon, the site of one of the attacks. A service of prayer was held in the chapel at 11 a.m. Then teams of students began making sandwiches to ferry to rescue workers at the Pentagon. On Saturday, September 15, a requiem was held in the Seminary chapel for Matthew Dyer. Kennard sang in the Seminary choir for that service and remembers, "thinking that in some way that event was making a community out of us and the privilege of just being allowed to be a part of that and how that might cement us."

Her middler year during a three-week period in October 2002, a sniper was on the loose in Maryland, the District of Columbia, and northern Virginia. He and his young companion killed ten people and critically injured three. The community was in crisis. It was hard to wait at a bus stop, buy gas for one's car, or go to a shopping mall for he gunned down people in those very places. Once again members of the Seminary community—students, faculty, and staff—drew strength from one another.

Then in the senior year of the class of 2004 came another catastrophe: On September 18, 2003, Hurricane Isabel roared ashore in northern Virginia. In monetary terms, it was the most expensive disaster in the history of Virginia. In human terms, world's were changed: Thirty-six lives were lost; residents coped with a 9.5 foot storm surge in Alexandria; and on the campus of the Seminary many trees came down, one landing in the middle of the garage of a faculty home and another taking out the ornate arch over the entrance to the cemetery. The campus was without power for several days; some faculty homes across Seminary Road, for close to a week. The community pulled together.

Of these complex three years, Kennard says, "I loved being in an academic environment for that three years….To wake up in the morning and to think, 'Reading Scripture all day, that is my job today,' and the great privilege of that….I loved coming to know the voices of all those different prophets and all those different evangelists….They were real voices to us by the end of that three-year period of time. It amazed me that faculty members of Virginia Seminary really desired to have friendships with us, real relationships with us. I always felt that the faculty looked on us as colleagues and that for the majority of our careers we would be colleagues, fellows of the Gospel. That was pretty amazing to me….On the last day of GOE's [General Ordination Examinations] Bishop Dyer stepped down [from the sanctuary of the chapel] and said he had a scripture to read to us from the middle portion of the first chapter of First Corinthians. He said, 'Before I read this I want you to know that this is how your teach-ers feel about you.' Then came this tear and then, 'I thank God for you everyday, that he has given you all the gifts you need, all the strength, all the knowledge. And our prayer for you is that you continue faithful on to the end.'[1] I can remember sitting there thinking, 'This whole thing has been worth it for just this one minute because now I understand how Scripture is alive, how it is a living, breathing word….It has a new word for every generation.'"

After seminary Kennard was assistant rector at a large, resource-sized congregation in Beaumont, Texas, for just over two years. She is now rector of St. Mark's parish in Bay City, Texas. "It is a pastoral-sized congregation in a

Susan Kennard at graduation

small town, but it has been a great experience. It has also been hard. What we do is hard. I think if I had gone to Camp Allen and said, 'I am going to have a giant retreat entitled "What We Do is Hard"' that it would be full in about thirty minutes because what we do is hard. I am on the Commission on Ministry now in the Diocese of Texas; so as we interview these people, I just cannot help myself from telling them it is the best life ever. I mean it is the best life there is. It is not the easiest life there is, but I cannot think of any place of privilege higher than the place we sit and serve.

---

[1] Paraphrasing 1 Corinthians 1:4-8a.

"I enjoy everything. I enjoy preaching, and I enjoy teaching. I guess what I like the best about this congregation is the broad range of ages. It is not a big congregation, but there are some of every single age….It is a hundred year-old congregation, and many of those founding families, the fourth or fifth generation, are still very active to this day."

Kennard was the first ordained woman St. Mark's Beaumont had ever called and is the first ordained woman at St. Mark's Bay City. In Beaumont "people actually said these words to me: 'We always said we would never have a woman, but you have changed my mind.' I think in both congregations [there was] a lot of angst about that, but I think both of these congregations as a core value have a very strong history of hospitality to the stranger; and they have a long history of respectful relationships with the clergy. Therefore, I think they did not know what to do with the whole woman thing. It was a big deal: what to call me and all of that, what to say. But I think the bottom line in both cases was they just fell back on what they did know which is, 'We know how to welcome the stranger. We know how to bring the chicken soup and the chili and the bread. We know how to make someone welcome who is new to us. And we know how to be respectful to that office.' So they fell back on those two things, and then the rest just took care of itself….In both of those communities there is a big [Roman] Catholic presence, and so I know that I am

Susan Kennard

widely thought to be a nun, still. I have had people take my money and say, 'Thank you, sister.' And it is easier to say, 'You're welcome' and just to be gracious about that."[2]

Thus, the horizon of wholeness has expanded from an interdependence witnessed on the campus of the Seminary to parishes in cities, towns, and villages around the world. Grounded in Christ, the Seminary's emphasis on community has empowered women and men to express more confidently their gifts and their differences. Enabled by God's grace, they are taking that vision of mutuality to the congregations they serve and, thereby, bringing new life to the Church.

With this wholeness have come new models of ministry. While women have often accepted assignments to small missions or half-time positions because there was nothing else open to them, increasing numbers of women are choosing alternative ways of combining vocational and familial responsibilities. Two young graduates of the class of 2004 provide examples.

St. Luke's, Atlanta, the home parish of Rebekah Hatch (VTS '04), has hired women clergy as associates for a number of years, though it has never had a woman rector; so seeing women at the altar was "a seamless presence in [Hatch's] life." On the advice of her uncle, a dean, she entered a diocesan discernment program. Throughout the year she spent in the discernment process, Hatch reflects, "I didn't really want to invest in it because I was sure that I was not going to be accepted. So I sort of kept my distance….I remember it just being very emotionally charged, and I had a rough time with it personally for different reasons….Entering seminary I still thought, 'I am still in discernment about this.' Being in seminary I had enough time to form and to be with people who were forming and to be with people who were formed in the vocational sense. I think that [VTS] is probably where I

[2] Interview with Susan Kennard, May 5, 2010.

finally accepted the call. I feel like I had sort of been dancing with the call, you know, for three years by the time I went to seminary…but it quickly became not only do I not know what else I would do with my life, but I am not sure how I haven't done this, since this is what I am going to do with my life forever. First, somebody else knew that, just not me.

"I think that the big challenge that I faced in CPE [Clinical Pastoral Education] and Field Ed, and even to this day in parish work, is not so much a gender issue but a gender issue coupled with age. I get a lot of, 'How old are you, and where are your children? Who is taking care of them? You are not with them. Are they running the streets?'"

After graduation from seminary, Hatch served as associate chaplain at St. Paul's school, the first ordained woman chaplain. "It was a great exercise in setting some boundaries. First of all, because I could not come near working as much as my supervisor, so I had to become more confident…to be able to say, 'This is what I am willing to do. This is what I am capable of doing….I was always very clear with [the students] that 'I am not here to take care of you. I am here to walk this journey with you, and we can share that conversation.' I taught there for two years, and there was a lot that was very challenging about it….I rarely had a day that was shorter than ten hours."

Hatch left that position when she became pregnant, then served a parish for three years when her first child was a baby. When her husband accepted a position at Georgia State, they moved to Atlanta. Now with two children she serves a parish five to six hours a week, "essentially just Sundays."

"I think one of the dominant themes in our life right now among my group of friends that are also clergy is this balancing children [and] dual-career families with how we are living out our ordained ministries. I am mostly thankful that there are other folks that are doing it….I feel like my call to ministry in this world is not exclusive to the four walls of a church, is not exclusive to my collar; and that at the end of my day, I find some sense of peace in feeling the pull between mom and wife and priest and citizen and child of God. I feel some sense of peace. I feel like I am simply doing all those things in order to live out my ministry, that loving the Lord with all your heart, mind, soul, and strength is about all of it, not just the piece where we lead the congregation or the piece where we raise our children. Loving your neighbor as yourself is something we hear a lot in church….I have really been challenged now that I am not working. If I am not as part of my job going to the Food Pantry and checking in or going to the hospital and checking in, then how am I doing that? The call to love your neighbor as yourself has changed for me because I don't, quote unquote, do it as part of my job. I had to figure out what that means for

SECOND FROM LEFT: Karin MacPhail
THIRD FROM LEFT: Rebekah Hatch

me and how I am doing that."[3]

As a child Karin MacPhail (nee Chambers) had been an acolyte in the Episcopal church in Odessa, Texas; but by the time she entered the University of Texas at Austin, she still had never seen a female priest. So on a Sunday morning her freshman year at All Saints Episcopal Church on the UT campus when she heard "an internal voice that said, 'That's what you're supposed to do,' it was very clear in the moment but very difficult to deal with or make sense of later." Subsequently, "there was some kind of women's conference at UT that brought in women in all different sorts of fields and had all these great speakers. One panel discussion was women in non-traditional roles. One of the panelists was a Methodist pastor who was a woman. She was very young, attractive, friendly, vivacious, just the kind of person I would want to be and very appealing in a lot of ways. So hearing her talk about this and seeing her up there—I think she wore her collar—she just looked like 'Oh. This is a normal person. This is a valid choice. This isn't, you know, an alien kind of idea.'

"So that started planting another seed. It really, though, was something that I think I needed a little more time to wrestle with, so I put it aside for a year or two at a time, not even really thinking about it and going on with other pursuits. Then something would happen that would make it all come back again and make me question and struggle and work things through...."

After three months in the Graduate School of Social Work at UT, "I just realized this was totally wrong. This was not what I wanted to be doing. There were so many problems I saw with the way we were being taught to help people...." So Chambers (her surname at the time) found a job in publishing in Manhattan, then made her way to Alexandria.

Subsequently, she left book publishing and went to work at the Close-Up Foundation where she was first an instructor, then moved into the office and helped run their program in Hawaii focused on international relations. "So I was working there, going to Immanuel [on the Hill]; and I think enough things were clicking into place in life and I was at the right church and I'd grown up some. And the call just became overwhelming to the point where I thought, 'I might still be wrong about it, but I've at least got to talk to my rector about it.' I was just at the point where I couldn't *not* do that anymore....

"The process went as smoothly, I think, as it goes for anybody. I can't think of anywhere along the way that I was ever discouraged except by myself because of my own lack of female clergy models and then later feeling unworthy, unsure, nervous or anxious about the process....It felt to me like they were going to unzip you, peel you open and absolutely everything, your credit report, your physical health, mental health, everything about yourself was just going to be out there; and that terrified me. It's not like I had a big secret....I talked with enough people finally that I decided, I'm not going to look at the whole thing anymore. I've got to just look at the next step. I'm not a saint, but I'm not the worst person in the world. And there's not really anything in particular for me to be afraid of. It's just the fear of being that inspected....

"I had a fantastic experience at VTS....I'd always gone to big schools; so to go to someplace where I actually knew everybody in my class and almost knew everybody in the whole school was great! I loved that. I loved this whole part of who I was that had felt like this weird kind of secret identity, strange thing about myself that was so different from most people [pause] Suddenly I was with all these other people who had gone through the same thing and we could be this kind of quirky thing together

[3] Interview of Rebekah Hatch by Jennifer Andrews-Weckerly, September 10, 2010.

and that was great! I loved really studying something I cared about, feeling like this was the right place….Things were clicking finally that I had tried to run away from for a long time. Then I met Alexander [MacPhail, a fellow student in the M.Div. program at VTS] and fell in love. That sort of casts a rosy glow. I got engaged during CPE, so that kind of makes my experience a little different from most!....

"We were married the third year….It was really affirming to me that third year to feel ready [to graduate] and feel like, 'This is enough. I can't live in that kind of laboratory and have so much attention and so much community. [But] terrible things happened: September 11th, the Sniper, Hurricane Isabel….How would we have made it through without each other….

"Post-seminary I've had one regular, full-time position which was as associate rector and chaplain at St. Paul's Memorial in Charlottesville. Half of my job was parish ministry, and half was campus ministry at UVA. It was a fantastic job. I loved it….The two other priests I worked with were really good mentors in a lot of ways. They were both quite a bit older than I….They liked the fresh perspective on things, so that was great; and I really had the sense that if I came up with an idea, I could go with it….

"Alexander and I both really liked the idea of my staying home for a few years if we were able to have children. Not forever, but we liked the idea that anyone under age three could be at home with Mom; and then after that, I could move back into (ideally) part-time for a long time until the kids weren't so little, and then back to full-time….So suddenly I've only been there [at St. Paul's] for a year, and I'm telling them, 'I'm four months pregnant. In December when this baby comes, I'm going to be leaving.' And both of the priests were very support-

ive….So I got nothing but support, but it was hard to only be there for a year and a half and then go…."[4]

In a 2010 article written for "Fidelia's Sisters," an online publication by, for, and about young clergy women published by The Young Clergy Women Project, MacPhail wrote, "I've been staying home for four and a half years now….This is a season of my life….I miss the stimulation of creative work. I miss grown-up conversation, and I miss bringing home a paycheck. I get exhausted and bored refereeing sibling squabbles all day…. But after each turned one, I started doing supply work (monthly at most) and took other opportunities that came along like writing book reviews and leading workshops and quiet days. I have found that doing something

Karin MacPhail

every couple of months makes a big difference in my happiness. This summer I have more work lined up than I've had since I was working full-time. I'm leading two weekend retreats, filling in at other churches on five Sundays, and working for a week as a camp chaplain….My daughter turns two at the end of June, and our plan is that I

---

[4] Interview with Karin Chambers MacPhail, October 12, 2010.

continue my patchwork ministry for another year or so before looking for a regular position somewhere, preferably part-time….Some days I can't believe that both dreams (to be a mother and to be a priest) came true. My cup runneth over, and I could use some help mopping up the mess!"[5]

As had Kit Carlson and Susan Kennard, these younger women reached a point of self-acceptance that allowed them to realize they had done their part along the path to ordination, could let go of the need to control, and let God chart the course of their ministries. Accepting one's weakness, not denying it, is openness to grace; and that kind of self-acceptance would continue to grow at VTS.

Christy Laborda (VTS '07) was a religion major at Bryn Mawr College. Her senior year a campus minister "sat me down and asked me if I had ever considered ordination, and I thought he was insane….One of my big perceptions was that you had to have everything figured out and you had to know what you believed and you had to be able to answer people's questions when they came to you. So that was a big thing for me to get around….The thing that made me most cautious entering VTS was the Southern culture, honestly, Southern with money….I think the Seminary would love not to be part of that culture, but I think it's still in the DNA. The churches in that area have a lot of that, and even our buildings speak of it. So I wasn't sure if I would be accepted or if I would fit in. I had Southern male classmates commenting, or at least one commenting, that I didn't walk like a lady, that I walked as if I had somewhere to go. I *informed* him that in fact I did have somewhere to go! I wasn't busy trying to float along the brick sidewalk. I was busy trying not to trip on the brick sidewalk just to get to class….The irony

is that I ended up having an amazing time at VTS. Ended up being a student leader, being asked to be a proctor of the dorm for two years. Ended up being vice president of the student body my senior year and holding positions both of the other years and being the unofficial party planner for a year or two….

"When I got to VTS, I think for the first time I realized that women were not very deep in the DNA of the Church….My Field Education was with Latino congregations, so there is a whole 'mother' issue [because so many parishioners in a Latino mission come from a Roman Catholic context]." She was told by the congregation, "Don't worry about your Spanish. Worry about the fact that you are a woman." She responded, "'I guess I will worry about my Spanish. I can't do anything about being a woman'….But just in general, in visiting churches, I would visit sometimes with some of my seminary friends who were also young. It seemed like people knew how to receive my male classmates in a way that they didn't know how to receive me. It felt a little like the old women of the churches just loved these young guys, and usually I was asked if I were a spouse. It was just assumed as we visited that I was a spouse….The first generation [of women seminarians] was a lot older because they had been fighting so long to get there. The second generation happened to coincide with the time when the Church wasn't ordaining young people: Very few made it through in their twenties; some, but not a lot. So I was twenty-three or twenty-four starting seminary and looked supposedly ten years younger is what everyone liked to tell me. I still get people thinking I am kidding that I am clergy or saying inappropriate things like, 'Wow! Are you twelve? When did we start ordaining twelve-year-olds?' and things that I don't think would be said to males.

---

[5] http://www.youngclergywomen.org/the_young_clergy_women_pr/20 (June 6, 2010)

"I think those comments can happen in general with women—more comments on hair and body and clothing—but I became very aware of that in seminary. I first started hearing the statistics about not only how few female bishops but [also] how few female cardinal rectors we have. It made me think, 'I am going to keep working even if I have babies. I am not going to get out of this rat race, even though I don't know if I want those things. I really don't think I do. Forget the rat race.' But at that point realizing that you really had to keep going to get there; and I just wanted to do it in general so that *women* would be doing it, not that *I* wanted to do it…."

After graduation Laborda was called to be vicar of

Christy Laborda

El Buen Pastor in Durham, North Carolina: "It was a great experience, and it was a really hard experience." The congregation more than doubled in her two years there, but it was in a neighborhood where she couldn't be alone in the building safely. "It was broken into on a pretty reg-

ular basis. The air conditioning had been stolen before I got there. We replaced it; it got stolen again….Most of my parishioners were undocumented, and their driver's licenses had expired; so they couldn't really even drive without fear of getting picked up. I couldn't put anybody else on the alarm system so that if it went off at night they could be called because I didn't want to put them in the position of meeting cops in the middle of the night at the church. The building was a disaster. It needed a lot of work. The last pastor was basically asked to leave, and there was a lot of damage around that. So almost every kind of challenge was there. The financial piece was okay. That was covered by the diocese and other congregations. So while it was great because I learned that I could do Latino ministry, the water was always up to just about my nose; so I was just always gasping. It didn't look like that from the outside, but that's what it felt like."[6]

From there Laborda went to Seaside, CA, to be vicar of San Pablo Apostol where she was the first female priest for almost every parishioner. She is now the rector of St. Stephen's Episcopal Church, Sebastopol, CA.

Another 2007 graduate, Arienne Davison, writes of her experience, "Attending seminary in Virginia reshaped how I understood who I was as a creature that happened to have White, Black, and Asian-American parents. I became increasingly conscious of my own need to honor the cultures that formed me as well as create spaces in the church [sic] for people (like me) and communities that don't fit neatly into racial, ethnic and language groups."[7] Davison began seminary without postulancy; and of that experience says, "I didn't really realize until after I had been granted postulancy that it had been like I was holding my breath. It felt like it could all be taken away until I had that approval. Then the formation

[6] Interview of Christy Laborda by Jennifer Andrews-Weckerly, September 1, 2010.
[7] "Diocese of Olympia Special Edition, on behalf of Bishop Greg Rickel," December 2, 2010.

worked in a different way, and I thought I could be a little more myself. I stopped worrying as much about if I was doing it wrong and just was able to participate more fully....Being in residential seminary with people who are at that same developmental space and doing formation was so important. It would be hard for me to do that with people who had teenaged kids or people that were retired....

"The thing that was challenging was my experience as an Asian American. I couldn't give words to it at first, and part of it was the elation of being there. Slowly I started to realize that it wasn't that I felt discriminated against. It was more like not being seen as fully who I was. For example, someone would say, 'Oh! I thought Asians were practically white,' not realizing that there is this whole multiplicity of experiences of the world that don't match. We would talk about the importance of ethnic diversity and anti-racism, but it would always be framed in the Virginia experience which was not about migrant farm workers, and it was not about building the railroads. It was about slavery. So if you didn't articulate discrimination or marginality in that way, you felt like you were crazy. Like you weren't being oppressed enough, like you did not have a legitimate experience....Sometimes you can't fix the problems, but I am going to be clear about when I have the energy to do the ministry of teaching [to correct your assumptions] and when I don't....If you read academic work that is from one cultural world and you are taught approaches that only work at one world view and that is not yours, it all just feels like you are insane. Like, 'The way I am thinking must be wrong,' and not different; so it takes a while to become comfortable with who you think you are. I have had a lot of people of color come through, whom I have talked to at VTS, who have shared that experience of being alienated and 'I'm just not

quite right' and finally realizing that actually they were ['right'], and it was another thing that they had to integrate. I think in some ways it is helpful because in so many cases most churches are still white and not just that the people are white but that is the norm of the Episcopal Church....There is a growing realization that maybe civil rights approaches which dominate the leadership of the Episcopal Church, because of the age of the leadership in the Church, are increasingly inappropriate for the cultural and demographic issues we face.... Racism isn't a Black or White issue. Racial and ethnic identity is really not that simple."[8]

After graduation Davison was hired as an associate during an interim period for a parish in western Washington state. She now serves as associate priest at Grace Church, Bainbridge Island, WA, and as Canon for Multicultural Ministries for the Diocese of Olympia.

FOURGROUND: *Phoebe Roaf*
BACKGROUND: *Robin Gulick Razzino*

Like others, Phoebe Roaf (VTS '09) has found that she most often sees how God has been active in her life in retrospect and not at the moment grace occurs. She notes, "Many people in many different contexts discerned my call to ordination years before I did....I did not have any interaction with either female priests or African American priests growing up. I was actually an adult in my mid-

[8] Interview with Arienne Davison, April 14, 2010.

twenties before I encountered either of those. So there was just nobody who looked like me."

Roaf had a successful career as an attorney and was very active in the Church. "By the time I was forty, there were many more people—family members and friends and even associates—saying, 'We really discern a call in you'….The challenge [was] I was in a diocese, the Diocese of Louisiana, which had never ordained an African American woman. So I said, 'Well, the answer's probably going to be "No" anyway. I'll just start the process, and then I can sort of tell God, "This is enough"'….When the answer was 'Yes. You're going to go to Seminary in the Fall of 2005,' I still wasn't convinced I was called to be a priest. But I was very clear that God wanted me to take the next step. So I said, 'At the very least, I'm going to get an M.Div.'….

"I think the thing which really convinced me was the summer following my first year, CPE and my first year in my Field Education parish. In both of those situations to be treated as if I had priestly authority, pastoral authority: patients on the ward calling for their chaplain. Even though I didn't have a collar, they viewed me in the role and even at St. George's, entering as a seminarian, being on the altar every Sunday and having people see me in that role and actually doing it, then I could begin to see it. It just felt right. It felt right….God knew all along that this was going to happen; and I have to say that God was absolutely right, and I was absolutely wrong, that I am very suited to this ministry. I've had a steep learning curve since I graduated; and there are many, many areas where I need substantial improvement. I'm sure my rector would tell you that. But it really is a case of God equipping those whom God calls….My number one role model is Jesus, but a close number two is Jonah….I'm so thankful that the Bible includes people who are stubborn and bull-

headed, who said, 'God wants me to do something, and I'm going to do the exact opposite' because I did that for many years…."

Asked about her three years at VTS, Roaf replied, "Oh great, great. Having Dean Martha Horne, Marge McNaughton-Ayers, and Mary Hicks—what powerful female role models for me….South Louisiana where I've lived since 1998 is overwhelmingly Roman Catholic, so we have a much lower percentage of female clergy than the nation-wide numbers because of the strong Catholic influence. Even among the Protestant denominations,

LEFT TO RIGHT: *Phoebe Roaf & Helen White*

there aren't many female clergy. So to be here [at VTS] with a class which was fifty percent female and to have so many female faculty members and administrators, it was wonderful. I think this place had a great role to play in shaping my vocation and my sense of myself. I'm very glad that I chose Virginia Seminary. It was definitely the right place for me….

"My vision for my ministry is to serve a multi-ethnic, multi-racial congregation with people from all backgrounds including all socio-economic backgrounds. That vision from Revelation of people of all races and nations and cultures around the throne praising God is the vision of heaven. And if that's what we will ultimately

Phoebe Roaf with female priests in Sudan

have why can't we do that here? You know, God isn't going to run from the Puerto Rican Church to the Korean Church to the West Indian Church to the Irish Church up in heaven. We're all going to be together. So that's my vision of my ministry. I don't know if that means ultimately becoming a church planter because, quite honestly, I don't know of many Episcopal Churches, certainly not in the deep South, that have that wonderful rich diversity."

Roaf is the first African American priest, male or female, to serve at Trinity Episcopal Church, New Orleans, a city which is predominantly Black. There are seven white male priests, a white female deacon, and Associate Rector Roaf. "The thing that amazes me," says Roaf, "is that there are still firsts in 2010. It just seems amazing. I don't think of myself as a trailblazer, but I suppose in some ways I am. So I am mindful of the fact that for future African American priests and African American women, in particular, how I carry myself will impact Trinity's willingness and the Diocese's willingness in the future to recognize and validate that call. I can't believe that I'm the first Black woman ever from south Louisiana who felt a call to ordained ministry. And I don't know what happened with all of those other vocations. I don't really know….

"I'm very happy in my ministry. Aspects of myself which weren't fully developed before I was ordained are being utilized, which is wonderful. I'm very analytical and very methodical. I like things to be in order, and I have surprised myself in this vocation: I've cried on the altar several times, which was very unexpected. My rector always says, 'Just keep breathing. If you stop breathing, you're going to faint. It's okay to cry, but just keep breathing!' I think of the enormity of the role. We have a Thursday morning healing service where we do anointing with oil blessed by the Bishop and the laying on of hands. Once when I had been at my parish for about a year, two women came to the service; and they both were clearly in the middle of either chemotherapy or radiation. They had no hair; I mean, no eyebrows, nothing. When those two women came to that rail for me to bless them, I couldn't say the words because I was crying. All I could do was take the oil and make the sign of the cross on their foreheads. It was a very powerful experience, and shows how important God is to us. So I think that it's good for me to have a deep emotional well which is being tapped into in this vocation, which was not the case when I was practicing law at a large corporate law firm. That served another purpose because that work is meaningful and very good, but this vocation is really plumbing some depths that had not been plumbed."[9]

Phoebe Roaf

The incarnation of grace reaches depths of which we have been previously unaware. On the horizon of

[9] Interview with Phoebe Roaf, October 14, 2010.

wholeness women and men express the fullness of their beings and present their gifts in service to the Church. Sharing a multiplicity of experiences creates spaces into which comes a new word for each generation. Journeying together with new perspectives, women and men as colleagues witness to revelation's diversity and to the grace of God.

GRACE
in Motion

CHAPTER THIRTEEN

"Therefore, if any one is in Christ, new creation; the old has passed away, behold, the new has come."

2 Corinthians 5:17
translated from the Greek

The new has come. A cross has been driven into the old order. A rood has separated strength from power, testifying that power belongs to God alone. Because a predicate is missing from Paul's proclamation of grace, one might ask, "Did Paul mean to say in verse seventeen of 2 Corinthians that whoever—male or female—is in Christ *is* a new creation? Did he mean that a new creation *is revealed* when anyone is in Christ? Was he suggesting that anyone in Christ *can see* a new creation? Was he perhaps talking about the *potential* for new creation when one is in Christ?" Could it be that the lacuna in verse seventeen of Paul's letter to the Christians at Corinth was intentional on his part, a means of suggesting dialogue with the reader and unending possibilities? Whatever the import of that omission, the context of this verse makes clear that new life is effected only by God: "All this is from God…" writes Paul, reminding us that power resides in God the singularly omnipotent one, unveiling grace in all its potency in motion.

Power can be separated from strength because these two attributes are not identical. To say one is powerless does not mean one is not strong. Power is control, dominion, and authority. Human power is most often exercised by those who seek prestige and to whom prerogatives have been granted. Strength, on the other hand, is toughness, fortitude, and integrity. Human strength is most often exercised by those able to withstand stress without breaking, those possessed of moral courage.

If moral courage begins with recognition of and resonance with the good, moral courage in action is the capacity to hold fast in the face of the storms of life. Moral courage on the part of those committed to Christ is

the ability to affirm that God's creative power gives birth to new life, that even human strength is a gift of God's grace, and that God's power is made perfect in human weakness.[1]

The first witnesses to Christ's resurrection, in all four gospels, were regarded as the weakest human beings in a stratified society: females. The dawning of a new creation was first proclaimed by women. What happened at that dawning was not readily apparent to the early disciples nor would it be for generations to come; for slowly, slowly, drop by drop does grace move via wisdom. But since, in the wisdom of God, the world did not know God through wisdom, it pleased God through the folly of what those women preached to save those who believed.[2] By their proclamation, and the preaching of men and women after them, grace was and is showered upon the followers of Christ at all points in the journey and is not a static process.

Of the over seven hundred and sixty women graduates of Virginia Seminary, only a representative group has been interviewed in a year's time—women typifying the geographic distribution of the influence of this seminary, women who serve small congregations and large, very young women as well as women of advanced years and experience, women whose vision of service has expanded from pastoral to liturgical to administrative roles, women who have dipped into and drunk refreshed from deep wells of tears within, tears of both sorrow and joy.

Some women graduates of Virginia Theological Seminary still cannot be ordained in the dioceses where they are resident. Women are still being marginalized,

[1] 2 Corinthians 12:9.
[2] Paraphrasing 1 Corinthians 1:21.

trivialized, and their lives being forfeited around the globe.[3] What has sustained the women graduates of Virginia Seminary in the face of discrimination and, in some cases, violence through the years? What reservoirs of strength have buoyed them as they confronted unfathomable strata of hierarchy? What theological ethos has enabled women to stay centered on the promises given them in baptism, their new creation?

Meditating theologically on the events that drew them to ordination and shaped their ministries, women have turned naturally to Scripture; and it is worth noting what Scriptures were *not* cited as formative by the women interviewed. There were no references to passages of self-abnegation, no stories of warfare, no books whose principal subject was a

Elisa DesPortes Wheeler

woman. No one offered Job as an example of guidance nor Lamentations nor Ruth nor Esther. The only minor prophets who motivated the ministries of these women to

any degree were Amos, Micah, and Zechariah. But there is one thing all the references have in common: Relying on the words contained therein gave the women courage to pursue new life in the face of challenges. Strength, not power, was what was sought and found.

Such strength is exemplified in the reflections of many of the women interviewed. "Not by might, nor by power, but by my spirit, says the Lord of hosts"[4] has been formative for Elisa DesPortes Wheeler: "I have tried to live those words in my ministry as a priest," she says. Mariann Edgar Budde contemplates, "The miracle of the loaves and fishes is the spiritual foundation of my life: God asks us, and perhaps even needs us, to offer what we have to give, even when we know our offering is insufficient; but God takes that offering and makes of it a miracle. The passage[s] from 2nd Corinthians about we do not proclaim ourselves[5] and we have this treasure in earthen vessels[6] [guide my ministry], and it's pretty clear

---

[3] At a six-day meeting of the Primates of the Anglican Communion in January of 2011, the Archbishop of Canterbury addressed the issue of gender-based violence originally broached by African bishops at their meeting in Uganda the previous year. As a result, the January meeting drew up a substantial statement outlining the responsibilities of the Church in combating gender-based violence throughout the world. In addition, from February 21 to February 27, 2011, women from the Episcopal Church, the Anglican Church of Canada, and many other Anglican Communion Provinces gathered in New York City for the 55th session of the United Nations Commission on the Status of Women. The 2011 theme of UNCSW was access and participation of women and girls in education, training, science, and technology, including the promotion of women's equal access to full employment and decent work.

[4] Zechariah 4:6.

[5] 2 Corinthians 4:5, New Revised Standard Version.

[6] 2 Corinthians 4: 7, King James Version.

Mariann Edgar Budde

where the power comes from." Similarly, Blanche Lee Powell has relied on "the passage in Romans about one's character and then the whole business about being strengthened…in Corinthians. There are things that hit you to the core: To be rejected gets to the core of your being. It was tough. But the other side is resurrection."

God's power for resurrection figures prominently in the minds of several: "God provides new life," affirms Betty Works Fuller, interpreting Jeremiah 1, "and will raise you up as on eagles' wings."[7] Katharine Babson reflects, "I feel like I've been resurrected so many times." For Patricia Merchant, "The Scripture that has stayed with me is from Luke. Marion Kelleran used it for her sermon at my ordination. 'Fear not,' the angels told the shepherds. This sentiment appears a lot in Gospel accounts. She reminded me that I would struggle with my fears all my life. She is right." And Patricia Thomas states, "I am very much a resurrection-centered person….Grace is in all of those different cycles that we do as Church…. God was with me always….God was with me, walking this walk; and the walk was to be an inclusive one." Ruth Kirk comments, "Samuel's story was always very powerful to me as a child, and I would always love to hear that story. I don't know if I asked my parents to tell it to me, but I have a memory of Samuel's story from early. Then in the last decade, the story of Jairus's daughter and the heal-ing of Jairus' daughter. Whenever I am feeling defeated or sick unto death, those words say to me, 'Little girl get up.' It's like, 'Okay, Jesus. I am going to get up. You are going to restore me, and I will continue the work you have given me to do.'" Elaborating on resurrection Kate Moorehead shares these thoughts, "I have two icons of Mary Magdalene preaching to the disciples in my office, the apostle in her red telling them all that Jesus is risen.[8] She for me is a great role model….So when I feel insecure, I look at her and think that God chose her to tell everybody even though she was a woman or because she was a woman. Who knows why?"

Shirley Smith Graham proffers an understanding of Scripture that sheds light on God's choosing the weak to make manifest God's power, the power of love: "The very short parabolic saying from Matthew, I think it is chapter 13[9]…where Jesus says there was a merchant who searched and searched and searched and found the pearl; and when he found the pearl, he sold everything that he had to obtain it….What that passage always meant to me was that God was the merchant and each of us is that pearl of great price. The record of salvation history: God chases us and pursues us for no good reason other than love. We are that pearl of great price and God gives up so much, metaphorically, all for us….It's the kenotic nomen. It's that God empties himself in that voluntary way of self-sacrificial offering for us. How can we do anything but bow ourselves?….That's my key to living, is to figure out how to be a well person and take care of my own needs so that I can offer of myself and give without anxiety and not run my resources so low that I'm not well for myself or my family or for the community I'm serving. And the voluntary bit has helped me in realizing that, you

[7] Paraphrasing Psalm 91.
[8] John 20:1-18.
[9] Matthew 13:45-46.

Shirley Smith Graham

know, I serve God best when I am loving myself the way God loves me. To spend myself down too much is to violate that love, and I can be of no use then."

Jesus' response to women figures prominently in the passages that give Christy LaBorda strength. "I think about John 4 a lot, the Samaritan woman. I see Jesus in many ways as coming in and putting love as the most important thing: love of self and of other and of God, and we demonstrate love of God by loving self and other…. The most important thing was [Jesus'] connecting with her….At the end of the day if I am up at the gates [of heaven], and I am told that I try to veer too much towards love…if I am being in trouble for understanding Jesus is too loving [pause]. My default is acceptance….I think a big part of my role is teaching to accept forgiveness."

Karin MacPhail speaks of her ministry as "trying to model God's love above everything else….You meet so many people who have been so hurt by life and by the Church….I don't have to save somebody; that's taken care of already." Her vision is "incarnational in that way of I'm a person just like you. Let's all walk this path together…. Other people have gifts I don't have, so working together as the body of Christ in this place, we all can pitch in and figure this out together….To everything there is a season[10] has really been part of envisioning my vocation as mother and priest…kind of hold their hand and be a reliable Sunday morning presence that lets them relax a little bit."

Susan Kennard draws strength from the witness of women in the Old Testament: "I love that whole [first] chapter of Exodus and the story of midwives Shiphrah and Puah who chose not to kill the baby boys….We are saying those names in Bay City, Texas, in the 21st century. I talk about it from the perspective of simply making the right decision with no idea whatsoever what the ramifications of that decision will be…no possible way of knowing that out of that tribe would come the parents of the Lord Jesus and just that notion that we make the decision on the day and then you just have to let go and the power in those very simple choices that we can just not imagine. Would it have been more difficult if they had been alone as opposed to a team of two who were able to look at each other and say, 'We'll see about that, of course we are not going to do that'….The whole call to Jeremiah and 'before you were in the womb I knew you, before you were born I set you apart.'[11] I always fall back on that in teaching, in formation, anything that involves Christian education in youth work of our absolute obligation to raise children up so that if the word of the Lord came to them in junior high school they would know what it was. And that the parents and teachers and mentors of that baby Jeremiah had no idea who had been given to them. He was not marked in some way, but that how in Anathoth they knew to raise them all up. And there again we are quoting Jeremiah in the 21st century. I love and fall back on constantly the 'I am' statements of Jesus from St. John's gospel…I love the concreteness of those images. I cannot function in my role leading a congregation if I let any distance go between myself and the letters of Paul…those Philippians and just those personal first and second Thes-

[10] Ecclesiastes 3:1.
[11] Paraphrasing Jeremiah 1:5.

Susan Kennard & parishioners blessing work done on mission trip

salonians, those straight from the heart 'this is how much I love you: you are my joy and my crown. Pray constantly. I pray for you without ceasing,' and just the love that he had for those people…that reminder of being a pastor and being a leader and how much of your heart it takes."

In addition to the first chapter of Jeremiah which is formative for many, there are other passages from the writings of that prophet that are meaningful to women. Both Ann Normand and Mary Wilson have been sustained by Jeremiah 29:11, "For surely I know the plans I have for you, says the Lord, plans for your welfare and not for harm, to give you a future with hope." "He has done that," says Wilson. To that passage Normand adds the admonition found in 1 Peter to tend the flock.[12]

"I became a Passionist because of my passion to the devotion of Christ," says Rosemari Sullivan. "So for me some of the guiding passages of scripture [are] in the letters of Paul: 'to me to live is Christ, to die is gain.'[13] 'I live no longer in Christ, but Christ lives in me'[14] That's

the core of the proclamation…resurrection…trinity."

"Life in the Christian community is centered and grounded in the life of the Holy Trinity…a divine dance (*perichoresis*) of beauty, truth, and righteousness…. God's action of 'reaching out and drawing in' is a call to the Christian community….Paul's letter (1 Corinthians 12:15) to live in the one body of Christ and to belong interdependently and equally, one should not exclude oneself from the body" sums up the view of Marge McNaughton.

Likewise, Katherine Grieb focuses on the writings of Paul: "It is important to me as a theologian and as a feminist to make a distinction between the letters that Paul wrote and the letters that are written in Paul's name….It's all in the canon. We owe it respect and consideration, but it's all part of the big conversation that began long before we were students of Scripture and will not end until long after we are all dead. And it's a privilege to be in that conversation. My thinking about Scripture has become more and more Jewish the more I teach. That is, the scriptures are alive, the conversation is rich and full, and the voices in Scripture are friends; but they are friends that you argue with sometimes; and they are friends that you want to know more about or want to say, 'I really can't see how you can say that.' That's very important for Scripture to be a living and active word. There needs to be interaction with it, so that the tradition of wondering what would have happened if, or looking at the places where there is a crack in the text and thinking, 'There is a story in there that hasn't come out…the power of God for good.'"

At Virginia Seminary "I got a sense of the living texture of scripture," says Nancy Hatch Wittig. "The ethos

---

[12] 1 Peter 5:2.
[13] Philippians 1:21.
[14] Paraphrasing Galatians 2:20.

of the New Testament, the story of the New Testament… is a historical document of God working through people for generation after generation. I think one of the things I have come to appreciate Paul for as the primary theologian after Jesus' ascension was the need to put down roots in various different places and to use some of the gifts of those people and of those places to help understand the gospel….to look at the New Testament as a whole, and not just as piece by piece, and see the development of the Church and to see the development of the stories and to make them our own, to find our place in those stories…. The wonderful thing about everything in Scripture, you find everything necessary for salvation, but not everything in Scripture is salvific. Things like that continually inform us to make the Gospel our own in our own time. The feeding of the hungry, the prisoners being let free…the lilies of the field: Don't worry about this stuff. You are going to be taken care of. You can't rely completely on God, but there is a lot God can do if you let Him. So a strong doctrine of the Holy Spirit….We need to be missionaries wherever we work, and that is what we are called to do: Preach the gospel, and do it with your life. Do it with the way you live…."

Significantly, awareness of God's judgment coupled with God's promises is echoed in each of the minor prophets quoted but was also a subtle subtext to conversation centered on verses that highlighted love of God and neighbor. As one might expect, "What does the Lord require of you but to do justice, and to love kindness, and to walk humbly with your God"[15] is mentioned by several women. While this passage is cited specifically by Alison Cheek, Jane Dixon, and Marge McNaughton, it is linked in the minds of many to passages that speak of empathy and interdependence with others. "Foundational to a theological ethos for the community and for me personally is Micah 6:8. These three mandates are a call to action and are the basis for the Church's mission and ministry," says McNaughton. The call to just and merciful action is also found in another passage cited by Elisa DesPortes Wheeler: "Jesus at the synagogue, Luke 4:16-19: 'The spirit of the Lord is upon me…to preach good news to the poor, release to the captives, recovery of sight to the blind, set at liberty those who are oppressed and proclaim the year of the Lord.' Those words are my charge as well. I still feel an intensity and urgency of the Gospel and the desire to carry out that charge." Likewise, liberation theologies are the "backbone" of Katherine Ragsdale's ministry.

Sheila McJilton reflects, "I have always resonated with the two great commandments. I go back to them in terms of ethics that I really feel that if we, in the Church, measured our behavior by loving God and loving our neighbor,[16] we wouldn't have some of the conflicts we have within the Church….I use as kind of Amos' plumb line[17] for my life 'Do I love? Is what I am doing a way of expressing love for God and neighbor?' If it isn't, don't do it. The other one is, for me, Luke's passage about to whom much is given, much will be required.[18] I have been aware of that for a lot of years because I have a number of wonderful gifts and sometimes I am not quite sure how I am being called to use them….I often rely on, in my instinctive work with people, common sense and also that sense of, I just felt for years that, I am still learning. I am still being prepared for a ministry, so that responsibility is al-

[15] Micah 6:8.
[16] Matthew 22:37-39.
[17] Amos 7:7-9.
[18] Luke 12:48.

ways there for me."

Feeling herself constantly being shaped, Rebekah Hatch is drawn to Jeremiah 18:1-11 and the potter. "But mostly on my stole from my ordination is a passage from Luke," says Hatch, "to 'Love the Lord your God with all your heart, soul, mind, and strength, and your neighbor as yourself.'"[19]

Still another linking of giftedness with responsibility is significant to Arienne Davison: "From James, 'be doers of the Word and not merely hearers' and all that follows up to the 27th verse of that first chapter because it is sort of a sense of we get this gift and then forget it. It is just a deep desire to be authentic to that, to who God made me to be and to that gift and to treat it with respect and to use it and that's the end to care for the widow and the orphan. That is the only logical result of seeing how God has gifted you is to go do the work....There are lots of things in this world that help us forget who we really are, and the Church is full of them too. So just figuring out how you are going to be faithful to that....God sometimes has to smash things apart for me to see it, so I think as an adult, as a developed faith, is to find ways to be more open and ready to accept rather than to wait so long for it to sink in."

Understanding the proper translation of "help meet" (King James Version) at Genesis 2:18 to be mutuality rather than subordination was transformative for Jane Dixon: "From Genesis about being created in the image of God, male and female, God created them into one, the counterpart. I'll always be grateful to Murray Newman for that. The second passage that I really got to know through Verna [Dozier] is Micah 6:8. Verna used to preach all the time about the fact that if we reverse those verbs, we do a lot of loving justice and doing mercy. I pray that my min-

istry has been about trying to do justice....The last passage that really has a major impact on me is from the first letter of John about you cannot talk about loving God whom you haven't seen if you don't love your brother and sister whom you do see."[20]

While judgment and promise figure prominently in the theologies of these women, so do diversity, hospitality, and an awareness of God's Kingdom at hand. "I've always been grounded in creation theology. We really are all created in God's image and likeness," ponders Anne Bonnyman. "All the imagery around parenting and birthing, all of those are powerful images for me. God is the source of life. That is powerful for me. Christ's images of hospitality, the expanded tableship that is breathtakingly inclusive and yet around which there's great accountability. The call to be in community and to be gathered around a table has rich, deeply layered meaning for us as a Church; and it's hard. It's really hard about who gets to be at the table and who gets to serve and who gets to be fed....Jesus' image of hospitality is profoundly moving to me, his risk-taking image of hospitality. It's not just the loosey-goosey thing. There's real accountability built into that. That's the hard part of community, is the inclu-

LEFT TO RIGHT: Rosemarie Sullivan, Bishop Penelope Jamison of New Zealand, Martha Horne, 1992

[19] Luke 10:27.
[20] 1 John 4:20.

sivity along with the accountability."

In the same vein, Martha Horne considers "an ethos of hospitality which was so important in both the Hebrew and Christian Scriptures. Within that hospitality, an ethos of diversity…representing different parts of the Christian tradition and from other religious traditions, as well as the Anglican tradition….The wonderful text from Revelation where 'every people, language, tribe and nation' gathered around the throne of God.[21] Dialogue is essential for understanding others, so it is dangerous, I believe, when the only voices we hear are those that sound like ours. It is not where God calls us to be, I believe. I believe that faith requires a tolerance for ambiguity."

Likewise, "I think probably the foundational belief or one of them is that we are all created in the image of God," says Christine Whittaker. "I have a longstanding and growing interest in comparative religion, particularly Islam and also in Tibetan Buddhism, but particularly Islam, which I have studied and observed in much of the Middle East over the last 15 or 20 years. It has informed this belief, but my conviction is that this is part of the gospel that Jesus preached—to enable us to see that we are created by God in the image of God and called to see the image of God in one another. Three Scripture verses that are important to me are the Romans 8 verse[22]—there is nothing, neither death nor life nor anything else in all creation that can separate us from the love of God in Christ Jesus—the new commandment in John's Gospel—love one another as I have loved you, by this people will know that you are my followers[23]—and that wonderful verse in Luke[24]—this man welcomes sinners and eats with them. What I find so moving and treasure about the Church are times when it is a community where barriers have broken down. When we gather in fellowship around all sorts of tables, we find that God is present for everybody; and we see the image of God in one another. I can think of example after example of times when I have experienced this. That's why hospitality for me is an extremely important Christian virtue."

Once again, justice and love of neighbor are linked. "The theological ethos that most guides me and shapes me as a priest in the church of God is that of Kingdom building," reflects Kim Coleman. "In a Kingdom theology—thy Kingdom come[25]—we no longer have options to see others as relative or not a part of God's picture of redeemed creation. Revelation 7:9 is the vision I hold before me: All around the throne, all nations and peoples and tongues. There is a diversity and inclusivity there, a welcome and a hospitality that says, 'Nobody can be undervalued. Everybody has a place.' So when I live into that vision of God's kingdom, it is easier to respond to questions that sometimes come up like what do we do about African American people or women or homosexuals or Hispanic people—what do we do? We say, 'Come to the table but don't stop there.' 'Come to' just opens up our thinking. It is a hard movement for us to make, but talking about the Kingdom of God coming here on earth and our preparations for that and our building toward that and our being prepared for that day when all nations and peoples and tribes will gather around the throne of God means there is a certain way I have to be in community and a certain design that I have to advocate. Again as God challenges me with different ways of feeding God's sheep, it just keeps coming back along with the question Jesus

---

[21] Revelation 5:9-10; 7:9.
[22] Romans 8:38-39.
[23] John 13:34-35.
[24] Luke 7:34; cf. Luke 5:30.
[25] Matthew 6:10; Luke 11:2.

raised of Peter and of us, 'Do you love me?'[26] The third guide that comes as a goad to remind me how complete and comprehensive God's redemptive work is 2 Corinthians 5:16-17, 'From now on, therefore, we regard no one from a human point of view,

Kim Coleman

even though we once knew Christ from a human point of view, we know him no longer in that way. So if anyone is in Christ, there is a new creation, everything old has passed away; see, everything has become new.' I sometimes need to be reminded that in Christ Jesus we no longer look to one another from a human point of view but celebrate the fact that in Christ Jesus we are one."

Similarly, the Revelation to John has particular meaning for Elisa DesPortes Wheeler: "Revelation 7:9-17. This passage is one of total victory. In the end Jesus, the shepherd, will walk among us and wipe away every tear from our eyes. I find this whole passage to bring me great comfort and spiritual power – that the victory has been won for us and after all is said and done, Jesus will be there to care for us and wipe away every tear from our eyes." Phoebe Roaf also relies on Revelation 7:9: "God equips those whom God calls....That vision from Revelation of people of all races and nations and cultures around the throne praising God is the vision of Heaven. And if that's what we will ultimately have, why can't we do that here?...In my reading of the Gospel, I see Jesus addressing issues of poverty and exclusion; and so when I see those things today, I think there has to be some way to comment on them without saying Democrat or Republican or Independent but to ask how is God calling us to respond to these situations based upon what we know about how

God himself responded."

How God himself responded was to offer himself in loving kindness [*hesed*]. "How much of your heart [loving] takes," mused Susan Kennard. But for human beings to choose to love is to choose to be vulnerable, to be available to being impacted and shaped by others, to change. How do Christians deal with change? They pray, and the change they seek to deal

Phoebe Roaf

with results in their own changing. The attitude of prayer, the attitude of encounter is willingness to be changed. They change, not because God has given them the answer to their dilemma. God does not give answers. He gives Himself. Those who pray change because in their own need and lostness, they meet the Christ. He meets them where they are when they are ready to be met there. Living in the assurance of His presence changes their frame of reference and brings them into a wider context, a greater perspective than their existent present. That greater perspective gives them the power to live in unaccustomed joy with the polarities of life.

Prayer is the expression of an inward music, the inner vision, trust, and commitment by which a person of faith may more fully live. Christians approach that vision because of the conviction that somehow life is more than animal instincts, more than personal values, more than self-control, more than conventional standards, more than a constant tension between what they would be and what they would do. And they experience the mystery of God's

[26] John 21:15.

giving them back themselves: renewed, strengthened, changed to proclaim, "Whoever is in Christ, new creation…behold, the new has come."

Carlyle Gill reflects, "Right now I'm very sustained by centering prayer…apophatic contemplative prayer has just been really important to me….I came here because Virginia expected people to worship together on a daily basis….I needed to be grounded in the biblical theology and the biblical story, so I loved it….The biblical story became very, very important to me, and chapel was my opportunity for theological reflection. That's where I learned [that] to reflect theologically was [to do so] in prayer, to really see how those stories and those words apply to me and what the connections were….Psalms have been important to me. My mother used to—we used to read psalms together at night when I was little, and the great thing I think about this, the theological vocation I got here [at Virginia Seminary], was that the biblical story is very easy for me to put my hands on. I can reach for it and get to it and use it….The liturgy has [also] always been really important to me and forming."

Prayer is also central to the ministry of Carolyn Irish. "On my bishop's ring is the prayer 'Abide in me.'[27] I believe it to be the prayer that Jesus offers and that I pray.

Carolyn Irish at prayer at her consecration as Bishop of Utah.

So I love looking at it each day and knowing that it will be with me always as a reminder of my desire and of God's desire for me….It is the one at the root of my heart and frankly, when I go there, I am okay. I know my way home. I know what to hear, what to do, what to offer, so that has been precious."

When asked what theological ethos guides her ministry, Kit Carlson replies, "My baptismal covenant. I came to believe before ordination that ordination is my expression of my baptism, that I didn't get a promotion or anything. I am a baptized follower of Jesus, and this is the particular way that Jesus wants me to minister in the world. So helping other people live into their baptismal ministry, whatever that may be….My other theological guide is a lot of the polytheology of this present evil age is passing away and the kingdom is coming and we live in a time between the times. How can we participate in the in-breaking kingdom of God, not let the present evil age dictate who we are and how we do our business. We are Kingdom people and the Kingdom is coming and that's the reality that we live in….I think those two: the sense of our individual ministry, but also our corporate participation is really incarnating the body of Christ in a world where the Kingdom is close at hand. Our job is to proclaim it, to body it, to live it out so that other people see that and be-

[27] John 15:4.

lieve it too. That's what I thought the Qur'an reading did. Yes, the Kingdom is at hand. The lions go lie down with the lamb,[28] and it's going to be great. And it was great."

The Advent readings from Isaiah[29] have also been important for Victoria Hatch; and she, too, considers the baptismal covenant central to her theology of inclusion. As Connie Jones says, "The passages in the baptismal covenant are most meaningful to me; so this is why I love that service, because we say them out loud as a congregation often. The two that I am thinking of are 'to seek and serve Christ in all persons, loving your neighbor as yourself.' That is the essence of it: Seeing Christ in the face of the other person. The other passage is 'Strive for justice and peace among all people, and respect the dignity of very human being.'"[30] Still another woman for whom the baptismal covenant is very important is Jane Dixon, "those last three promises that we make about loving."[31]

The baptismal covenant is humanity's way of responding to the fact that the new has come. The promises of new life in Christ, given in baptism, sustain those who

Kit Carlson & Pere Jeannot

believe. Baptism is an individual's principal and primary response to the covenantal promise God first made to us, a human answer to God's gift of grace. Baptism is a commitment to God in Christ which indicates one's willing participation in the life of the Spirit. The baptism of each of the women interviewed freed them for wholeness and new life. If in baptism these women have found strength to continue, perhaps it could be said that they have tangibly found that the sacraments as outward and visible signs of inward and spiritual grace are real for them. These signs of something beyond themselves have given them hope. These women have taken unto themselves the promises of God; and in that process, their lives have become grace in motion.

---

[28] Isaiah 11:6-9.
[29] Isaiah 2:1-5; 11:1-10; 35:1-10; and 7:10-17 in Year A of the *Book of Common Prayer*. Isaiah 64:1-9a; 40:1-11; 65:17-25 in Year B of the *BCP*. These have been slightly changed with the publication of the *Revised Common Lectionary*.
[30] *The Book of Common Prayer*, p. 305.
[31] *Book of Common Prayer*, pp. 305-306.

CLASS OF 2010 GIFTS TO THIS BOOK

Anonymous Donor
The Rev. Mary K. Babcock, '10
The Rev. Gillian R. Barr, '10
The Rev. Barbara A. Bassuener, '10
The Rev. Pierre-Henry Buisson, '10
Mrs. Sophie Buisson
Ms. Lynn M. Campbell, '10
Class of 2010
The Rev. Robert F. Coniglio, '10
The Rev. Philip H. DeVaul, '10
The Rev. Geoffrey D. Doolittle, '10
The Rev. Geoffrey P. Evans, '10
The Rev. Christine M. Faulstich, '10
Mr. and Mrs. John T. Faulstich
The Rev. Leslie C. Ferguson, '10
The Rev. Stephen D. Foisie, '10
The Rev. Kenneth N. Forti, '10
The Rev. Willis R. Foster, Sr., '10
The Rev. Lauren M. Kilbourn Gaudette, '10
The Rev. Patrick J. Greene, '10
The Rev. Matthew R. Hanisian, '10
The Rev. Dr. J. Barney Hawkins IV
The Rev. Linda Wofford Hawkins
The Rev. Catherine D. Hicks, '10
The Rev. Marian T. Humphrey, '10
The Rev. Kimberly S. Jackson, '10
Ms. Tracey E. Kelly, '11

The Rev. Jessica T. Knowles, '10
The Rev. Catherine C. L. Lemons, '10
The Very Rev. Ian S. Markham, Ph.D.
Mrs. Lesley Markham
Mr. Jackson McDaniel
The Rev. Dr. Judith M. McDaniel
The Rev. Richard D. Meadows, Jr., '10
The Rev. Julia Weatherly Messer, '10
Ms. Sayama Naw Lwin Thida Myint, '10
The Rev. Sara E. Palmer, '10
The Rev. Dr. Susan M. Prinz, '10
The Rev. Christopher M. Robinson, '10
The Rev. Narcis J. Sebikwekwe, '10
The Rev. Benson E. Shelton, '10
The Rev. Janis H. T. Shook, '10
Ms. Julie A. Simonton, '10
Mrs. Sonya K. Sowards, '10
The Rev. William M. Sowards
The Rev. Susan R. Sowers, '10
The Rev. Richard A. Tucker, '10
The Rev. Amy P. Turner, '10
The Rev. Brian W. Turner, '10
The Rev. Matthew Venuti, '10
The Rev. Alexander H. Webb II, '10
The Rev. Cornelia M. Weierbach, '10
The Rev. Janis E. R. Yskamp, '10

ACKNOWLEDGMENTS

Hearing the stories of women whose journeys in faith exhibited grace has been a profound blessing, an opportunity provided by Ian Markham for which I am deeply grateful. I am also indebted to Jennifer Andrews-Weckerly who interviewed eight of the women whose stories are contained herein. The time and support the members of the reading committee offered were invaluable: Rose Duncan, Sam Faeth, Christine Faulstich, Barney Hawkins, Ian Markham, Bob Prichard, Julia Randle, Susan Shillinglaw, and Allison St. Louis all read first drafts of the book and made generous comments. As always, my family was a source of ever-sustaining love. Finally, I want to thank the women and men who entrusted their stories to me. Not all are directly quoted here, but their reflections provided helpful context. I pray this account does them justice.

- Judith M. McDaniel
St. Barnabas Day, 2011

Judith M. McDaniel joined the VTS faculty in 1990. She is currently the Howard Chandler Robbins Professor of Homiletics. She completed her Interim Ministry Certification, Interim Ministry Network, Baltimore, MD in 2004; her Doctor of Philosophy from University of Washington, Seattle, WA in 1994; Master in Divinity, cum laude, General Theological Seminary, NY in 1985; a Certificate of Graduation, Diocesan School of Theology, Seattle in 1977 and her Bachelor of Arts, cum laude, University of Texas at Austin in 1961.

Before joining VTS, Professor McDaniel served as Rector, St. John's Parish, Gig Harbor, WA; Associate Rector, St. John's Parish, Olympia, WA; Priest Associate, St. Mark's Cathedral, Seattle, WA; Deacon, St. Mark's Cathedral, Seattle, WA; Deacon, St. Barnabas Parish, Bainbridge Island, WA and from 1977-78, Parish Administrator, St. Barnabas Parish, Bainbridge Island, WA.

Professor McDaniel has served on many educational boards and organizations, including the Interlochen Alumni Organization on the Board of Trustees. She is the author of many works, including Homiletical Perspective: Day of Pentecost, Trinity Sunday, Proper 3, Year B, Feasting on the Word, (Westminster John Knox Press).